SCENIC DRIVING

INDIANA

Barns on local family farms are an iconic feature of the Indiana landscape.

SECOND EDITION

SCENIC DRIVING INDIANA

Including Brown County, Bloomington, and the Whitewater Valley

PHIL BLOOM

Globe Pequot

Essex, Connecticut

All the information in this guidebook is subject to change. We recommend that you call ahead to obtain current information before traveling.

Globe Pequot

An imprint of The Globe Pequot Publishing Group, Inc.
64 South Main Street
Essex, CT 06426
www.globepequot.com

Distributed by NATIONAL BOOK NETWORK

First edition published 2001
All photos provided by the Indiana Destination Development Corporation unless otherwise noted.

British Library Cataloguing in Publication Information available

Library of Congress Cataloging-in-Publication Data available
ISBN 9781493089031 (paperback) | ISBN 9781493089048 (epub)

Printed in India

Contents

The Scenic Drives

SOUTHERN INDIANA

CENTRAL INDIANA

NORTHERN INDIANA

Overview

South Bend
Angola
Gary
Nappanee
Plymouth
Warsaw
Fort Wayne
Huntington
Rensselaer
Lafayette
Thorntown
Conner Prairie
Indianapolis
Richmond
Rockville
Greencastle
Terre Haute
Cataract
New Trenton
Bloomington
Columbus
Lawrenceburg
Ohio River
Bedford
Vincennes
Montgomery
Troy
Tell City
Evansville
0 25 50 Kilometers
0 25 50 Miles

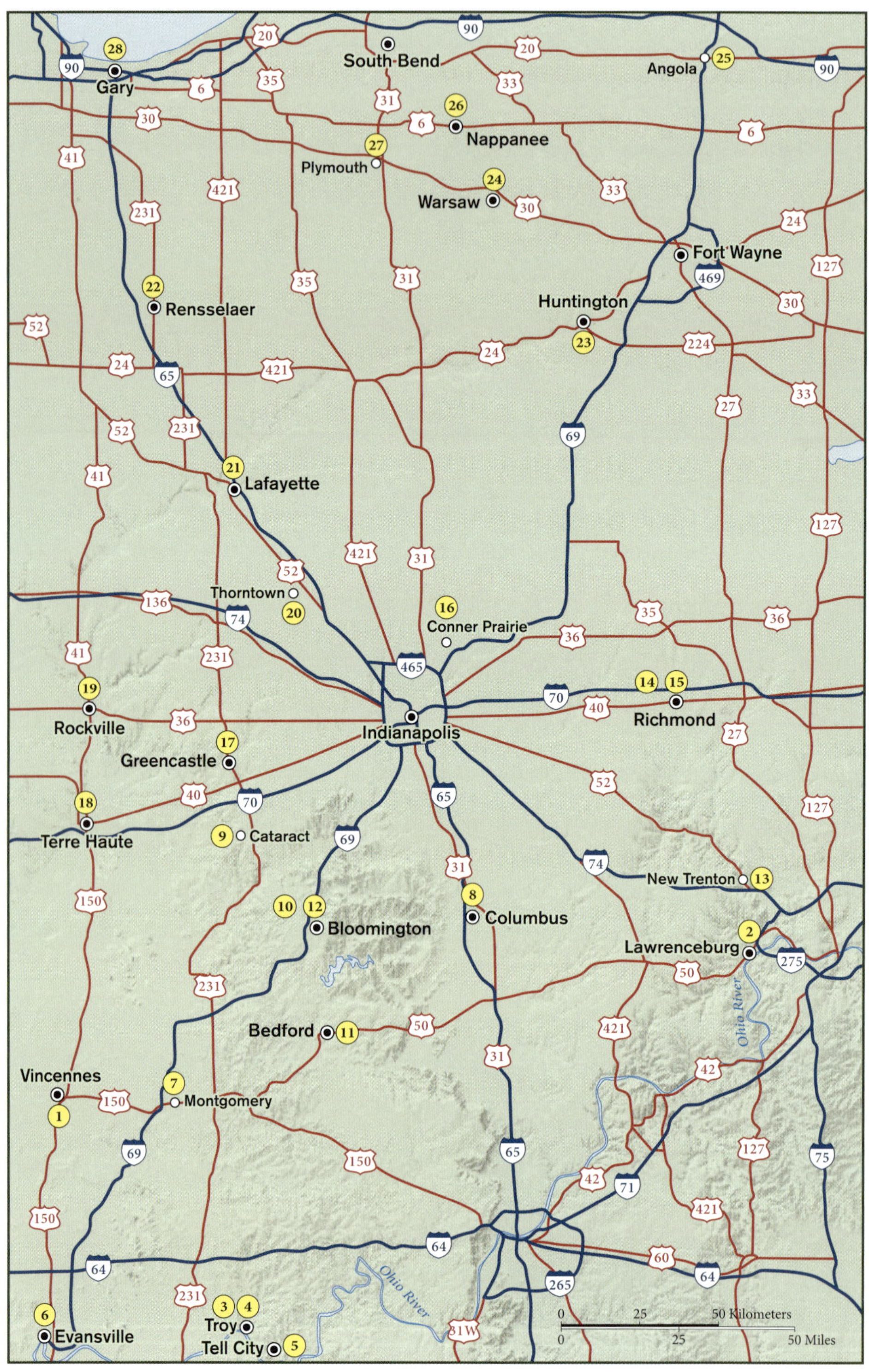

Map Legend

Interstate Highway/
Featured Interstate Highway
64
95
State Highway/
Featured State Highway
57
62
US Highway
41
231
Trail
Forest Service Road
Building or Structure
Capital
City
Lighthouse
Mountain Peak
Town
Route Location
1
Lodge
Bridge
Steps/boardwalk
Coastal Flood Warning
Campground
Ferry
Glacier
Dam
Ski Area
Point of Interest
Waterfall
Museum
River, Creek, or Drainage
Reservoir or Lake
International Border
State Border
National Park
Wildlife Sanctuary/Reserve
State Forest/Park

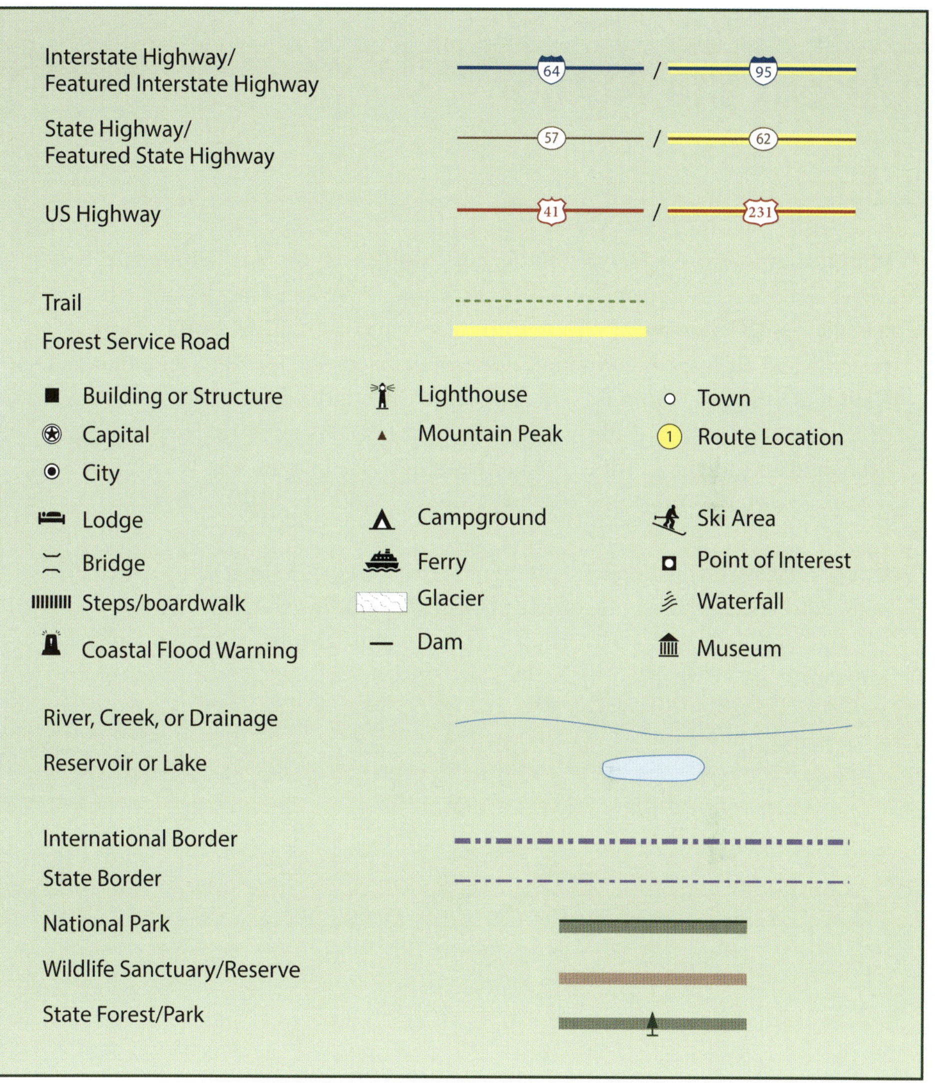

About the Author

Phil Bloom is a native Hoosier and lifelong resident of Indiana. He enjoyed two careers before retiring from both—33 years as a newspaper reporter and editor (the last 18 as an award-winning outdoors editor at the *Fort Wayne Journal Gazette*) and 10 years as communications director for the Indiana Department of Natural Resources. Bloom is a life member of the Outdoor Writers Association of America and served as the group's president in 2008 and 2018. He is an Eagle Scout and an Indiana Certified Master Naturalist. He lives in Fort Wayne and is a volunteer with the American Red Cross.

Doug Wissing wrote the first edition of *Scenic Driving Indiana* upon which this updated version is based. Doug has published a wide array of articles regionally and nationally. He is a freelance writer and journalist based in Bloomington, Indiana.

Acknowledgments

The many city, county, and regional tourism groups across the state, along with the Indiana Destination Development Corporation and the Indiana Department of Natural Resources, deserve special credit for their assistance in bringing a fresh look to *Scenic Driving Indiana*.

Maple trees and split-rail fencing add beauty to Indiana's fall foliage.

Introduction

What is the song of Indiana? Perhaps it's a Cole Porter or Hoagy Carmichael tune, a song by John Mellencamp, or "Moonlight on the Wabash." Maybe it's a Gregorian chant from the St. Meinrad monks or a Tibetan chant from Bloomington or a Beanblossom bluegrass lament or a Shipshewana Amish hymn. Or maybe it's the jingle of the reins as the draft horses pull through the fields or the murmur of a brook or the shush of Lake Michigan waves, the pushy cry of a red-winged blackbird, the heart-rend of a whippoorwill, or the chuff of a train, the silence of a Quaker service or the scream of an Indy racer. Or maybe it's all these things.

I've driven from one end of this great state to the other, zigzagging across the dimples and folds and flatlands of Indiana, winding down countless country lanes. And I can testify there is a lot of Indiana to experience. The glint of the dawn on the Ohio River, the sugar-powder hills of the dunes, canal boats, vintage cars and old-time trains, fireflies dotting a summer field into a pointillist canvas, forests ablaze with autumn color stretching to the horizon. The smell of new hay, old wine, and campfires flickering on a cool evening.

Ah, Indiana. Here's to your rivers and roads and endless prairies. To your expansive forests and deep lakes. To your layers of history and the energy of your many cultures. And especially to your people, who twang out their greetings and take the time to tell you how to get there.

The Landscape

Indiana is a long state, stretching from the pine forest lands near Lake Michigan down to the cypress bogs of the Wabash and the lower Ohio River. Across its 36,420 square miles, an almost unimaginable diversity thrives: hardwood forests and fertile wetlands, glades, barrens, savannas, and prairies.

There are several distinct natural regions in the state. The southern hill country is a rumpled swath of limestone hills and ravined forest. Caves, rushing streams, and dense forests are part of the ecology and culture of the region. With sprawling floodplains and unique aquatic life, the watersheds of the major southern Indiana rivers—the lower Ohio, the Wabash, and the White—are themselves a distinct natural region. The southern lowlands in the southwestern section of the state are bottomlands where rich agricultural land coexists with teeming wetlands and the state's best oil and coal deposits. It is the hottest part of the state, and the one closest to America's Deep South in both climate and culture.

The central flatlands display quite graphically the impact of glaciation, in some places lying flat as a poker table on the landscape, in others, rolling in swells and swales like a kindly sea. The Grand Kankakee Marsh, which stretched for 5,300 square miles across northwestern Indiana, is mostly a memory, but a collection of state wildlife areas along the Kankakee River give a hint as to the wonder of the wetlands once described as the Everglades of the North.

The lakes region in northeast Indiana is pocked with hundreds of kettle lakes, liquid memories of the ice blocks left by the retreating glaciers. The Calumet Region's dunes at the Lake Michigan lakeshore are among the most diverse environments in the world, where the tenets of ecology were parsed out by pioneering biologists in the early 1900s.

Diversity—there's diversity here in Indiana.

Indigenous people found Indiana a nice place to make a home. The state is blanketed with evidence of their exuberant lives—mounds and mussel banks, millions of potsherds, arrowheads for thousands of hunters. Their descendants roamed the state from one end to the other—the Miami, Delaware, Potawatomi, and Iroquois tribes, to name a few. When the Europeans found the land, they came in droves. First the French hunters and trappers, then the British "long knife hunters," followed by the settlers of northern Europe, and then the great waves from eastern and southern Europe that populated the burgeoning industrial cities. In one way or another, they're all still here, and they make Indiana what it is.

The first European settlements were along rivers—Vincennes on the Wabash River, Clarksville on the Ohio, and Fort Wayne at the convergence of the St. Marys, St. Joseph, and Maumee Rivers—and accordingly the towns with the longest history and finest vintage architecture are found there. The canal boom of the 1830s left a string of port towns along its path that are intact memories of a short-lived boom, when the commerce of the world floated to their docks.

The first great national road ran straight as a die across the belly of the state, and towns like Centerville still tell the story. The coming of the silver railroad tracks changed the face of Indiana, withering the river and canal towns and accelerating the development of hundreds of others. Dozens of small Hoosier towns still radiate out from their timeworn stations—sometimes poignantly empty, more often converted to shops and visitor centers.

When the automobile age arrived, Indiana took to it with a passion. Hoosiers pioneered the infant industry, creating many of the nation's early models, along with legendary ones like Cord, Auburn, Stutz, and Duesenberg. The mythic brick racetrack (Indianapolis Motor Speedway) in Speedway, Indiana, and the near-ubiquitous car museums across the state live to tell the tale. That and the small-town root beer stands, the post–World War II motor hotels now used as transient housing, and the swooping '50s-style signs that hang on the fronts of buildings that are a hundred years older. They tell the story of an Indiana on wheels too.

Driving is easy here. With a few exceptions, the routes in this book are on paved roads, mainly highways. I've aimed down the two-lanes for the most part, leaving the big highways for those in a hurry. Campgrounds and services abound in this well-settled state. You'll seldom be far from our modern world, though sometimes it may seem as though you are a long way from anywhere.

Most of the drives in this book are day trips, though any of them lend themselves to overnight jaunts or saunters that can last a week. There are plenty of delights for those who take the time to explore a bit.

The weather in Indiana is classified as temperate continental, but any native will tell you that is only part of the story. "Hang around awhile if you don't like the weather," they say, "it'll change soon." And they are right. The mid-latitude westerly wind belt that passes over Indiana, and the jet stream and hemispheric storm track associated with it, guarantee lots of different things happening weatherwise, often in a short period. In general, there is about a 25°F shift in annual average temperatures from the north (40°) to the southwest (67°).

What the north and south have in common is humidity. The great waves of moisture that boil up from the Gulf of Mexico ensure this is a well-watered place, essential for our dense forests and rich agricultural lands, though somewhat wilting for humans at times. Indiana gets almost 40 inches of rain a year, with the south getting most of its precipitation in the winter, the central and north in the early spring. For all, the driest month is October.

While there are ample reasons to visit the state throughout the year, spring and fall are particularly inviting. In the spring the blooming redbud and dogwood trees turn the forests into ethereal landscapes. Fall foliage is almost iconic, with hundreds of thousands of acres on fire with reds, oranges, purples, and yellows—exotic biotic changes happening for our viewing pleasure. Indian summer in Indiana is a special time after the first frost. Days are warm and sunny with low humidity, the nights cool and crisp—another ideal time for touring.

Recommended Reading

The Natural Heritage of Indiana, edited by Marion T. Jackson (Indiana University Press, Bloomington, Indiana, 1998), is a beautiful exploration of Indiana's extraordinary natural diversity.

Indiana's Wildlife Viewing Guide, by Phil T. Seng (Falcon Publishing, Helena, Montana, 1996), showcases eighty-nine of the best wildlife-viewing spots in the state.

The Indiana Way, by James H. Madison (Indiana University Press, Bloomington, Indiana, 1986), is an overview of Indiana history written by one of the state's most respected historians.

Indiana: A New Historical Guide, edited by Robert M. Taylor Jr., Errol Wayne Steven, Mary Ann Ponder, and Paul Brockman (Indiana Historical Society, Indianapolis, 1989), is a guide to the compendium of the state's history.

From Needmore to Prosperity, by Ronald L. Baker (Indiana University Press, 1995), explores the folklore and origins of Indiana place names.

Hiking Indiana, by Phil Bloom (Globe Pequot Press), is a guide to the best trails in the state.

Indiana: Across the Land, by Lee Mandrell and DeeDee Niederhouse-Mandrell (Indiana University Press, 2017), is a photographic tour around the Hoosier State.

Oddball Indiana: A Guide to 350 Really Strange Places, 2nd edition, by Jerome Pohlen (Chicago Review Press, 2017), highlights unusual finds, from an outhouse collection to Johnny Appleseed's gravesite.

SOUTHERN INDIANA

1

River to River

Vincennes to the Falls Cities

General description: The 112-mile drive follows the path of the old Buffalo Trace blazed by vast bison herds migrating from Illinois prairies to the salt licks of Kentucky. The trip commences in Vincennes and concludes in the Falls Cities of New Albany, Jeffersonville, and Clarksville.

Special attractions: George Rogers Clark National Historical Park, Old Cathedral Complex, The French House, Grouseland, Indiana Territory Capitol, Fort Knox II, West Baden Springs Hotel, French Lick Resort, Falls of the Ohio State Park, Culbertson Mansion State Historic Site.

Location: Southern Indiana.

Drive route numbers and names: US 50 and 150.

Travel season: The roads are drivable in all but the worst of winter weather. Spring and fall are particularly beautiful.

Camping: New Vision RV Park (812) 745-2125, Oubache Trails Park (812) 882-4316, and Vincennes RV Park (812) 890-2034) in Vincennes; Glendale Campground (812) 644-6107 near Washington; Hudsonville Family Campground (812) 486-6215 and Ruritan Park Campground (812) 486-3255 in Montgomery; West Boggs Park (812) 295-3421 near Loogootee; Martin State Forest (812) 247-3491 near Shoals; Buffalo Trace Park (812) 738-8236 near Palmyra; Louisville North Campground (812) 282-4474 in Clarksville.

Services: Gas, food, and lodging in most towns from Vincennes to Clarksville.

Nearby attractions: Indiana Military Museum, Red Skelton Museum of American Comedy, Vincennes Brewing Company, Vincennes University, and Yonder Spirits Distillery in Vincennes; Glendale Fish & Wildlife Area near Montgomery; Hindostan Falls near Loogootee; Martin State Forest, the Jug Rock and Bluffs of Beaver Bend Nature Preserve near Shoals; French Lick Scenic Railway; Wilstem Wildlife Park, Pioneer Mothers Memorial Forest near Paoli; Patoka Lake; Squire Boone Caverns at Mauckport; Corydon Capitol Historic Site; Louisville, Kentucky.

The Drive

The oldest town in Indiana, Vincennes was founded in 1732 as a French fur-trading outpost. The town is located at a strategic ford in the Wabash, which connected the Great Lakes and the St. Lawrence with the Mississippi. For many decades the village was a remote part of the far-flung French North American empire. Each spring hardy voyageurs canoed down from Quebec to exchange trade goods for the beaver pelts that fired so much conquest and exploration in the New World.

Vincennes to the Falls Cities

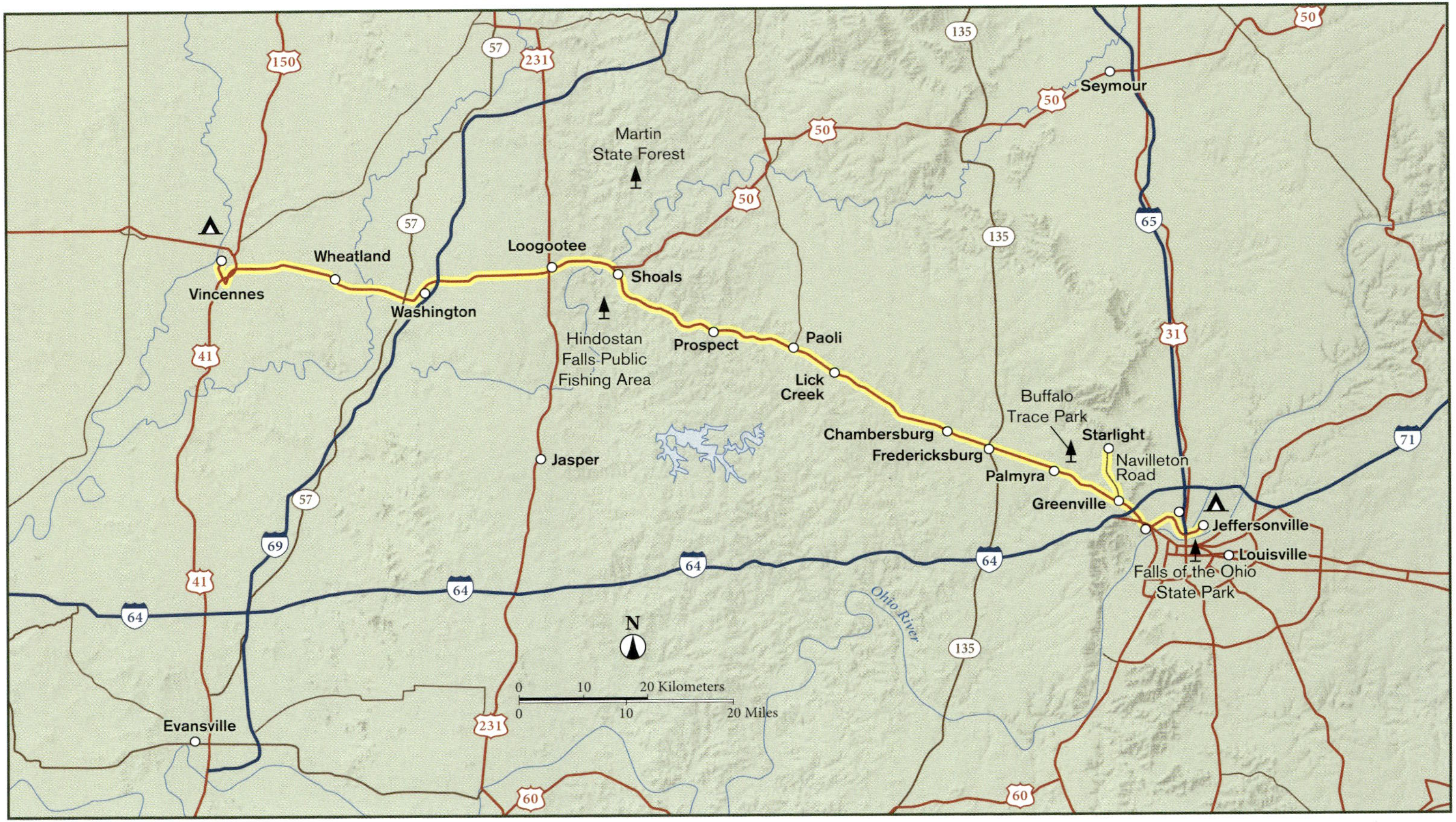

Martin
State Forest
Seymour
Vincennes
Wheatland
Washington
Loogootee
Shoals
Hindostan
Falls Public
Fishing Area
Prospect
Paoli
Lick
Creek
Jasper
Buffalo
Trace Park
Starlight
Chambersburg
Fredericksburg
Palmyra
Navilleton
Road
Greenville
Jeffersonville
Louisville
Falls of the Ohio
State Park
Ohio River
Evansville
N
0 10 20 Kilometers
0 10 20 Miles
150
57
231
50
135
65
31
71
41
69
64
60

French culture remained intact in Vincennes well into the twentieth century. Today there are still remnants of the old French days. When the French parishioners began building the Old Cathedral in 1826, it was the third in the little town, and the first to be constructed of logs. It remains a spiritual lodestone of the community. The basement crypt, accessible by stairs to the right of the altar, is the final resting place for the pioneer bishops. The adjoining French and Indian cemetery is the final resting place of many of the original families, with gravestones dating back to 1800. The Brute Library is the state's earliest library, with volumes dating back to the twelfth century.

The George Rogers Clark National Historical Park celebrates the great Revolutionary War victory of the Americans that recaptured **Fort Sackville** in the Battle of Vincennes and won the Northwest Territory for the young republic. Clark resurfaces at the end of this drive in Clarksville.

The Old French House at 509 N. First St. is a fine example of an early fur trader home. Michel Brouillet constructed his log home in 1806. Every May the French Commons resounds to the sounds of a Revolutionary War battle and the fifes and fiddles of eighteenth-century musicians at the annual Spirit of Vincennes Rendezvous.

Grouseland at Park and Scott Streets is the anchor of a group of historic structures that represent Vincennes's heyday as a great inland frontier political

George Rogers Clark Memorial commemorates the Revolutionary War general.
National Park Service

capital in the post–Revolutionary War period. Grouseland, a Federal-style house built from 1802 to 1804, was the home of William Henry Harrison, the first governor of the Indiana Territory. From this structure he negotiated five treaties with the Native Americans that opened the Middle West to European settlement. On the lawn the fabled Shawnee chief, Tecumseh, met with Harrison. Harrison later was elected the ninth president of the United States. There is a visitor center in the log cabin behind the house.

Vincennes is chock-full of history. The two-story Red House on Park Street served as Indiana's capitol from 1805 to 1813. The Western Sun print shop next door was Elihu Stout's frontier newspaper and printing company, which began in 1804. The tiny white house across the street is the birthplace of famous turn-of-the-century author Maurice Thompson, best known for the novel *Alice of Old Vincennes*. The Vincennes University (VU) campus to the east is the home of the first institution west of the Alleghenies and north of the Ohio River, founded in 1801.

Fort Knox II is a 44-acre park that is the site of Fort Knox, one of several military forts built near Vincennes.

More recent additions to Vincennes attractions are the **Indiana Military Museum** and the Red Skelton Museum of American Comedy. Both opened in 2013, the former to commemorate Indiana's role in conflicts, from the Civil War to Desert Storm, and the latter to honor the legacy of laughter from the native son whose comedy career spanned vaudeville to television.

Follow the river road on the west edge of the VU campus 0.4 mile to Portland Avenue. Turn left and proceed 2 blocks to Oliphant Drive, then turn north 1 mile to Fort Knox Road and drive 1.9 miles to the Fort Knox site. Ouabache Trails Park adjoins the site.

The River-to-River Scenic Drive follows US 150, the historic path formed by the buffalo herds' migrations across Indiana from the Illinois prairie to the Falls of the Ohio at today's Clarksville, where they crossed in low water to the Kentucky salt licks. It was the first natural highway in the region, beaten 6 feet deep into the earth in some places, used by Indians, frontiersmen, invading armies, and militia. Take Sixth Street northeast to the edge of town and the intersection of US 50/150. Proceed south on US 50/150, then east 10 miles to Wheatland.

Wheatland, founded in 1806, was the home of James "Blue Jeans Bill" Williams, the fourteenth governor of Indiana. In 1876, when he defeated Benjamin Harrison, grandson of William Henry Harrison, it was considered the first election of a common man over the blue bloods of the early state. There is a 30-foot memorial to Williams at Walnut Grove cemetery south of Wheatland. Harrison rebounded from the gubernatorial loss to win election to the US Senate in 1881 and 8 years later as the twenty-third US president.

The road continues through rich agricultural land, part of the Southern Bottomland Natural Region. In 1817 Daviess County was termed "the garden spot of Indiana" and it remains among the state's leaders in agricultural production.

Washington, Indiana, 8 miles east, flourished with the arrival of the railroad in 1857. By 1889 the town was a major refurbishing depot for the Baltimore and Ohio Railroad, employing more than 1,000 workers, though little remains of the previous bustle.

Take US 15/150 to IN 57 and turn left/north to arrive in downtown Washington. On Hefron Street, a block from the Daviess County Courthouse square, the Helphenstine House is a fine example of Greek Revival architecture, built at the height of the style in 1847. The Robert Graham House on Maple, owned by an Indiana car manufacturer, is a 1912 example of Frank Lloyd Wright's Prairie School of Architecture, with marble fireplaces, crystal-glass French windows, parquet floors, and a billiards room.

The Daviess County Historical Society Museum on East Main Street is a fifteen-room collection of Daviess County and Indiana history, including a vintage schoolhouse, bank, church sanctuary, parlor, and embalming room.

Return south to US 50/150 and continue east as the route goes through a region of Amish farms. More than 7,000 Amish live in the eastern half of Daviess County.

Loogootee, 15 miles east of Washington, is part of Martin County, where the lowland region begins to give way to the dramatic topography of the Crawford Upland, a region of cliffs, deep valleys, dense forests, and towering ridges.

Shoals, 8 miles east, is the county seat. Just before the city limits, the 60-foot-tall Jug Rock is on the north side of the highway, a natural formation that is the wonder of the county. It is the largest free-standing "stand rock" east of the Mississippi. The 1877 county courthouse and jail 4 blocks south of the highway on Capitol Street is the site of a famous lynching. The Archer boys, accused of torturing and killing a local farmer, were hung from the trees in front of the jail in 1886.

Shoals's greatest claim to fame was its near monopoly of mother of pearl buttons in the years around World War I. The buttons were made from freshwater mussels harvested from the rich White River beds. There were seven button factories in the Shoals area at one time. Today the town depends on the deep gypsum mines discovered in the mid-twentieth century for employment. Two major producers employ more than 400 workers. The National Gypsum mine 2 miles east of Shoals is the nation's deepest at 515 feet.

Continue east 13 miles to IN 56 in Prospect, then turn south in 0.9 mile to West Baden Springs and French Lick. Springs Valley, as the two towns are collectively known, is the home of renowned turn-of-the-century mineral springs spas. The French Lick Resort still operates as a golf and tennis resort with a casino added in 2006. Two notable events occurred at the resort. In 1917 chef Louis Perron created tomato juice. Discovering he was out of oranges to make juice for breakfast guests, he improvised with tomatoes and the new drink was a hit. Later, New York governor Franklin D. Roosevelt used the national governors conference in 1931 at French Lick as the launching point for his first presidential campaign.

The nearby West Baden Springs Hotel, once dubbed the eighth wonder of the world, has gone through a remarkable renovation to restore its grandeur after years of neglect. It features a dome spanning 200 feet over the atrium. Both hotels are listed on the National Register of Historic Places.

Return to US 150 and continue 9 miles east to Paoli, an old Quaker town with a historic Greek Revival courthouse built between 1848 and 1850. Quakers were instrumental in the operation of the Underground Railroad, which transported runaway slaves from the South to freedom in Canada in the years before the Civil War. One branch of the road ran through Paoli. One mile south of the Paoli Square is a trailhead for the Pioneer Mothers Memorial Forest, an 88-acre old-growth forest of oak and hickory trees. Joseph Cox and his heirs owned the hillside forest from 1816 to 1940 but left the trees untouched. When the last Cox family member died in 1940, a lumber company bought it, but a community fundraiser and the US Forest Service struck a deal to buy it back and preserve it forever.

US 150 continues southeast through the Hoosier National Forest, past a couple of nineteenth-century villages, Rego and Hardinsburg, then on to Fredericksburg, founded in 1805 as a toll road on the New Albany–Vincennes plank road. Tolls were collected according to the number of wheels and horses. People going to church, funerals, muster, or elections were exempt. The town also sat astride the Blue River, which empties into the Ohio, affording flatboat transport in high-water springs.

Palmyra, 4.9 miles to the east, dates to 1810. The town is at the junction of two of Indiana's earliest roads: the Mauckport Road (IN 135) and the Buffalo Trace (now US 150), which crossed Indiana from Vincennes to New Albany. Buffalo Trace Park, 0.7 mile east of Palmyra, celebrates the historic trail. Harrison County Parks manages the 146-acre site, which includes recreational facilities, modern and primitive campsites, and cozy cabins.

Greenville, 7 miles east, was first settled in 1807 and was a manufacturing center for barrels, wine kegs, and wooden clocks, due to the fine white oak forests that surrounded the town. It also was a toll stop on the old pike, which operated from the 1820s to the 1880s despite the emergence of the railroads.

To the east 2.9 miles, Galena, originally called Germantown, was another toll stop on the road. The old mill, built in 1857, was a steam-powered flour mill. Because of the many nearby streams, the area abounded with Native American villages and burial grounds. Just east of Galena on IN 150 is Mt. St. Francis Center for Spirituality, a retreat center and outdoor sanctuary offering 400 acres of hiking trails free and open to the public from dawn to dusk.

The scenic drive passes through the Knobstone Escarpment, Indiana's most prominent physiographic feature, which rises nearly 600 feet from the Ohio River valley below. The knobs above New Albany are a longtime truck farming area for the Louisville market. For many generations, the mostly German farm families hauled berries, melons, and tobacco to the Louisville wholesale market. The Starlight area is known for agritourism. Huber's Orchard and Winery, established in 1843, is at 19816 Huber Rd. in Borden. Take Star Valley Road off US 150 to Rake Road, then to Huber Road. In addition to award-winning wines, Huber's spinoff—Starlight Distillery—is gaining attention for its bourbon, brandy, rye whiskey, and gin. Joe Huber's Family Farm, 2421 Engle Rd., has seasonal fruits and vegetables, pickled items, signature jams, jellies, and butters, and a farm restaurant rated four-star by the *Louisville Courier-Journal.*

North of New Albany 2 miles on US 150, the Mary Anderson Center is a nationally renowned artists' retreat focused on providing a haven for creative work. Continue on US 150 to I-64 and proceed east into New Albany.

The Falls Cities—New Albany, Clarksville, Jeffersonville, and neighboring Louisville, Kentucky—got their nickname from the Falls of the Ohio. In the Ohio River's 981 miles from the Allegheny Mountains to the Mississippi, the Falls of the Ohio were the only obstacle, where the river dropped 24 feet in 2 turbulent miles. The Ohio raced over the falls in a series of rapids and chutes and waterfalls for thousands of years until canalization and damming in the nineteenth and twentieth centuries subdued it. This immense natural barrier has created a node of ecology, history, and commerce over the last 12,000 years. The Falls of the Ohio neatly divided the river into the Upper and Lower Ohio. East to Pittsburgh was the Upper; from the Falls west to Cairo, Illinois, at the junction with the Mississippi, was the Lower.

New Albany was the first town below the falls, located in a lowland east of the Knobstone Escarpment. Three Scribner brothers arrived from New York in 1813, bought the platted town, and named it after the capital of their home state. The Scribner House at 106 W. Main, owned by the Daughters of the American Revolution, was built by brother Joel in 1814.

Steamboat building was the primary industry in New Albany until the Civil War, with four to seven shipyards working constantly. Town Clock Church, now the **Second Baptist Church**, at 300 E. Main St., is a remnant of river days. It was built with a tall steeple in the mid-nineteenth century, a landmark for river pilots since.

New Albany's Mansion Row Historic District was named to the National Register of Historic Places in 1983. It includes Main bounded by State and 15th, and Market Street between 7th and 11th. The stately homes range in style from Federal to Italianate to French Second Empire. A centerpiece among mansion row is the Culbertson Mansion State Historic Site, a three-story Second Empire mansion built by businessman and philanthropist William S. Culbertson.

The Floyd County Carnegie Library Cultural Arts Center in New Albany, one of many libraries Andrew Carnegie supported, opened in 1904 and served the community for 65 years. The center is open year-round and offers permanent and rotating exhibits as well as arts and culture.

Jeffersonville was influenced by a proposal from Thomas Jefferson incorporating an alternating checkerboard of green spaces and buildings to protect the town from yellow fever and other pestilences that plagued the early settlers.

The nineteenth-century Old Jeffersonville Historic District was listed on the National Register of Historic Places in 1983. The district is bounded by Court and Graham Streets, the Ohio River, and I-65. Within the district, the quirky 1837 Grisamore House at 111–113 W. Chestnut and the 1832 Henry French House at 217 E. High are on the National Register of Historic Places. Gustav Schimpff's Confectionery at 347 Spring St. has been serving candy since 1891, and you can enjoy soda fountains under their old pressed-tin ceiling and catch a free candy-making demonstration. The **Clark County Museum**, 725 Michigan Ave. in Jeffersonville, is filled with artifacts dating to the settlement of the area as well as Native American artifacts from tribes that traveled the buffalo trace paths.

The business of government has always been a major part of Jeffersonville. It was the early county seat and home of Indiana's second land office. The 1874 US Quartermaster Depot at 10th and Meigs was the major dispensary for the armed forces from the Civil War to the Korean War. The depot warehoused everything from mule saddles to army shirts—71,000 different items in all. Since the depot closed in 1957, it has become home to Jeffersonville's City Hall, restaurants, and local businesses.

The Howard Shipyards dominated Jeffersonville from 1848 until well into the twentieth century as the largest inland shipbuilder in the United States. On the 52-acre site along the historically deepest section of the Ohio River, the Howard yards produced more than 3,000 boats. At 1101 E. Market, the Howard Steamboat Museum brings this world to life with a collection of steamboat memorabilia relating to the golden age of river travel, a wide array of bells and whistles, ship wheels and models, tools, photographs, and documents. The museum is housed in the Howard family mansion dating from the 1890s. Many of the rooms are decorated in high-style Victorian furnishings and elaborate trappings brought from Chicago's World Columbian Exposition.

Across the street, the giant Jeffboat complex continued Jeffersonville's maritime tradition until closing in 2018. Through World War II, the shipyards produced many of the landing craft used in the invasions on both fronts, with 13,000 workers laboring in the yards by 1944. In 1976 it launched a $20 million floating palace, the *Mississippi Queen*, a seven-deck steam-powered stern paddle wheeler with a forty-four-whistle calliope. It went out of service in 2008 and was scrapped.

The Big Four Pedestrian Bridge in Jeffersonville has quickly become a regional attraction after opening in 2014. The former railway bridge for the Cleveland, Cincinnati, Chicago, and St. Louis Railway (hence "Big Four") was converted to pedestrian and bicycle traffic and connects Jeffersonville to Louisville.

Take Riverview Drive 0.7 mile west to Clarksville, the oldest American town in the Northwest Territory. It was chartered in 1783 by George Rogers Clark, Revolutionary War hero and brother to William Clark, who joined Meriwether Lewis here to begin assembling the Corps of Discovery for their journey of exploration to the Pacific. There is a marker at the location of George Rogers Clark's home site west of the corner of South Clark and Harrison Avenue. The log cabin, a replica of Clark's original home, was destroyed by arson in 2021, but the grounds around it remain preserved. Officials are planning to restore the site. The Clarksville Museum in the Town Hall at 230 E. Montgomery has a collection of memorabilia relating to Clark.

Clarksville was also the site of one of the first instances of government privatization. The old Indiana Reformatory for Men was the First State Prison for Men, built in 1821 with publicly subscribed funds and then leased to private individuals

Statue of explorers Lewis and Clark in front of Falls of the Ohio interpretive center.
SoIN Tourism

who incarcerated the prisoners on a per capita basis. The first prison operator, Captain Seymour Westover, was killed with Davy Crockett at the Alamo. The redbrick Romanesque complex was sold in 1923 and remodeled into a Colgate-Palmolive-Peet Company soap factory. The factory closed in 2007, but the Colgate Clock remains on the building as the second-largest timepiece in the world at 40 feet in diameter.

The most unique aspect of Clarksville, however, is the Falls of the Ohio State Park, 201 W. Riverside Dr. In 1981 the United States Congress declared the Falls of the Ohio the country's first National Wildlife Conservation Area, a 1,404-acre site that is a favorite of birders. The conservation area protects the habitat of migrating birds who visit the falls to feed in the wetlands and potholes of the limestone reef. Over 270 species of birds throng the falls area. In the river below the falls, 125 species of fish swim, including the endangered paddlefish.

Congress also protected the immense fossil beds that constituted the limestone reef, the largest exposed Devonian Age fossil beds in the world. More than 600 species of fossils and 250 species of coral have been identified on the beds. The Indiana state park opened in 1990 on 68 acres, overlooking the fossil beds and offering a dramatic view of the Louisville skyline. A few feet down from the park's interpretation center, visitors can hike the 220 acres of fossil beds through a landscape of tiny canyons, fossilized coral, and clusters of miniature crinoids and trilobites. Adventurous souls can cross the McAlpine Dam spillway to explore the outer fossil beds.

The interpretation center encapsulates much of the history of the Falls of the Ohio area. A multiscreen video explains the epochal geologic story of the falls. There are immersive exhibits on everything from coral reefs and fossil beds to mastodons and early humans, steamboats, George Rogers Clark, the legendary Welshmen, and the ecology of today's falls. Three aquariums show the varied life of coral reefs and the Ohio River.

2

Whiskey and Wine

Lawrenceburg to Madison

General description: A 68-mile drive along the Ohio River shore through a series of 19th-century towns that are a national treasury of architectural styles and small-town life. The route follows the nationally celebrated Ohio River Scenic Route.

Special attractions: Madison's National Register of Historic Places district; Lawrenceburg, Aurora, Rising Sun, Vevay; riverboat casinos at Lawrenceburg, Rising Sun, and Florence; and cruise boats on the Ohio.

Location: The extreme southeastern corner of Indiana.

Drive route numbers and names: IN 56, 156, and 62.

Travel season: The roads are drivable in all but the worst of winter weather. Spring and fall are particularly beautiful. Traffic is heavier during the Madison Regatta in early July.

Camping: Lake in the Pines (812) 623-2136 in Sunman; Camp Shore Campground (812) 438-2135 in Aurora; Arnold's Creek Campground (812) 438-3012, Beyonder Getaway (812) 438-4500, and Shawnee Campground (812) 290-1141 in Rising Sun; Clifty Falls State Park (812) 273-8885, Canby Ferry Campground (812) 292-4159, and Riverview Campground (812) 265-8303 in Madison.

Services: There are services in Lawrenceburg, Aurora, Rising Sun, Vevay, and Madison, as well as numerous spots along the route.

Nearby attractions: Ross & Squibb Distillery in Lawrenceburg; Perfect North ski slopes at Lawrenceburg; Guilford Covered Bridge Park in Lawrenceburg; Great Crescent Brewery in Aurora; Hillforest Victorian House Museum in Aurora; Veraestau Historic Site at Aurora; Red Wolf Sanctuary in Rising Sun; Markland Locks & Dam; Mad Paddle Brewstillery, New Madison Brewing Co., and Righteous Brewing Co. in Madison; Lanthier, Stream Cliff Farm, and Thomas Family wineries in Madison; Big Oaks National Wildlife Refuge north of Madison.

The Drive

The drive begins in the old riverport town of Lawrenceburg and neighboring Greendale. The scent of fermenting mash has hung over this part of the valley since the towns' early days, as the area is known for whiskey production. By 1809 the region's abundant grain and clear, cold well water stimulated whiskey production as the pioneers discovered the ease of transport and profitability of the distilled elixir versus raw grain. As late as 1941, there were still three major distilleries in town. Joseph E. Seagram and Sons was the last remaining distillery before MGP Ingredients purchased it in 2011. MGP produces spirits sold under fifty different brand names and owns Ross & Squibb Distillery in the former Seagram's facilities.

Lawrenceburg to Madison

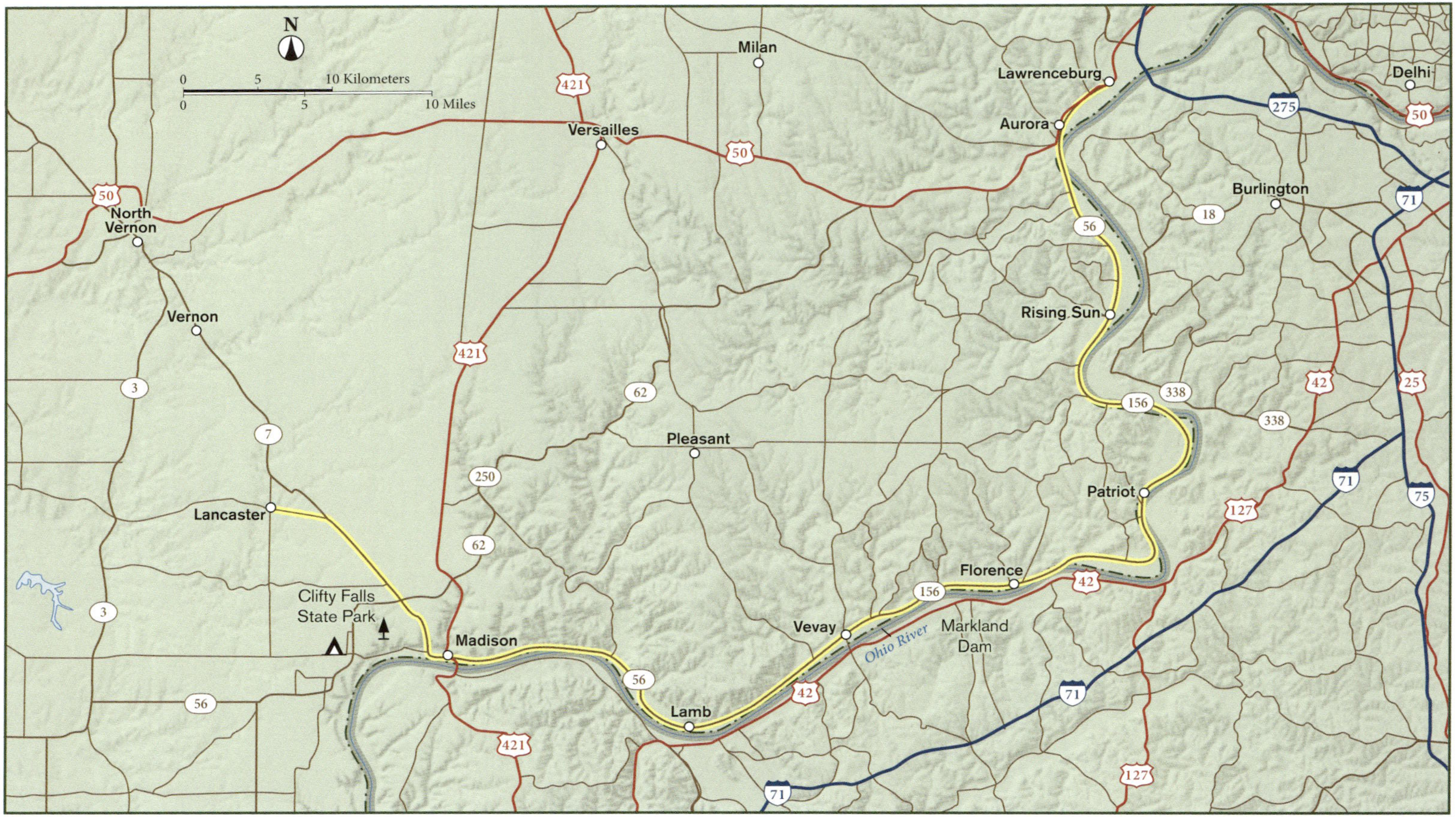

In Greendale turn 0.5 mile north on Nowlin Street to Greendale Cemetery. The cemetery was founded in 1867 on land given to Colonel Zebulon Pike in 1803 for service in the Revolutionary War. His son, Brigadier General Zebulon Montgomery Pike, was the famed explorer of the American West for whom Pikes Peak in Colorado is named.

Lawrenceburg, founded in 1802, is the fourth-oldest city in Indiana. In the heyday of the steamboat era, Lawrenceburg was a favorite port of call.

The architecture of Lawrenceburg is still a remarkable example of a nineteenth-century mercantile center. In 1984 the entire downtown district, bounded by Charlotte, Tate, William, and Elm Streets and the railroad tracks, was added to the National Register of Historic Places and includes more than 250 buildings.

There are at least thirty significant historic buildings in the downtown area. Among many historic structures in Lawrenceburg, the Dearborn County Courthouse on High Street is an exceptional example of Greek Revival architecture. The Dearborn County Historical Society is in the 1818 Vance-Tousey House at 508 High St. It was considered the finest house between Cincinnati and Louisville, a Federal-style structure built with plans brought from England. The 1818 Jesse Hunt three-story brick building at Walnut and High was Indiana's first "skyscraper," an awe-inspiring sight to the pioneers. It now houses a bank. A group of Federal row houses are located at 124–136 E. High St. The commercial Italianate building at 316–318 Walnut was jacked up one story in the nineteenth century.

At 229 Short St., the Queen Anne–style Presbyterian Church was the first congregation ministered by famous abolitionist Henry Ward Beecher, the brother of Harriet Beecher Stowe, author of *Uncle Tom's Cabin*. Beecher was ordained here in 1837 and served as its minister until 1839.

The American Legion at the corner of Front and Second has the Flying Red Horse "Peggy" in a glass case outside the club. The customized Model T Ford fitted with Mobile Oil's iconic Pegasus was built by two World War I vets who wanted a parade vehicle. Peggy's giant wings flapped as she reared on her hind wheels and spun at American Legion parades all over America from 1936 to 1972. She was put out to her glass pasture in 1994.

Amid the collection of historic Lawrenceburg buildings is the Hollywood Casino on Hollywood Boulevard. The immense Las Vegas–style complex boasts one of the world's largest floating casinos, with 150,000 square feet of gaming space.

Two miles south, the town of Aurora was founded in 1804 on a picturesque bluff above the river bend. In its heyday, steamboats constantly pulled to the public dock to unload passengers and load the manufactured goods of the town: foundry work, whiskey, furniture, and caskets.

The downtown area, bounded by Importing, Water, Market, Fifth, and Exporting Streets, is a National Historic District. There are several exceptional examples of Gothic Revival structures in Aurora, commingling with other nineteenth-century styles. They include the 1878 St. John's Lutheran Church at 214 Mechanic St., the mid-1870s First Evangelical Church at 113 Fifth St., and houses at 318 Fourth St. and 403 Judiciary, the latter a Queen Anne hybrid built between 1870 and 1890.

The crown jewel of Aurora is the grand Hillforest Mansion at the end of Main Street. It's as though an enormous steamboat ran aground high on the hillside. Built in 1855 for local financier and industrialist Thomas Gaff, Hillforest served as his family's home until 1926. The circular porches wrapping the semicircular front, the rooftop cupola resembling a steamboat pilot house, the slender columns and arched windows all contribute to the steamboat effect. Designated a National Historic Landmark, the mansion is owned by the Hillforest Foundation and open for public tours.

Even higher on the hillside, the landmark 1810 Veraestau displays more than 200 years of Greek Revival enthusiasm. Original owner Jesse Holman named his home by combining the Latin words for spring, summer, and fall. The house was owned by two families, who maintained the original style through two major renovations, before it was donated to Indiana Landmarks Foundation in 2004.

Veraestau, built in 1810, rests high above the town of Aurora. INDIANA LANDMARKS

At the west edge of town, look for Riverview Cemetery. Laughery Creek is at the southern end of the cemetery, where Mohawk leader Joseph Brant and one hundred warriors attacked and soundly defeated Colonel Archibald Lochry and 107 Pennsylvania volunteers in August 1781. The troops were enroute to join George Rogers Clark. Lochry and approximately half of his troops were killed and the survivors taken prisoner. There is a memorial to the Lochry Massacre in the cemetery, and another at the south end of the new Laughery Creek Bridge (the creek name was misspelled when it was recorded and was never corrected).

The old Laughery Creek Bridge, built in 1878, is an extremely rare iron triple-intersection Whipple through-truss span, hence the nickname Triple Whipple Bridge. It was converted to a pedestrian bridge in 2009 and is the only example of this truss type in the world.

Rising Sun is 6.5 miles west in Ohio County, the smallest county in Indiana at 86 square miles. Platted in 1814, Rising Sun boomed in the 1830s and '40s with as many as 2,500 people thriving in the town. Each spring 300 to 400 flatboats left Rising Sun daily, headed downriver. There were eight factories, two steam-powered mills, three potteries, a newspaper, a clutch of churches, and a seminary for teachers.

Today, the population is about the same. The sprawling Rising Star Casino (formerly the Grand Victoria Casino & Resort by Hyatt) sits a few blocks east of downtown, connected by the town's Riverwalk along Front Street. The casino is decorated like a vintage gambling palace, with gilded corbels and wooden turnings. It has a 300-room hotel, another nonsmoking lodge, an 18-acre Scottish-links-style golf course, and two entertainment venues that have drawn such acts as the Oak Ridge Boys, Charlie Daniels Band, America, and the Guess Who. Unlike the Hollywood Casino boat in Lawrenceburg, the Rising Star boat actually cruises down the river for about a mile and a half before returning.

The Ohio County Historical Society Museum at 212 S. Walnut is a good starting point for a walking tour of the town. Housed in a former plow factory, it has a collection of quilts and farm implements, diverse and sundry music machines, and the town pride: the famous 1920s "Hoosier Boy" speedboat. Be sure the tour guides tell you about Smith Riggs, a local blacksmith who invented the first modern electric chair.

The Ohio County Courthouse, an 1845 Greek Revival structure on Main Street, had no inside stairs until a 1980s restoration.

Perhaps the most unusual business in Rising Sun is a harp factory, relocated here from California in 2000. Housed in a refurbished 1881 building, Rees Harps produces concert-quality stringed instruments that are shipped to customers around the world.

Two blocks south of Main Street on Front Street stands the Empire Hotel, a historic six-room hotel built in 1817 and still serving guests. Next door is the Olde Post Cabin, one of the few original log structures still standing in Rising Sun. Built with rough-hewn exterior logs in the early 1800s, the two-story cabin has been a private residence, hat shop, and post office.

Take IN 156 south out of Rising Sun. The road runs through the floodplain along the Ohio with cabin cruisers and coal barges coursing down the river almost at the level of your car. Sand and gravel quarries dot the roadside.

The Switzerland County line is 4 miles west. A land of steep and rolling hills, the county sits at an elbow of the Ohio. Switzerland County was separated from Dearborn and Jefferson Counties in 1814, at the behest of Swiss-French settlers who migrated to Indiana to pioneer wine production in America. The vineyard prospered, becoming the first commercially successful vineyard in the country. By the mid-nineteenth century, more than 30,000 acres of grapes were in production along Indiana's Ohio River shore, from the eastern border over to the Falls of the Ohio at Louisville, which became known as "The Rhineland of America." By 1880 Indiana was a top-ten grape producer in the nation, but black rot, phylloxera, and the inevitable death knell of Prohibition devastated Indiana production. The industry was moribund until passage of the Indiana Small Winery Act of 1971, which permitted wineries to sell directly to the public. Currently, there are more than 200 wineries, cideries, or meaderies scattered throughout the state and ten winery trails. Ironically, there is only one in Switzerland County.

Ohio River traffic declined through the nineteenth century, and the railroads and major highways passed Switzerland and Ohio Counties by. People migrated to more economically vibrant areas as the soil showed signs of depletion and the river markets dried up. The lack of modern transport deterred large industries and preserved the historic air of the region.

On the right side of the highway, 1.2 miles from the county line, the Federal-style brick Merit-Tandy-Tillotson House sports a balustraded widow's walk on its roof, a somewhat incongruous folly for a one-story cottage. It sits in a stretch of countryside known as Mexico Bottoms that commemorates the Mexican-American War veterans who cleared the bottom of the giant trees.

Patriot, 2.8 miles west, looks worse for wear, as befits a town that has suffered from numerous catastrophes. At one point, Patriot had several mills and distilleries and substantial river traffic. A fire in 1924 destroyed most of the commercial district. The disastrous 1937 flood swept away the wharf, bank, boats, mills, and distilleries, and the town never recovered. Several structures are scattered through the village from Patriot's boom years, including Queen Anne buildings and a couple vernacular buildings worth noting: the tiny whitewashed old stone jail at 106 First St., and a nineteenth-century tavern on Fifth and Front Streets.

At the junction of IN 156 and 250, there is a marker to Patriot native Dr. Elwood Mead, "the engineer who made the desert bloom." He built the Hoover Dam, and Lake Mead was named for him. Traveling south on IN 156, the lowland is called Egypt Bottoms because the fertility of the soil yielded corn crops of biblical proportions. It is an area of upright I-houses (named because they are most often found in states that start with I—Indiana, Illinois, and Iowa), hand-hewn rock walls, and clapboard Country Gothic churches.

Florence, founded in 1817, is 11 miles southwest of Patriot. At one time it was the home of the Anti-Swearing Society which fined its seventy-five members for profanities. West of Florence, the 608-room Belterra Casino Resort & Spa, opened here in 2000, is owned by the same company that operates Hollywood Casino in Lawrenceburg.

The Markland Locks and Dam and generating station are 4.5 miles west. Constructed in 1956 and 1963 near the village of Markland, the dam is 1,416 feet long, with two parallel locks on the Kentucky side of the river that are 110 feet wide. Across the bridge in Kentucky, an observation tower overlooks the locks. An information signboard presents a history of Army Corps of Engineers projects that dammed the Ohio.

Vevay (pronounced VEE-vee), a tidy town with well-kept nineteenth-century buildings, is another river town that deserves a stroll. When architects surveyed Vevay in 1980, they discovered that 86% of the structures in the town were more than 50 years old, and nearly two-thirds were built before 1883.

The Knox House at 302 W. Main has New Orleans–style iron grillwork, as does the Grisard-Sieglitz home at 306 E. Main. The Switzerland County Historical Museum is in a hundred-year-old Presbyterian Church at Main and Market.

At 209 W. Market St., the Ulysses P. Schenck House was built with the best elevations facing the river, the important avenue of the day. Schenck was called the "Hay King" due to his success in dealing timothy hay from the Switzerland County fields downriver on flatboats. The Dufour Cottage to the east is one of several houses in Vevay built by Jean François Dufour. It was Dufour's brother, Jean-Jacque, who established the successful vineyard in Vevay.

The unusual fish scale–shingled Vevay Christian Church on Market was built as a Unitarian Church in 1863. The 1817 Morerod homestead on Arch Street still has a 500-gallon wine cask in the cellar to vint the grapes from builder Jean Daniel Morerod's extensive vineyards. The clapboard Armstrong Tavern at 201 W. Market was built in 1816. Slaves were ferried over daily from Kentucky to work in the tavern in the early days. The Edward Eggleston and George Cary House at 306 W. Main is on the National Register of Historic Places, as is the Old Indiana Theater at the corner of Ferry and Cheapside.

The magnificent 1870s Benjamin Schenck Mansion sits on a hill overlooking the town. It boasts the finest furnishings of the day, including walnut tin- and copper-lined bathtubs. Down at the end of Market Street, Pleasants Rose Mansion Inn bed-and-breakfast is another restored merchant prince home, lavishly furnished with period antiques.

But Vevay's most unique entry in the Historic American Buildings Survey is the Switzerland County Courthouse privy, a hexagonal brick outhouse built in 1864 with a louvered cupola. The courthouse, a Greek Revival structure, is nice too. The basement has a deep cellar that served as a way-stop on the Underground Railroad.

At the west end of town, the contemporary Ogle Haus Hotel is a good place to sit on the terrace and watch the river traffic. The tall stacks of the Markland Generating Plant and the endless lines of passing river barges are a reminder that the Ohio is sometimes known as "America's Ruhr."

Scattered about **Vevay** are goat statues decorated in different ways. They are a tribute to Fred, a white 4-H billy goat that escaped and freely roamed the area for years before dying in 2013. Later that year, someone placed a concrete goat statue on the hillside that Fred frequented. The town has capitalized on its mascot with more goat statues, and the tourism bureau offers numerous goat-themed souvenirs.

Lamb, 16.5 miles west on IN 56, is the site of Indiana's oldest existing brick house, the George Ash House, built at the turn of the eighteenth century. Turn left at the town sign and proceed 0.25 mile to the dead end, then go left 0.3 mile along the river. The upright little house is on the north side of the road.

Cedar Cliffs parallel the highway a few miles west of Lamb, offering a 12-mile view down the river for those energetic enough to make the climb. Four miles farther west, look for an old rusting red crane on the north side of the highway. The roofless, two-story fieldstone house on the hill behind the crane is the home of Chapman Harris. The Underground Railroad came through here, as it did at many places along the river, sheltering the refugees following the North Star. Chapman Harris was an ex-slave who worked as a minister and blacksmith. During the day, he preached of the evils of slavery and the joys of heaven for the righteous. Come nightfall, Chapman Harris went to his anvil on the river shore. As his hammer rang out across the wide waters, the fugitives on the far bank knew it was safe to cross to the other side, and the skiffs set out on the voyage to the promised land of Canada.

Madison, 0.5 mile west, is known as "The Williamsburg of the West." The town was founded in 1810 in a bend where the Ohio curled the farthest to the north. The 133 blocks of Madison's National Historic Landmark District—the longest in the country—are an extraordinary ensemble of Greek Revival, Federal,

Italianate, Queen Anne, Bungalow, and vernacular architecture, most well maintained and in everyday use. While much of vintage Madison is in private hands, there are several outstanding historic buildings open for tours, including the 1844 James F. D. Lanier mansion

By 1839 the pioneering Madison-Indianapolis Railroad, the first railroad in Indiana, conquered the high bluffs that surround the old town and reached the town of Vernon. The 311-foot climb over 1.3 miles was the steepest standard-gauge track in the world. The incline can be seen at the corner of Main and McIntire. The matrix of river, rail, and road funneled the region's raw goods into Madison for manufacture and processing and shipment out into the larger markets.

In a brief period, the town became a bustling industrial city with brick smokestacks belching and dozens of products being produced. There were wagon, tack and spoke factories, shipyards, six wharves, castor- and linseed-oil factories, distilleries, and breweries. Madison was a major pork-packing center, rivaling Cincinnati. By 1850 Madison led the state in manufacturing capital and total number of products shipped. Banks, mansions, stores, and stately churches rose where only wilderness existed a few decades before.

The brick commercial architecture of the downtown area was constructed during Madison's heyday from 1830 to 1850. After that, new railroads linking Louisville, Indianapolis, and Cincinnati de-emphasized river traffic, sending Madison into a slump. A burst of economic activity in the 1870s "modernized" Main Street with cast-iron fronts that added Italianate touches like elaborate cornice brackets. Today, even the bars and cafes are historic: The Historic Broadway Hotel and Tavern at 313 Broadway is Indiana's oldest family tavern, serving customers since 1834. The town is rich with bed-and-breakfasts in lovely old homes.

The Madison Area Convention and Visitors Bureau, 301 E. Main St., has a wealth of information about the town. The 1818 Jeremiah Sullivan House at 304 W. Second is considered one of the finest examples of Federal architecture in the old Northwest Territory. It is open to the public, as is the Schofield House at 217 W. Second St. The 1820 Talbott-Hyatt House has extensive restored gardens and outbuildings.

At Poplar and First Streets, the Shrewsbury House radiates the austere grace of classical antiquity. Magnificently proportioned, the Shrewsbury House has a spectacular spiral staircase that rises through the house's three stories, unsupported except by its own thrust.

Schroeder Saddletree Factory Museum at 106 Milton St. is one of twelve Madison companies from the late 1870s that once made more than 150,000 carved wooden frames for crafting riding saddles.

At 511 W. First St., the grand James F. D. Lanier Mansion overlooks the broad Ohio. The "crown jewel" of Madison's historic district, the Greek Revival structure was considered the finest house on the Ohio in its day. Neo-Corinthian columns soar 30 feet to the 50-foot-long portico, and the meticulously restored interior features a self-supporting spiral staircase from the ground floor to the cupola. The mansion, open to public tours, is a National Historic Landmark managed by the Indiana State Museum & State Historic Sites.

Behind the Lanier House, the charming John Eckert cottage at 510 W. Second St. was built by a local tinsmith in 1872. The octagonal building at 615 W. First St. was Madison's railroad terminal and now houses a museum. The Jacob Shuh House at 718 Main St. is a Greek Revival structure built from 1837 to 1838 and reminiscent of the town houses of Salem and Portsmouth.

Main Street has a fine collection of mid- and late-nineteenth-century commercial buildings, many with Italianate facades. Mulberry Street has a remarkable collection of unaltered 1830s commercial buildings.

Seven miles north of Madison, the Eleutherian College sits proudly on a ridge. Founded by New England Baptist abolitionists, the three-story fieldstone structure built in 1854 was the first college in the United States where African American

Madison's stately Lanier Mansion is among the river town's many historic buildings.

and white students of both genders could study together. To reach the college, travel north from Main Street on Cragmont Street, a.k.a. IN 7, for 7.8 miles. Turn west on IN 250 and drive 2.5 miles to the village of Lancaster. The college building is on the south side of the road.

At the west edge of Madison on IN 62, Clifty Falls State Park has a rugged terrain of deeply cut canyons, waterfalls, scenic walking trails, campgrounds, and a lodge overlooking the Ohio River.

When the nearby Clifty Creek Generating Plant was opened in 1955, it was one of the largest power-generating plants in the world. It burns on average 12,000 tons of coal daily and produces enough electricity to power a city of 1 million people.

3

The Haunts of Young Abe Lincoln

Southern Indiana hills, valleys, and forests

General description: The 47-mile drive winds through the hills of southern Indiana where Abraham Lincoln spent his formative years and where his beloved mother and sister are buried.

Special attractions: Troy, where Lincoln first arrived in Indiana and later argued the law; Lincoln State Park and Lincoln Boyhood National Memorial; Holiday World and Splashin' Safari in Santa Claus; and Lincoln Pioneer Village at Rockport.

Location: Southern Indiana.

Drive route numbers and names: IN 66, 70, 245, and 162; US 231.

Travel season: Summers can be blistering in Spencer County, but the entertainment complex at Santa Claus can offer respite with its water park. The roads are drivable in all but the worst of winter weather.

Camping: Hoosier National Forest (812) 547-7051 at Buzzard Roost, German Ridge, Indiana-Celina Lakes, Saddle Lake, and Tipsaw Lake; Lincoln State Park in Gentryville and Lake Rudolph Resort in Santa Claus.

Services: There are services in Troy, Grandview, Santa Claus, and Rockport.

Nearby attractions: Scenic Lincoln Railway in Tell City; Tell City Brewing Co.; Blue Heron Vineyards in Cannelton; Winzerwald Winery in Bristow; Benedictine monasteries at St. Meinrad and Ferdinand; Huntingburg for antiquing and league baseball; Eagles Wings Zipline in Leopold; Jasper for German culture and food (see Drive 4).

The Drive

Abraham Lincoln arrived in Indiana with his family in 1816 as a 7-year-old boy and trundled down the old buffalo trail by oxen cart to Illinois in 1830 as a robust raw-boned man. "There I grew up," he said of his formative years in Indiana, pioneering on a farm on Little Pigeon Creek. Surrounded by the cabins of Kentucky yeomen like his father, he earned his keep by farming the land and clearing the woods.

The scenic drive begins in Troy, where Lincoln landed with his family in 1816. The Lincolns crossed the Ohio River at Troy on Thompson's Ferry and followed a wagon trail to Hurricane, the township where Thomas Lincoln had staked his claim. The wilderness road passed within 4 miles of the Lincoln homestead, and Thomas felled trees the rest of the way to make a path for the wagon. Abraham Lincoln later said he "never passed through a harder experience than he did going from Thompson's Ferry" to their home site.

Southern Indiana Hills, Valleys, and Forests

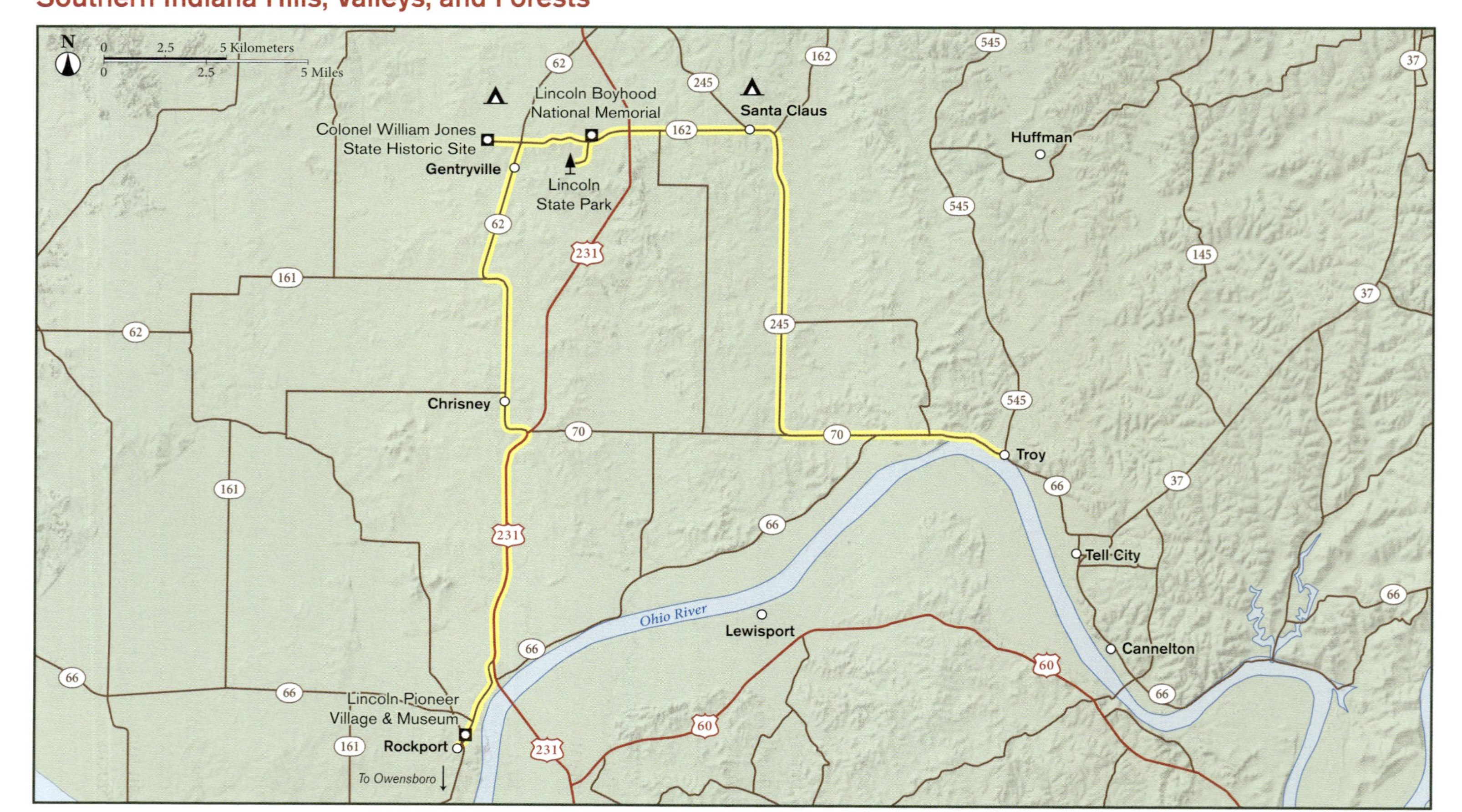

At the age of 17, Abe was back working in Troy, helping on a ferryboat and picking up extra money selling wood for 50 cents a cord to the steamboats. He also hauled passengers out to midstream to catch the passing steamboats in a small skiff he built. A Kentucky ferryman lodged a complaint and hauled Abe into court for operating a ferry without a license. Lincoln, at the time, studied the law and pled his own case before Justice of the Peace Samuel Pate across the river in Kentucky. Lincoln argued that since he only traveled to midstream and never crossed the river, the law didn't apply. He won the case, and his success cemented his interest in the law and learning.

The old trail to Hurricane that the Lincoln family traveled when they arrived in frontier Indiana is no more, so this route will take a more circuitous but ultimately far easier way. Proceed west on IN 66 along the Ohio River 1 mile to Lincoln Ferry Park, where Lincoln toiled on the ferryboat. An open-air shelter overlooking the river makes for a pleasant picnic area.

Continue west on IN 66 for 2.2 miles to IN 70. Stay to the right on IN 70 for 2 more miles to IN 245. Turn right on IN 245 and go 8 miles to Santa Claus.

Being the only town in the country named Santa Claus, the post office prepares for an annual December onslaught of 400,000 pieces of Christmas mail needing the special postmark compared to 13,000 the other eleven months of the year. Beginning in 1914, local postmaster Jim Martin began responding to the "Dear Santa" letters that made their way to Santa Claus. Today, the entire town is involved in the yearly task, responding to up to 30,000 letters from around the world. "Everyone around here is so aware these letters have to be sent out," said Pat Koch, queen mother of the Holiday World and leader of Santa's Elves, the organization that coordinates the letter-writing.

Santa Claus Land, the original name of Holiday World, began in 1946, the first themed amusement park in the world, predating even Knott's Berry Farm in California by a bit. The Kochs' theme park was renamed Holiday World in 1980 and boasts the wooden Raven roller coaster, one of three "world class" roller coasters according to American Coaster Enthusiasts. State-of-the-art amusement rides share the park with charming vintage rides that are lovingly preserved. The park also has a collection of Lincoln memorabilia. The Splashin' Safari water park features a wave pool, water slides, and an action river.

Drive 4.5 miles west on IN 162 to Lincoln State Park and the Lincoln Boyhood National Memorial. The 196-acre complex encompasses the 100-acre farm that Thomas Lincoln sold when the family moved to Illinois in 1830. The Memorial Building houses a museum dedicated to the life and times of Lincoln, a visitor center, and auditoriums, designed with the aesthetics and culture of the Lincolns in mind. The nearby gravesite of Nancy Hanks Lincoln, Abraham's mother, is the focus of the park.

Abraham Lincoln's boyhood home is a national park site, complete with a replica log cabin. National Park Service

The National Park Service developed the Living Historical Farm in 1967, one of only two in the park system. The farm is a well-interpreted working pioneer farm, portraying life on the Indiana frontier. Self-sufficiency was the rule, with nearly everything consumed on the farm needing to be grown or made.

Across the road, Lincoln State Park is an extensive 1,750-acre recreation area with two lakes, 240 campsites, cabins, hiking trails, and a nature center. Many of the park's original structures and trails were constructed as part of the Depression-era Civilian Conservation Corps (CCC) program.

The 1,500-seat Lincoln Amphitheater within the park presents theatrical performances such as *Young Abe Lincoln*, Broadway musicals, tribute bands, and other musical acts under the management of the Indiana Destination Development Corporation.

Nearby, a historical reproduction of the log-constructed Little Pigeon Primitive Baptist Church is erected on the site of the church that served the Lincolns as a spiritual haven. The gravestone of Sarah Lincoln Grigsby, Abe's beloved older sister, is in the church cemetery. Sarah died in 1828 during childbirth. She and her stillborn child are buried together.

Proceed 1.4 miles west on IN 162 to a marker for the site of the James Gentry homestead. Gentry was a pioneer entrepreneur, the founder of Gentryville, and a friend of the Lincoln family. The crossroads hamlet of Gentryville is 0.1 mile farther west. For several decades, Gentryville has been most famous for the creative antique clutter of Polen's Antique Shak, housed in an old general store, and other buildings at the junction of US 231. It was at this crossroads that Abe Lincoln began his political education, absorbing the banter and bluster of the days' issues at Gentry's Store as the Whigs of the area debated the Democrats.

Turn south on US 231 to the next road west, County Road 1575N, and proceed 0.7 mile to the Colonel William Jones House, Lincoln's political tutor. The 1834 Federal-style brick home reflects Jones's economic position while his neighbors were housed in log cabins. Lincoln State Park oversees the Jones House, which is listed on the National Register of Historic Places.

Return to the intersection of US 231 and turn south, traveling 17 miles south to Rockport. Before reaching Rockport, the mammoth AK Steel Plant looms, which is having a dramatic economic impact on the area. Twin 1,040-foot towers and boiling vapors in the distance are part of the AEP (American Electric Power) generating plant. In 2021 AEP announced plans to shut down the two coal-fired units.

The early nineteenth-century settlers of Rockport clustered at the bottom of the bluff on which Rockport now sits. The riverside bluff is also where Abraham Lincoln cast off on a flatboat journey to New Orleans. A marker at the intersection of South First Street and Second Street commemorates his trip to the South. In 1828 James Gentry decided to send trade goods down the river to New Orleans, and he contracted 19-year-old Abraham Lincoln to work on the 65-foot-long flatboat. During the three-month journey, Lincoln saw slavery firsthand, first along the plantations on the Mississippi River where they stopped to trade, and later in the New Orleans slave markets. To return to Indiana, Lincoln and his crew churned back up the rivers on one of the steamboats. If their trip was like most, it probably took about nine days.

The **1867 Mathias Sharp House** at 319 Second is listed on the National Register of Historic Places. The Federal-style Rockport Inn at 130 S. Third was built as a private residence in 1855. The current Spencer County Courthouse features a large interior stained-glass dome. Built in 1921, it is the county's fifth. A marker at Second and Main Streets denotes the site of the Rockport Tavern where Lincoln spent the night in 1844 when he was stumping for Whig candidates.

Just south of Ninth and Main, the Lincoln Pioneer Village is in the city park. The 4-acre plot has an inn, church, school, law office, store, and homes. A museum was added in 1950 that includes one of Thomas Lincoln's cherry-inlaid corner cupboards, his specialty as a frontier craftsman. The Pioneer Village was built in the 1930s by the Works Progress Administration and was added to the National Register of Historic Places in 1998.

South of Rockport on US 231, the nostalgic Holiday Drive-In Movie Theater shows the latest Hollywood films on six huge screens every night in the summer and on weekends in the fall.

4

Land of the Indiana Germans

The heartland of Indiana's German colonies

General description: A 48-mile drive through the heart of Indiana's Old Country, where small towns and farmland retain its traditional appeal due to the strong, family-oriented German culture and the importance of the Catholic Church in the area.

Special attractions: The Ohio River at Troy, St. Meinrad Archabbey and Monastery, Monastery Immaculate Conception, Jasper's Germantown culture and Schnitzelbank Restaurant, Huntingburg's Victorian delights.

Location: Southern Indiana.

Drive route numbers and names: IN 545, 62, and 162; US 231.

Travel season: The route is along all-weather roads. Fall, with the magnificent hardwood forests, is a good time to visit. The region's festivals bring in thousands to share in the fun.

Camping: Patoka Lake (812) 685-2464; Ferdinand State Forest (812) 827-2857; and Sun Outdoors Lake Rudolph (812) 937-4458 in Santa Claus.

Services: There are services in Troy, St. Meinrad, Ferdinand, Jasper, and Huntingburg, as well as numerous spots along the route.

Nearby attractions: Patoka Lake; Holiday World and Splashin' Safari theme park; Lincoln Boyhood National Memorial and Lincoln State Park; Patoka Lake Brewing in Birdseye; St. Benedict's Brew Works in Ferdinand and Jasper; and Yard Goat Artisan Ales in Huntingburg; Spirit of Jasper Train; Dubois County Museum in Jasper.

The Drive

In 1815 Virginian families platted Troy at the mouth of the Anderson River, one of the earliest towns below the Falls of the Ohio at Louisville.

The Nester House at 300 Water St. is a remnant of Troy's nineteenth-century commercial heyday along the riverfront. The rough-cut sandstone Greek Revival building dates to 1863 and has served as a grocery, tavern, hotel, museum, and now a private residence named Riverplace. Local lore has it that the basement served as a way stop on the Underground Railroad and featured a tunnel from the cellar to a barn 2 blocks away.

A Greek Revival house on Market Street at Harrison was built in 1840, as was the gable-fronted Greek Revival in the next block east and I-house at 525 Walnut St. Vintage structures ranging from Queen Anne to Craftsman are dotted throughout the tiny town.

Indiana's German colonies

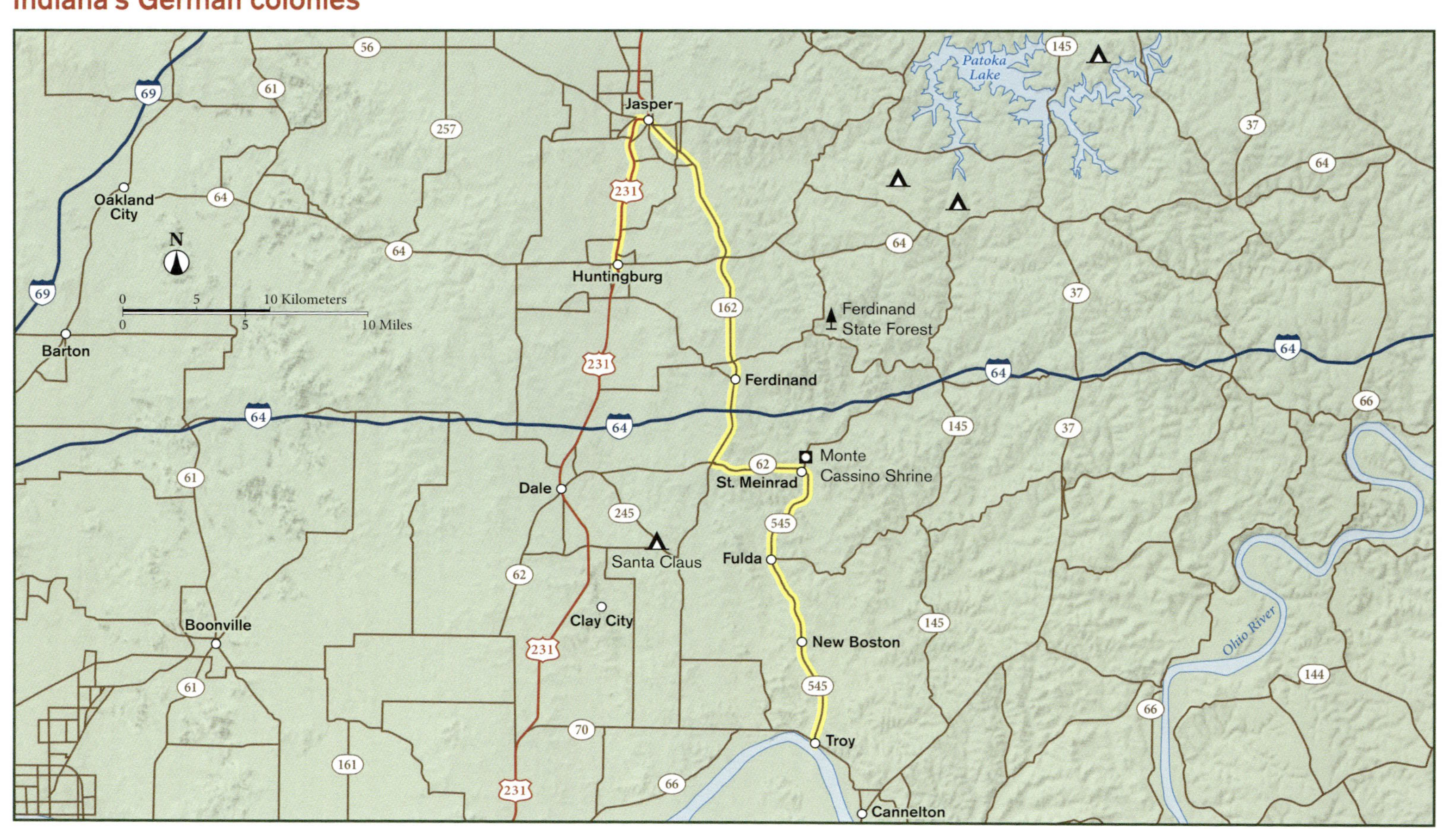

The Nester House in Troy has been a grocery, tavern, hotel, and private home since 1844. Jane Hayden

Troy was Perry County's first seat but lost the honor when the county was reorganized in 1818. The town continued to prosper through the nineteenth century as a port town for the road that ran north along the Anderson River into the German colonies. St. Pius V Church, with its 142-foot bell tower, is the most visible landmark in the town. Built from 1881 to 1884 to serve the area's German Catholics, the new church replaced one built in 1847 when waves of German immigrants were arriving at the waterfront.

The 18-foot-high Christ of the Ohio statue stands atop a bluff overlooking the Ohio River. It was fabricated from Colorado travertine limestone by an ex–German prisoner of war, Herbert Jogerst, who returned to Indiana to practice his art after being incarcerated in Kentucky during World War II. It has been a landmark for boaters on the Ohio since its dedication in 1957. The statue is located on Market Street, 1 block north of IN 66 off Spring Street.

There were once many potteries along the river, across the road from the statue. Potters used local clay for much of the nineteenth century, manufacturing utilitarian Bennington-type pottery.

The bluff affords a 30-mile view of the river. The hilltop is known as Fulton's Bluff because Robert Fulton's brother Abraham died building a house on the hill when an enormous log rolled onto him. There is a marker to Fulton on the west edge of Troy. He arrived in Troy in 1814 to build a woodyard and manage his brother's coal mine. It is said when Robert Fulton's smoke-belching *New Orleans* puffed past Troy in 1811, the Troy residents took to the bushes in fear. Abraham Fulton is buried in the Troy Cemetery at the end of Washington Street, the first European buried in what was an old Indian burial ground.

IN 545 North follows the trail that pioneer priest Father Joseph Kundek, a Croatian, blazed along the Anderson River to the German colonies he founded. The towns of Fulda, Ferdinand, and Jasper were laid out a day's ox cart ride apart, or about 10 miles.

The New Boston Tavern, 3 miles north of Troy on IN 545, is an old roadhouse serving regional fare like smoked pork chops and catfish fiddlers on the weekends.

A few miles north on IN 545, the 150-foot steeple of the mid-nineteenth-century St. Boniface Catholic Church rises from the landscape. The Romanesque interior has sixteen stained-glass windows, a 535-pipe organ dating from 1898, and seating for 300 on oak pews installed in 1896. Come summertime, the parish puts on a renowned turtle soup dinner, with hundreds of gallons being served in a few hours.

Louie's Tavern in Fulda is another roadside attraction, regionally famous for its turtle soup and boasting of "the best pizza in southern Indiana."

The Archabbey of St. Meinrad, 5 miles north, appears to have been levitated from the Fatherland. The Benedictine monastery was begun in 1854 when two priests came from Switzerland to minister to the growing German population. Their work continues today. In 1872 the monks began construction of the sandstone complex of buildings you see today. The **Archabbey's Church of Our Lady of Einsiedeln**, with its 168-foot steeples, was built from 1899 to 1907. Local craftsmen and monks carved most of the stone with sandstone from a local quarry.

The monastery at St. Meinrad remains one of the great centers for Gregorian chant, a singing style that dates to the Middle Ages. The monks' daily singing of the medieval Gregorian chants rises into the lofts of the vaults. The monks' daily religious services, from 5:30 a.m. to Vespers at 6 p.m., are open to the public.

Half a mile north of St. Meinrad on IN 62, the tiny sandstone chapel at Monte Cassino is a paean to devotion, the site of an annual pilgrimage commemorating relief from an 1871–1872 smallpox epidemic. Each January since that date, hundreds of monks, seminarians, townspeople, and other devotees have climbed to the tiny chapel at the top of the hill to offer prayers of thanks for their miracle. The interior of the church is adorned with verses from the Litany of the Blessed Virgin Mary that were painted by German artist Gerhard Lamers in 1931.

The companion monastery of the Benedictine nuns, Monastery Immaculate Conception, is located about 6 miles away in Ferdinand. It can be reached by driving west on IN 62 to IN 162, then north 2 miles to Ferdinand. The massive redbrick Romanesque has stood on the hill in Ferdinand since 1915, added to structures that were built from 1883 to 1887. Trimmed in Bedford limestone and Italian terra-cotta, the building has an interior dome that rises 87 feet above the floor. The monastery and its grounds were listed as a National Historic District in 1983.

Ferdinand is among the more traditional towns in the region. *Indiana: A Guide to the Hoosier State*, written by the Works Progress Administration's Indiana Writers Project (1941), notes, "Ferdinand is a German Catholic community retaining the language and customs of the Fatherland. English, of course, is understood and spoken, as is a strange admixture of the two languages. Rathskeller signs bear names such as Kunkler, Schnellenberger, and Hoppenjans. Many of the citizens carve and wear wooden shoes, or fashion wooden beer mugs and holders for pretzels."

Jasper, the region's largest town, is 13 miles north on IN 162. It was laid out in 1830 as the county seat at a good mill site on the banks of the Patoka River. By 1841 there were a hundred German families in the vicinity of Jasper. The dense stands of oak that surrounded the town formed the basis of the town economy

The redbrick Monastery Immaculate Conception in Ferdinand has been home to Benedictine nuns for more than 100 years.

as Jasper became the nation's wood-office-furniture capital by the next century. The Jasper Desk Company began in 1876 and is still the nation's oldest operating furniture factory but now part of the Jasper Group. Kimball International Inc. of piano and furniture fame is headquartered here, as are a number of other well-respected furniture manufacturers.

The heart of the town is St. Joseph Catholic Church on Newton Street between 11th and 13th Streets. It is a tall, brooding, brown sandstone structure built between 1867 and 1880 by the parishioners and topped by a 235-foot-high bell tower designed to look like London's Big Ben. The walls are 4 to 6 feet thick, and the foundation is 10 feet deep. Swiss stained glass, Austrian mosaics, carved oak pews, and Italian marble altars grace the interior. To the south of the church, the first Deliverance Cross was erected in 1848 by George Bauman, who survived a raging ocean storm by promising to erect the statue in exchange for divine intercession. The original was destroyed by lightning in 1928, and the current cross was erected in 1932.

The Gramelspacher-Gutzweiler House on 11th Street between Newton and Main is the oldest house in town and is listed on the National Register of Historic Places. Built in 1849, the Federal-style, two-story brick building was designated the state's most imposing Federal structure by the sagacious architectural historian Wilbur Peat. The stepped gables are a throwback to Jacobean and Flemish buildings, seldom seen on Federal-style buildings of this age and location.

The town square is the site of several Strassenfest activities, Jasper's frenetic German festival. Dubois County Courthouse on the square was built in 1909 and 1910 to replace an 1845 structure. The John Opel House, built in 1850, also known as the Green Tree Inn on St. James Street at the south edge of town on IN 162, is another fine Federal brick building on the National Register. Green Tree Antiques, located in buildings on the premises, is one of the best shops in the region. Nearby on IN 162, on the Vincennes University regional campus, the Indiana Baseball Hall of Fame honors Hoosier baseball greats. The dedication in 1979 was attended by Yankee great Mickey Mantle.

Another Jasper lodestone is the glockenspiel-topped Schnitzelbank Restaurant at 393 Third Ave. (IN 162). The original Schnitzelbank opened in 1903 but was replaced in 1971 with a new building. The restaurant has served specialties like beef rouladen, sauerbraten, Wiener schnitzel, kassler rippchen, turnip slaw, and beer in goldfish bowl–sized glasses. It is the best in Indiana German cooking.

A 75-acre urban renewal project turned a private nine-hole golf course and the surrounding woodlands into the Parklands of Jasper, featuring walking trails, ponds, a tree fort, a splash park, and a 120-seat pavilion.

Huntingburg is 7 miles south on IN 231, another small German manufacturing town, specializing in furniture and decorative arts. The many brick homes date from the days when the town brickyards bustled with orders. The brick William Geiger Home, 511 Geiger St., was built in 1854 and 1855. The town's pride is the restored Italianate Huntingburg Town Hall, built in 1866, and Fire Engine House at 311 Geiger St., scene of everything from civic business to wedding receptions. It was listed on the National Register of Historic Places in 1975.

The Victorian Fourth Street is the home of several well-stocked antique shops. The vintage architecture of the street has been an attraction in several movies including *A League of Their Own*, starring Geena Davis, Madonna, and Tom Hanks, which celebrated the women's baseball leagues of the 1940s and 1950s. The filming of the baseball movie prompted an extensive restoration of Huntingburg's League Stadium, now the home field for the Prospect League's Dubois County Bombers. The semi-pro games are held from late May to mid-August.

5

Hoosier Forest Loop

Along the scenic Ohio River and into the rugged uplands

General description: The 138-mile loop courses through Perry and Crawford Counties' charming Ohio River towns and hamlets and then up through the Hoosier National Forest and the Crawford Upland, a region of forests, caves, and scenic rivers. A portion of the drive is along the Ohio River Scenic Route.

Special attractions: The historic Swiss-German town of Tell City; Cannelton, an early Industrial Revolution town with its famous cotton mill; historic southern Perry County; the Hoosier National Forest; Leavenworth's Overlook Restaurant; nationally renowned Wyandotte and Marengo Caves; scenic Blue River.

Location: Southern Indiana.

Drive route numbers and names: IN 37, 62, 64, 66, and 166, and I-64.

Travel season: The route is on curvy and hilly two-lane state highways through the most dramatic topography in the state. The roads are drivable in all but the worst of winter weather. The Hoosier National Forest offers great flowering tree displays in the spring and a phantasmagoria of fall color.

Camping: O'Bannon Woods State Park (812) 738-8232 near Corydon; Newton-Stewart State Recreation Area (812) 685-2464 at Patoka Lake near Birdseye; Dubois County Park (812) 482-2434 at Huntingburg; Ferdinand State Forest (812) 827-2857 near Ferdinand.

Services: Gas, food, and lodging are available in Tell City, Cannelton, Derby, and Leavenworth. There is gas and food at Rocky Point and Marengo and numerous places along the route.

Nearby attractions: Holiday World and Splashin' Safari; Spencer and Dubois Counties' German-flavored towns and villages.

The Drive

The drive starts in Tell City, founded in 1858 as a Swiss-German manufacturing community and named after the thirteenth-century Swiss hero William Tell. In 1857 a group known as the Swiss Colonization Society purchased 4,154 acres of land between Corydon and Troy to create a planned community.

Almost 50 years earlier, it was the site of the first coal extraction west of the Appalachians. In 1809 an associate of steamboat inventor Robert Fulton, Nicholas Roosevelt (great-uncle of President Theodore Roosevelt), spotted the coal seam while descending the Ohio by flatboat to scout out fuel for Fulton's maiden steamboat voyage down the river 2 years later. Roosevelt contracted with the locals to

Along Ohio and the Rugged Uplands

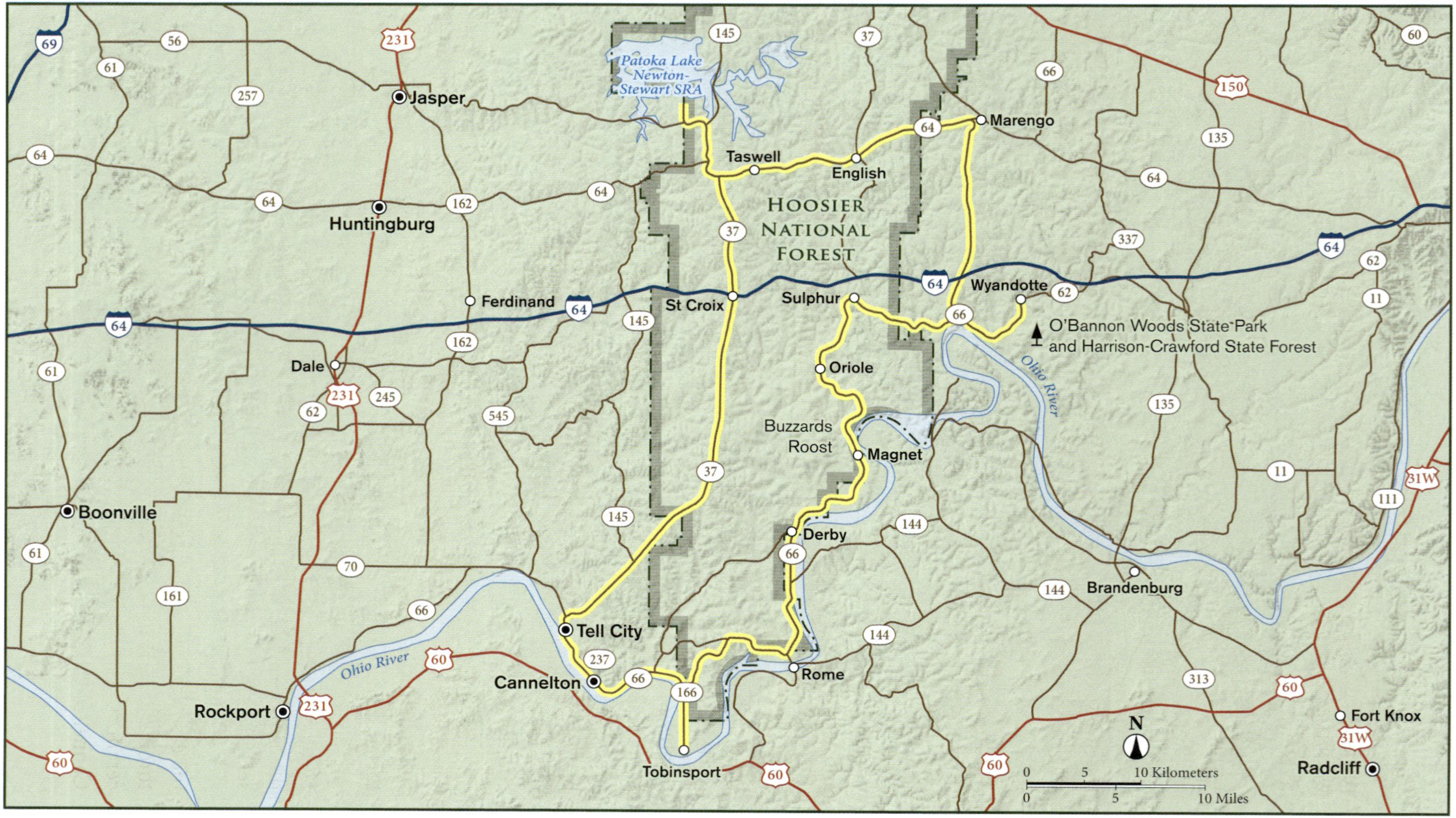

dig out the coal. The locals piled it on the riverbank, where the coal remained until Robert Fulton's steamboat *New Orleans* chuffed down the stream on the way to New Orleans.

When the Swiss arrived, they laid out the city in 400 town blocks with 7,600 residential and garden lots. By 1885 the town bustled with more than two dozen factories, including flour and grain mills, a plow and wagon factory, breweries, a distillery, furniture makers, sawmills, and brickyards.

Tell City's 80-foot-wide, 2-mile-long Main Street trumpets the ambitions of the Swiss settlers. The grand boulevard, wide enough to turn a horse team and wagon, was to be the main thoroughfare for the city.

The Perry County Visitor and Convention Bureau is in the Southern Railroad Depot at 333 Seventh St. The Tell City Industrial Historic District encompasses most of the south end of the city's business district from Blum to Humbolt and is a collection of industrial buildings dating from 1860 to the 1960s. The William Tell Woodcrafter building on Seventh Street has flood-level marks painted on the northwest corner of the building, showing the levels of the 1883, 1884, 1907, 1913, and 1937 floods.

The brick-and-limestone City Hall, built in 1896 at Main and Mozart Streets, was a tad large for a city hall, but Tell City anticipated wresting the county seat from next-door Cannelton—which they did, but not until 100 years later. Parts of the building were used through the decades as a school, library, church, and town theater.

The Tell City Pretzel Company, which began making traditional German pretzels here in 1858, was sold in 2009 and has relocated to nearby Jasper. The hand-twisted pretzels are a teeth-challenging bit of yesteryear. They are still made the old-fashioned way with a closely guarded recipe and shipped all over the country.

There are several fine examples of commercial architecture on Main Street. The Victorian flourishes reflect the burst of affluence that followed the arrival of the railroad. The 1950s glass and stainless-steel facades reflect the florescence of the auto era, as does the 1955 Frostop Drive-In at 947 Main.

Sitting obliquely on a rise above the uniformly level surroundings, the Old Stone House at 1239 13th St. predates the right-angle planning of the Swiss. It is the earliest house in town, a double-pen constructed of rough-cut sandstone. It served as an early meetinghouse and school.

Cannelton is a mile east of Tell City on IN 66, founded in 1837 to exploit the easily mined coal for steamboats and manufacturers. Cannelton prospered through the nineteenth century with coal mining, brick yards, and pottery and ceramic tile manufacturers. The most important industry, however, was the Cannelton Cotton Mill, founded in 1849. The austere sandstone building with

Cannelton's Cotton Mill, built before the Civil War, has been converted to apartments. LINCOLN HILLS DEVELOPMENT CORP.

100-foot Italianate spires still looms over the town today. The cotton mill was the largest industrial building in pre–Civil War Indiana. The mill is listed on the Registry of Historic American Engineering Records and the National Register of Historic Places. In 1991 it was listed as a National Historic Landmark and has since been converted to apartments.

The town still bears the mark of the early New Englanders. The Cannelton Historic District is bounded by Richardson, Fourth, Washington, and Adams Streets and includes examples of architecture from 1837 to 1936. The spare mill building and the fine ashlar stone houses on IN 66 (Seventh Street) speak of the aesthetics and architectural traditions of New Hampshire. In use since 1869, the Free School—also known as Myers Elementary—is the oldest school building in continuous use in the United States. At the corner of Sixth and Taylor Streets, it is part of the Cannelton School system. The congregation of the 1845 St. Luke's Church at 101 East Third St. were early recyclers. The windows are from a church in England, circa 1800, and the congregation salvaged the bell from the steamboat *Major Barbour*, which sank in the Ohio River off Troy in 1848 after colliding with another steamboat, the *Paul Jones*. The church is listed on the National Register of Historic Places.

The Perry County Courthouse was built in 1896 of yellow brick and Bedford limestone. Cannelton wrested the county seat from Rome in 1859 but lost it to archrival Tell City in 1994. The stately sandstone St. Michael Church at Eighth and Washington Streets was started in 1858 for the German Catholics in the town and completed 12 years later. The 1937 flood inundated the town, filling some of the buildings with water up to the second floor. At one point, a local man rowed through town, towing a pair of swimming 400-pound hogs behind him.

The Bob Cummings Bridge at the east edge of town is named after a Cannelton newspaperman. It leads to Hawesville, Kentucky's Riverview Restaurant on Old Highway 60 East, which serves regional fare on an overlook over the Cannelton Locks and Dam.

Proceed east 1.1 miles on IN 66 from Cannelton to the Cannelton Locks and Dam. Replacing three smaller dams upstream, they were built between 1963 and 1974 for $99.6 million, taking as much concrete to build as 70 miles of interstate highway. The high-lift dam created a vast, 114-mile-long, 87,000-acre lake that extends to Louisville, the longest on the Ohio.

The riverbanks begin to flatten in this section of the drive, and the bottoms are furrowed into rich corn and tobacco fields. Proceed east on IN 66 about 0.8 mile to the Lafayette Spring marker where the steamboat *Mechanic*, carrying Revolutionary War hero Marquis de Lafayette, snagged a floating tree and shipwrecked on a dark night in May 1825.

IN 166, 1.6 miles farther east of the marker, runs down the Tobinsport peninsula, the earliest settlement in the county, dating from 1802. In 1960 a Chicago-Miami flight carrying sixty-three people fell apart in midair and crashed into a hillside soybean field. The plane hit the ground at 600 mph, burying the nose 50 feet deep. Parts were strewn from German Ridge to Gatchel 10 miles north. Proceed 1.6 miles down IN 166 to Millstone Road, then turn east a mile to the Air Crash Memorial.

Rome, 10 miles east on IN 66 from the IN 166 turnoff, was Perry County's first seat of government, founded in 1818. The stately public square that surrounds the classical brick courthouse reflects the town's early importance. The Rome courthouse was built between 1818 and 1822, a Federal-style building based on the new state capitol at Corydon. It is listed on the National Register of Historic Places and is considered the state's oldest existing courthouse.

The Connor and Shoemaker cemeteries dating from early in the nineteenth century have exceptional folk art–carved gravestones. The Conner cemetery is located at the end of the river road to the north of the village. The Shoemaker cemetery is 2 miles west of Rome.

Northwest of town, German Ridge Road runs north 3.2 miles to the German Ridge Recreation Area in the Hoosier National Forest, a rugged landscape palisaded with spectacular cliffs. This was the first campground built by the Depression-era Civilian Conservation Corps (CCC) in the Hoosier National

Forest. This county road to German Ridge follows the earliest Indian and pioneer trails in the region, running from Vincennes to the Sinking Creek in Kentucky across from Rome.

The farm of Nancy Alice Martin is 1.5 miles east. Martin returned home in 1929 after a celebrated career as Alice DiGarmo, circus trapeze artist. In 1934 hired-hand Ernest Wright argued with her over back wages of $2.75. Evidently, the employee conference was not to Wright's liking as he slit Martin's throat with a folding pocketknife and buried her in the barnyard, where her body was discovered a week later. Martin is buried in the Lower Cummings Cemetery 2 miles to the north.

Proceed on IN 66 to Derby, a tiny town laid out in 1835. Named after Derby, Ireland, it prospered as a river port, shipping lumber-related products such as barrels, chairs, and railroad ties. In the town's heyday, there were 103 people, three stores, two banks, and two saloons. A disastrous fire in 1893 ended its golden age. After that the town was a declining spot on the river until an influx of people building second homes began to have an impact in the 1970s and 1980s. Today, there are several pristine riverside cabins for rent and recreational facilities in the area.

The Hoosier National Forest's Tell City District surrounds the area, with 80 miles of hiking trails, numerous lakes and ponds, hundreds of camping spots, and eight mountain biking trails. The entire county is a bicyclist's haven with hundreds of miles of quiet country lanes and trails to tour. A fine bike touring map is available through the tourism information office in Tell City. The Mano Point Fishing Area's boat ramp is in constant use, launching craft to cruise the river's 18,000-acre Cannelton Pool. Oil Creek is a bayou-like canoeing stream, a pristine home to thousands of waterfowl. The Mulzer County Park in Derby offers a shady riverside picnic area.

Magnet is a bucolic little spot on the river 7.5 miles east of Derby off IN 66. The Magnet Overlook north of town is a nice picnic location, affording a long sweep down the river. It is a particularly good vantage point to watch the river traffic, including the giant excursion boats like the *Delta Queen* and *American Queen* when they make their regal way down the waterway.

In August 1865 the steamship *Argosy III*, carrying home a roster of mustered-out Civil War veterans, ran aground in a storm, killing ten Union soldiers. Their ten white grave markers can be seen, along with a historical marker, 0.5 mile south of Magnet along the river.

A few miles upriver, the US Forest Service maintains Buzzard Roost Recreation Area as a scenic overlook. In 1857 a slaughterhouse and commercial smokehouse were built nearby. Since only half of a carcass could be used for smoking, the balance became the provender for the flocks of buzzards who were attracted to the site. Today, it is a good place to spot bald eagles.

Return to **Magnet**, turn right (northwest) on Parks Road, and drive 1.5 miles to the former Sacred Heart Catholic Church, which was built in 1837 and served parishioners until the mid-1970s. It now operates as a community center that bills itself as "Perry County's least exclusive gated community."

Continue past the church on Parks Road to Ultra Road and turn left to reconnect with IN 66. Drive 13 miles north to the Crawford-Perry county line.

The two counties have been among the poorest along the Ohio River shore from Pittsburgh down to Cairo. However, they are among the richest in the state in natural beauty, both above and below ground. Half of Crawford County's acreage is forested, with more than 30,000 acres in state and national forests; there are more than 60,000 acres of Hoosier National Forest land in neighboring Perry. Tourism is rapidly becoming an important part of the economy.

The ghost spa of Sulphur Springs is just north of the county line, one of the bustling mineral water spas that flourished in Crawford County at the turn of the century. The White Sulphur Spring Hotel, a three-story structure that served up to 250 health seekers at a time, prospered for years before burning in 1909. As late as the 1940s, Sulphur Springs was still a popular resort, with cabins and rooms in private homes.

IN 66 connects with IN 62 in Sulphur, 1.4 miles north, which has a general store selling gas, refreshments, and Uncle Donnie's Chili.

Turn south on IN 62 and drive 6.5 miles, then stay right on East Indian Hollow Road to the intersection with South Fredonia Road. Turn right and drive 1.5 miles to Fredonia, Leavenworth's longtime rival for ascendancy in the county. **Fredonia** was the **Crawford County** seat from 1822 to 1843. Despite its picturesque setting, Fredonia never prospered because the steep cliffs that provided scenic views were too precipitous to construct a landing on the Ohio River.

Backtrack to IN 62 and drive 1.5 miles to reconnect with IN 66. Turn right toward Leavenworth.

Leavenworth basks high on an Ohio River bluff. The original town was founded in 1818 and became one of the principal shipping ports along the Ohio River, but after a 1937 flood devastated the town, it was moved uphill. A tidy town of frame houses, most dating from construction in the 1930s and 1940s, Leavenworth sports antique and craft shops and Stephenson's General Store on the town square, which all invite browsing. The Overlook Restaurant at the western edge of town has been a landmark for many decades, offering Hoosier-style cooking with the best view on the Indiana shore. The Dock Restaurant and Bar is another popular dining spot, located at the corner of Dock and Front Streets near the Leavenworth boat ramp.

O'Bannon Woods State Park is 7 miles east, a 2,300-acre property that includes the world-renowned Wyandotte Caves, home of some of America's largest subterranean rooms and columns. Two tours are offered, from a short introductory tour of Little Wyandotte Cave to the Big Wyandotte Cave tour, which takes visitors past rare twisted and spiraled cave formations to one of the world's largest underground structures: Monument Mountain.

O'Bannon Woods is located within the 24,000-acre Harrison-Crawford State Forest. Across the road from the caves, the park and forest complex features 80 miles of horse trails and eleven hiking trails, including the long-distance Adventure Trail. Campgrounds and cabins are available for rent. The Blue River, named for its clear, spring-fed water, courses through the hill country, past caves and bluffs and wooded glades, foremost among Indiana's Natural and Scenic River System. "The Blue is the most natural stream of its size in Indiana," renowned ecologist Alton Lindsey wrote in the 1960s, and it remains so today. The stream is the only habitat in Indiana of the hellbender, a giant salamander that can reach 15 to 20 inches in length. The hellbender is a flabby, wrinkled specimen with a wide head that is among the largest salamanders in the world.

Wyandotte Caves has some of the largest underground structures in America.

Return to IN 66 North at the west edge of Leavenworth and drive 12 miles north to Marengo, home of another famous Indiana cave. Discovered in 1883, Marengo Cave, with enormous cavern rooms like the Queen's Palace and the Crystal Palace, is one of the nation's most beautiful caves and was designated a National Natural Landmark by the National Park Service. There are two tours through the cave, and the cave operators recently added a digitized historical presentation in one of the caverns. The cave facility also offers canoeing, horseback trail riding, hiking, fishing, and a picnic area. Marengo Cave features courses on cave exploration, a cave simulator, gemstone mining, and a climbing tower.

Milltown on the Blue River is 5 miles east of Marengo on IN 64. Cave Country Canoes rents hundreds of canoes and kayaks for trips down the limestone-bluffed valley.

Proceed west 16 miles from Marengo on IN 64 through **Taswell**, where the state highway merges with IN 37. Taswell was supposed to be named Laswell after a pioneer family, but the US Post Office misspelled the name when it established a station there in 1882, and the name stuck. Continue west to just northeast of Eckerty.

Patoka Lake, Indiana's second-largest lake, is 3.5 miles north of **Eckerty** on IN 145. The US Army Corps of Engineers partnered with the Indiana DNR to create the 8,800-acre lake by damming the Patoka River, at a cost of $65 million. Besides the lake itself, there are four state recreational areas around the lake covering an additional 1,700 acres devoted to wildlife. The Newton-Stewart State Recreation Area on IN 145 north of Eckerty offers nature interpretation in its solar-heated center, along with camping, swimming, and boat launching.

Drive 7 miles south from Eckerty on IN 37 to I-64 and pass under the four-lane highway to St. Croix. **Holy Cross Catholic Church**, built in 1855, is the lone landmark in St. Croix.

Tell City is 23 miles south. There are four Hoosier National Forest lakes off IN 37—Celina, Indian, Tipsaw, and Saddle—all offering a pleasant break from the road.

The turnoff for the French-Belgium hamlet of Leopold, named after King Leopold of Belgium, is 8 miles south of the IN 37 intersection with I-64. The Gothic Revival **St. Augustine Catholic Church** was built between 1866 and 1873. A statue of the Virgin Mary holding baby Jesus was carved in Luxemburg and still stands in the church.

Proceed south on IN 37 to the loop conclusion at Tell City.

6

The Road to Utopia

Urban Evansville to historic New Harmony

General description: The 38-mile drive courses through the lowlands of southwestern Indiana, from the bustling city of Evansville through the Victorian river port of Mount Vernon to the renowned wetlands of Hovey Lake. The tour concludes in the early 19th-century Utopian town of New Harmony.

Special attractions: Angel Mounds State Historic Site; Mesker Park Zoo and Botanic Garden; Bally's Evansville casino riverboat; Evansville Museum of Arts, History & Science; Children's Museum of Evansville; Evansville African American Museum; Evansville Wartime Museum; Reitz Home; Wesselman Woods Nature Preserve; and the nationally celebrated historic town of New Harmony.

Location: Extreme southwestern Indiana.

Drive route numbers and names: IN 66, 62, and 69.

Travel season: The roads are drivable in all but the worst of winter weather. The attractions at New Harmony are open year-round.

Camping: Harmonie State Park (812) 682-4821 near New Harmony; Burdette Park (812) 435-5602 and Rocky Falls RV Park (812) 746-7907 near Evansville; Weather Rock Campground (812) 867-3401 near Haubstadt.

Services: There are full services in Evansville, Mount Vernon, and New Harmony, and food and gas at numerous places along the route.

Nearby attractions: Hovey Lake Fish & Wildlife Area; Harmonie State Park; Twin Swamps Nature Preserve; Log Inn in Haubstadt (Indiana's oldest restaurant); Ellis Park Racing and Gaming.

The Drive

The drive begins at the eastern edge of Evansville at Angel Mounds State Historic Site—*really* one of Indiana's beginnings: a 103-acre Middle Mississippian village that prospered in the fourteenth and fifteenth centuries on a palisaded bluff above the Ohio River. One thousand Native Americans erected twelve significant earthen mounds, the largest rising 44 feet high and covering 4 acres. From 1939 until his death in 1964, Indiana archaeologist Glenn A. Black supervised excavation at the site, where more than 2.5 million artifacts were discovered.

Angel Mounds was declared a National Historic Landmark in 1964, the nation's highest designation. An interpretation center offers exhibits, an informational slide show, and a simulated archaeological excavation. A replica village gives the visitor a sense of urban life in America while Europe was still in the Medieval Ages.

Urban Evansville to New Harmony

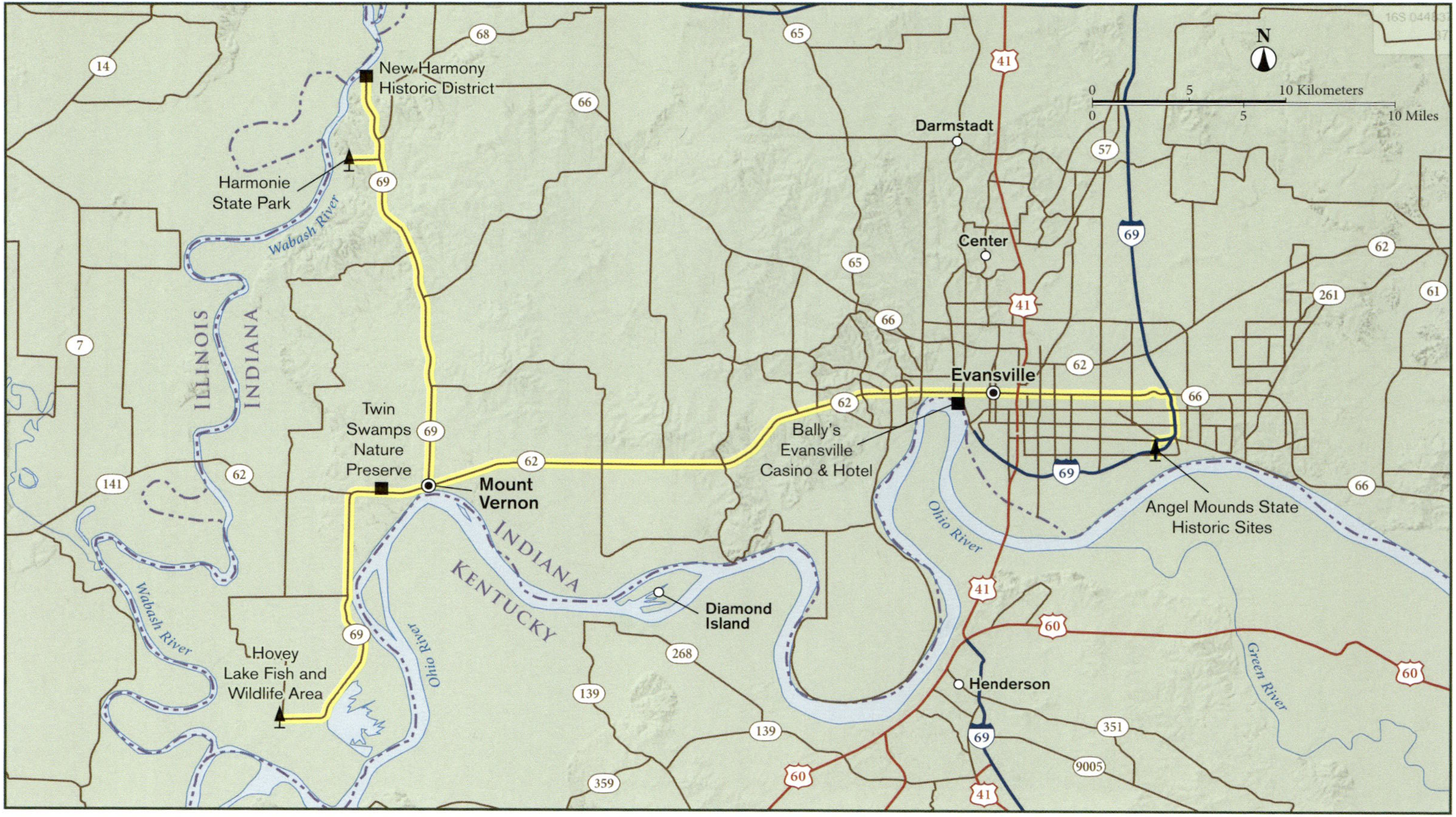

Angel Mounds State Historic Site was a prosperous village in the fourteenth and fifteenth centuries. Indiana Department of Natural Resources

Thanks to excellent rail connections, progressive business, and civic leaders, Evansville is the preeminent city in the tri-state region. Indeed, Evansville is the largest city on Indiana's entire Ohio River shore (115,300 people in 2024) and the third-largest city in Indiana. The city has several outstanding parks, as well as the vintage Ellis Park horse-racing track. The calendar is crowded with festivals, from the thrilling Thunder on the Ohio hydroplane racing festival to the Teutonic charm of the Volksfest at the 125-year-old Germania Maennerchor, from Native American Days at Angel Mounds to the West Side Nut Club Days, second only to Mardi Gras in attendance. There are eight historic districts and eighty-one individual structures on the National Register of Historic Places. It's a prosperous place with industrial parks, large manufacturing facilities, regional shopping centers, and affluent suburban neighborhoods.

Evansville has never turned its back on the Ohio, celebrating its river heritage with a 2.5-mile riverfront promenade along the levee built after the 1937 flood. War memorials dot the riverfront, which also features an amphitheater, boat ramp, and a whimsical 1913 tile-roofed Japanese-style pagoda that houses the Evansville Area Trails Coalition.

Bally's Evansville casino on the riverfront was Indiana's first gambling boat and offers 940 slot machines and 14 blackjack tables along with a plethora of gaming options. Nearby, the Evansville Museum of Arts, History & Science at

411 S.E. Riverside Dr. is a cultural mainstay of southwestern Indiana, showcasing more than twenty-five exhibits annually, along with a fine permanent collection that covers everything from a cabinet that Abe Lincoln built to sixteenth-century paintings to a collection of locomotives and train cars.

Across Riverside Drive, nineteenth-century timber barons' mansions rise like giant wedding cakes in the Riverside Historic District, with the 1871 Reitz Home Museum at 224 S.E. First St. as the centerpiece of the neighborhood. The Reitz home is open for tours.

Evansville and **Vanderburgh** County have embarked on a remarkable outdoor project that encompasses recreation and healthy living. The Pigeon Creek Greenway Passage is a 10-foot-wide paved trail for walkers, joggers, and bikers that stretches nearly 7 miles along Pigeon Creek and the riverfront. It eventually will include more than 40 miles of multiuse trails that will link parks and neighborhoods encircling Evansville. The National Park Service designated the Passage a National Recreation Trail in 2004.

Also located on the riverfront, across from Bally's Casino, is the LST-325 Ship Memorial, a WWII Landing Ship Transport that was used in the invasions of Sicily and Normandy. It is the last fully operational LST in existence and is open to guided tours and scheduled excursions on the Ohio River.

Evansville's downtown has an outstanding collection of historical architecture, from the neo-Baroque treasure of the Old Courthouse at Fourth and Vine to the 1930s Art Deco sleekness of the Greyhound Bus Terminal—now home to a burger restaurant—at Third and Sycamore Streets. The 1913 Alhambra Theatre at 50 Adams Ave. is a Moorish Revival fantasy, while the Old Vanderburgh County Jail and Sheriff's residence are a crenelated Gothic Revival interpretation of Lichtenstein Castle in Germany. The Old Post Office Place at 100 N.W. Second St. housed federal offices, the customs office, and the post office when it was built from 1875 to 1879. After an extensive restoration, it now houses the Evansville Chamber of Commerce, offices, and a restaurant.

The African American Museum, 579 S. Garvin St., tells stories of the city's Black residents from 1820 to the present.

Evansville has two sports venues of note—Ford Center, a $127.5 million multipurpose arena opened in 2011, and Historic Bosse Field, the third-oldest baseball stadium in the country behind Fenway Park (Boston) and Wrigley Field (Chicago).

Wesselman Woods Nature Preserve is a unique urban forest at 551 N. Boeke Rd. It encompasses the largest virgin, old-growth woodland in any city in the country. While the woods are protected from development, an adjacent recreation area offers tennis, ballparks, picnic grounds, and a playground. The Mesker Park Zoo, on Bement Road, was Indiana's first when it started in the late 1920s with a few small animals, a couple of lion cubs, and Kay, the elephant purchased in 1929 after a citywide fund drive. Today, after a multimillion-dollar renovation in 2008, more than 700 animals cavort and congregate on the zoo's 50 acres, making it one of the state's largest. Drive west on IN 62 out of Evansville across the Posey County line. "Everything is near the river in Posey County," former state tourism official and Posey County native Marianna Weinzapfel said. "We've got two to pick from." The Ohio curls along the southern border and the Wabash wiggles down the western side. The road is through a flat lowland with Evansville's sprawl alternating with prosperous farms tilling the rich soil and perpetually pumping oil wells.

There are several archaeological sites scattered along the route; none are open to the public. There are four archaeological sites in Posey County listed on the National Register of Historic Places, including the Mann site just east of Mount Vernon, which was the largest Hopewell town in Indiana, probably a satellite town of Angel Mounds to the east.

Mount Vernon, 20 miles west of Evansville, is a throwback to the Hoosier small town of yesteryear, with a courthouse square surrounded by rococo Victoriana and its turn-of-the-century neighborhoods. Founded in 1805, the town grew rapidly after it was named the county seat in 1825. Courthouse Square and its 1876 courthouse is a historic district on the National Register of Historic Places, as is the Welborn Historic District bounded by Ninth, Locust, and Second Streets, and the alley between Walnut and Main Streets. The 1895 William Gonnerman House at 521 W. Second is on the National Register of Historic Places, a fine example of the period.

At the foot of Main Street, Shelburne Park provides public access to the Ohio River. The town is also the home of the Ports of Indiana–Mount Vernon, Indiana's largest port, opened in 1976 to handle cargo traveling the inland waterway system from the Great Lakes to the Gulf of Mexico. The center includes a mile of riverfront designed to handle mooring, fleet assembly, and drydock repair.

At the west edge of town is IN 69, aka Graddy Road. Proceed 8.2 miles south to Hovey Lake State Fish and Wildlife Area. The Nature Conservancy calls the pristine environment one of the "Last Great Places." The enormous wetland in the pocket of southern Posey County where the Ohio joins the meandering Wabash is a slurry of sloughs and swamps reminiscent of the Deep South. Bald cypress trees poke their bony knees from the swamp water as blue herons stalk among the water lilies. Turtles bask on their favorite log as warblers and gnatcatchers flit through the wild grapes. Deer peer from behind the moss hanging on the cottonwoods and wild pecans. The refuge is a nesting place for bald eagles, along with double-breasted cormorants and great blue herons.

Hovey Lake's 7,400 acres are a magnet for hunters—5,200 hunters, the majority waterfowl hunters, used the property in 2023–2024.

The nearby Twin Swamps Nature Preserve is an unsullied 597-acre wetland with some of the Midwest's most intriguing flora and fauna. One section of the Indiana DNR–managed site features overcup oak and the other, America's northernmost stand of bald cypress. Some of the old stand remains—massive trees, hundreds of years old, stately among the buttonbush and swamp rose. Moonseed, rare American featherfoil, and spider lily are scattered through the swamp, with wild blue orchids flaring here and there. Three miles farther down IN 69 from the Hovey Lake office, the John T. Myers Locks and Dam is at the lowest point in Indiana. The first boat passed through the locks in 1970. This is considered a high-lift dam, raising vessels an average of 18 feet. Four million to five million tons of cargo move through the locks monthly.

Backtrack to downtown **Mount Vernon** and turn left on IN 69, also labeled Main Street. Proceed 11.3 miles north and pass the Posey County Fairgrounds before turning left on CR 325. Continue west for 1 mile to Harmonie State Park. The park stretches along a series of rapids in the Wabash and offers visitors campsites, a nature center, picnic areas, and an assortment of trails.

Return to IN 69, turn left, and proceed 2.9 miles to IN 66. Turn left to enter New Harmony, site of famous Utopian communities. Early in the nineteenth century when most of Indiana was still a vast untamed forest, Harmony, and later New Harmony, was the site of two remarkable Utopian experiments, unique in that it harbored both sacred and secular communal societies. The first, the Harmonists, led by George Rapp, were waiting for the Second Coming of Christ. The second, the Owenites, rejected religion completely. The Harmonists' legacy is New Harmony's magnificent historic buildings and town layout dating from 1814. In turn the Owenites' left a remarkable scientific and intellectual legacy a decade later.

Jane Blaffer Owen, married to a descendant of Owenites' founder, Robert Owen, arrived in New Harmony in 1949. She immediately recognized the extraordinary possibilities of the sleepy little town. Inspired by the town's intellectual and spiritual history, she set up the Robert Lee Blaffer Trust in 1959 and embarked on the next Utopian journey, the longest to date.

She envisioned New Harmony as a place of spiritual awakening, where the mystical and spiritual could commune with a well-nurtured built environment. The town became the destination for assorted clergy, writers, and artists, co-evolving in an atmosphere of seminars, think tanks, liturgical ceremony, and secular expression.

Architect Richard Meier's Atheneum visitor center at Arthur and North Streets is the starting point for most tours. Visitors can orient themselves with an informational film and pick up maps and literature. The multilevel building offers New Harmony visitors exhibits and great vistas of the Wabash and the town.

The Harmonist labyrinth is one of many remnants of two New Harmony utopian communities.

Across North Street from the visitor center, Cathedral Labyrinth and Sacred Garden is based on the sacred geometries of Cathedrale Notre Dame de Chartres in France. The brick wall next to the labyrinth encloses the Harmonist Cemetery, where 230 Harmonists are buried in unmarked graves alongside a ninth-century Hopewell burial mound. The wall was built by Harmonists who returned in 1874 to raze the original Harmonist church, which had deteriorated, and used the church's bricks to build the wall. Proceed down North Street past austere frame houses that the Harmonists left unpainted, since they believed the Second Coming was imminent. The David Lenz House at West and North Streets is typical of the Harmonist period. A cluster of log cabins across the street speak of the structures lived in by Harmonists' neighbors in the hinterland. They are not original to the site but were moved in from the county. The Barrett-Gate House at Main and North Streets is one of only two existing log-and-frame Harmonist structures.

Across from the Barrett-Gate House, the Roofless Church is modernist architect Philip Johnson's interdenominational paean to spirituality, designed with the thought that only the sky is a big enough roof to shelter all faiths. The church includes sculptures and gates by Jacques Lipchitz and the recently installed *Pieta* by Stephen de Staebler. Next door to the church on North Street, the small white building is the Richard Meier–designed Pottery Studio, completed in 1978. New Harmony's premier restaurant, the Red Geranium, and the New Harmony Inn are farther to the east on North Street.

One block south at Granary and Brewery Streets, the 1823 Salomon Wolf House contains an entrancing diorama of New Harmony as it appeared in 1824. The house was moved from another site in 1975, and the original bricks were rotated so the unweathered side was exposed. Nearby is the five-story brick and sandstone Harmonist Granary. Because the upper windows were mistakenly thought of as gunports, old accounts of New Harmony call it the "Rappite Fort." In fact, it was a wool and cornmeal mill until being converted to a granary. Geologist David Dale Owen used it as his laboratory and museum. It was the headquarters for the US Geological Survey during his tenure as chief geologist.

On Main between Church and Granary Streets, the mammoth brick Dormitory No. Two was built in 1822 by the Harmonists to communally house both men and women. During the Owenite period, the building housed a Pestalozzian school and a tavern. It later served as a newspaper office for the *New Harmony Register.*

The greensward on Church Street is the site of the two Harmonist churches. The brick church that later formed the cemetery wall was built in 1822 and was a marvel to travelers of the day. The Workingman's Institute at Tavern and West Streets is a remarkable holdover from the era of endowed public libraries, before Andrew Carnegie dispersed his library buildings throughout the land in the twentieth century. It is Indiana's oldest public library. Today, it is a repository of manuscripts and artifacts relating to the communalist days, as well as a quirky town museum.

The gingerbread brick house across the street is the Schnee-Ribeyre-Elliott House, built in 1867 by a saddlemaker who made his fortune in the Civil War. The corner of Tavern and Brewery Streets has a clutch of historic houses, including the brick Georgian 1830 Owen House. The other three corners include a National Register Harmonist shoemaker's house, now used for historic exhibits, and the Keppler House, now used for geology exhibits.

New Harmony's Main Street reflects Indiana's boom time in the Victorian era. There are several interesting shops, galleries, and cafes along the tidy street. On Church Street, Thrall's Opera House was important to New Harmony through the decades. Originally built by the Harmonists as Dormitory No. Four, it served as a singles dorm and boardinghouse during the Owen period. In 1828 the building began its life as a theater. In 1888 the facade was given an up-to-date look and operated as a theater and cinema until 1914, when it became a garage. The state of Indiana bought the opera house in 1964 and restored the structure to its 1888 splendor. It reopened as a theater in 1968 and operates today under the management of the University of Southern Indiana.

7

Brown County Loop

The hills and hamlets of Brown County

General description: The 49-mile drive is through the dramatic hills and valleys of Brown County, nationally known for its scenery and artist colony.

Special attractions: Picturesque scenery throughout; the Story Inn in Story; Brown County Historical Society Museum Complex in Nashville; Brown County State Park; shopping.

Location: South Central Indiana.

Drive route numbers and names: IN 46, 45, and 135; county roads, W. Youth Camp Road, Bellsville Pike, Christiansburg Road, Plum Creek Road, Lanam Ridge Road, and Owl Creek Road.

Travel season: This is a rumpled landscape with some precipitous hills, best avoided in snowy weather. The autumn brings staggering amounts of traffic into Nashville and Brown County State Park, but the back roads can still be enjoyable driving. Avoid the state highways into Nashville and the park on peak leaf-season weekends unless you enjoy sitting in traffic jams.

Camping: Brown County State Park (812) 988-6406 in Nashville; Yellowwood State Forest (812) 988-7945; numerous private campgrounds near Nashville; Woods-N-Waters Campground (812) 342-1619 in Columbus.

Services: There are full services at Columbus and Nashville. There is gas and food enroute including Pikes Peak and Beanblossom.

Nearby attractions: The architectural haven of Columbus begins the route, and the university town of Bloomington is 15 miles west of Nashville. T.C. Steele State Historic Site; Yellowwood State Forest; Bill Monroe's Music Park & Campground in Bean Blossom (home to the annual Bill Monroe Bluegrass Festival); Bear Wallow Distillery in Gnaw Bone; Brown County Winery in Nashville; Hard Truth Distilling Co. in Nashville.

The Drive

Brown County is as much an idea as a place, an icon of bygone days that's been merchandised and packaged a thousand different ways. Yet despite all the hype, the county remains an extraordinary destination for scenic driving, a roller-coaster ride of dramatic hills and serpentine roads, charming hamlets and beautiful vistas.

The spectacular scenery for today's visitor was anathema to the early settlers. The hilly, rocky terrain made all but subsistence farming impossible. Roads and place names speak of poverty and isolation: Scarce O'Fat Road, Gnaw Bone, Milk Sick Bottom, Needmore, Stoney Lonesome. Scarce O'Fat was said to have soil so poor the starving cows had to lean against the fence to bawl. Timbering, salt

Hills and Hamlets of Brown County

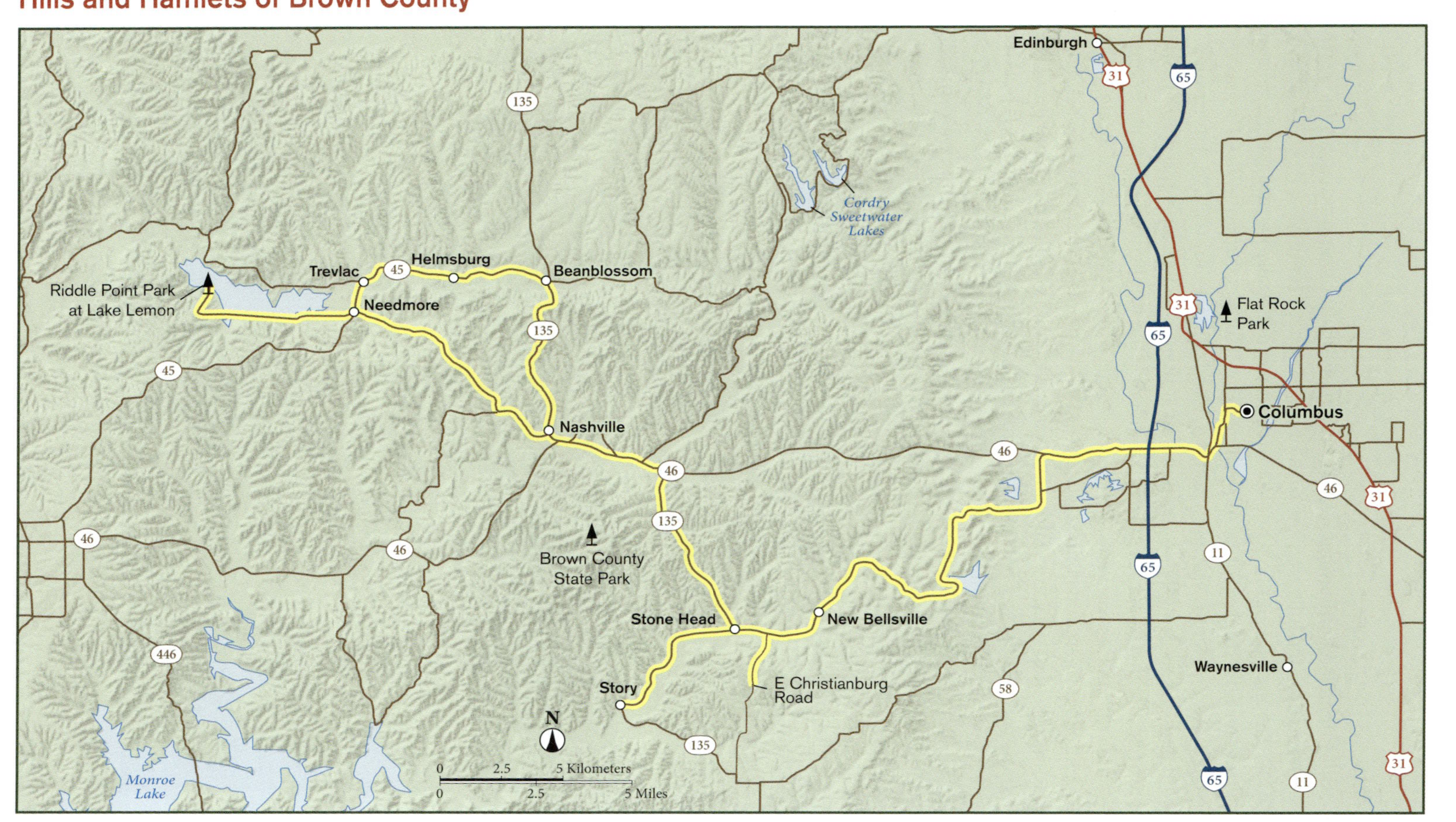

collection, and goldmining were the main occupations until urban artists began filtering into the hills after the turn of the twentieth century.

The Brown County School of Art became nationally known, a regionalist outgrowth of the Impressionist movement. The "Hoosier Group"—T. C. Steele, Marie Goth, Adolph Shulz, C. Curry Bohm, Genevieve and Carl Graf, V. J. Carriani, and others—found Brown County to be "an authentic American landscape," in Shulz's words, and they spent their careers rendering the soft light and hazy air in thousands of romantic canvases. By the late 1920s Brown County was a locale at the confluence of art and commerce. Up to twenty painters were full-time residents with twice that working seasonally. Nashville enjoyed a national reputation, and the artists bustled to keep up with demand, with the results sometimes speaking of creativity and sometimes of business realities.

Tourists followed soon after, and the county has depended on tourism since. Millions today still trundle down the two lanes into the hilly county to enjoy the combination of rusticity and sophistication that Brown County has been known for since Model T days.

The uplands and steep ravines of the area are part of the limestone karst topography of the Mitchell Plain. The Mitchell Plain is in turn part of the Interior Low Plateaus Physiographic Region that extends northward from northern

Brown County State Park is renowned for its colorful scenic overlooks.

Alabama to south of Indianapolis, some of the nation's most rugged terrain east of the Rockies. The complex erosion patterns of the V-shaped valleys and high "knob" hills are courtesy of the glacial ice sheets that slid down to the northern edge of the county, the runoff cutting through to the shale and siltstone beneath the limestone. Southern Brown County was never glaciated, and it is where the most dramatic scenery is found.

Black walnut, wild cherry, and sycamore line the stream banks, and oak, beech, sugar maple, and hickory thrive on the hilltops and slopes. Wildflowers and berry bushes light up the understory. Painted sedge, a grasslike plant that is rare in the rest of the state, covers most of Brown County's dry slopes.

The drive begins in Columbus. From I-65, proceed west on IN 46 for 2.8 miles to CR N 525 W. Turn south and proceed 1.4 miles to a T intersection with W. Carr Hill Road to the left and CR 150 S to the right. Take a right turn on CR 150 S, alternately labeled West Youth Camp Road. Hulking forested hills loom on the horizon.

At CR 750 West, turn left and proceed 0.8 mile until the road becomes South Poplar Drive and winds through a ravined, sun-dappled forest and wraps around the west side of Grandview Lake before reaching Bellsville Pike, a vital trade route for rural communities along is path. Turn right and continue west as Bellsville Pike parallels the South Branch of **Salt Creek** and then the Middle Fork of Salt Creek, which feeds into **Monroe Lake**, a 10,750-acre reservoir southeast of **Bloomington**.

New Bellsville is the first small town reached on Bellsville Pike, its namesake. Founded in the 1800s by Joseph Campbell, it is emblematic of the quaint villages scattered throughout Brown County

The hamlet of Pikes Peak is 1.8 miles farther southwest. A frustrated gold rusher named James Ward founded the town. Intent on getting to Colorado, he placed a sign on his wagon that read "Pike's Peak or Bust." He didn't get far before he abandoned the plan and returned to the hills of Brown County to start a general store. In jest, customers began calling the place Pikes Peak.

Continue 1 mile west on the valley road from **Pikes Peak** to **Stone Head**, a quirky crossroads at the junction of IN 135. It's marked by a benign stone head carving that presides over a road marker noting Columbus is 17 miles in one direction and Fairfax in the other. Henry Cross, known in the area for crafting fine gravestones, carved the roadside bust and two others in 1851 in lieu of meeting the obligation of paying county road taxes versus working off the tax with donated labor. Cross proposed three road makers featuring busts in the likeness of the county road commissioner.

The surviving Cross sculpture has endured years of abuse, having been stolen several times and shot once by a drunk. Both the stone head marker and the nearby Thomas A. Hendricks House built in 1895 are on the National Register of Historic Places.

Tucked-away Story Inn's slogan is "One Inconvenient Location Since 1851." Rich Hofstetter/Story Inn

Follow IN 135 South from Stone Head and drive the hairpin road 4.4 miles to Story. The same overlogging that caused the Brown County timber industry to go bust in the 1930s caused Story to lose its several hundred inhabitants. Story was nearly a ghost town when a young couple found it in the 1960s and began buying it up. Today, the old grocery store with a couple of vintage pumps out front is the Story Inn, a gastronomic destination with the slogan "One Inconvenient Location Since 1851." Founded by Dr. George Story in 1851, the town thrived quickly with a church, one-room schoolhouse, grain mill, sawmill, slaughterhouse, blacksmith, post office, and two general stores, but the Great Depression in 1929 put an end to Story's prosperity. In the mid-1980s one of the general stores was converted to the Story Inn, now the centerpiece of a town turned business turned National Historic District. When all the bed-and-breakfast rooms are filled, the town may be bulging with a population of nearly twenty.

Return to Stone Head and turn north on IN 135 as it parallels **David Creek** before intersecting with IN 46. Turn left on IN 46 to reach the north entrance to Brown County State Park, Indiana's largest park at nearly 16,000 acres. Visitors are greeted by a two-lane wooden covered bridge that is the oldest in a state that boasts nearly one hundred such historic structures. Henry Wolf built the bridge in 1838, but its original location was over Ramp Creek nearly 70 miles north in Putnam County. When the bridge was scheduled for demolition in 1932, state officials moved it to the park. Its 7-foot overhang at each end prohibits passage for recreational vehicles, large trucks, and vehicles towing trailers, which are directed instead to the park's west entrance.

The state park is blessed with miles of hiking, mountain biking and horseback trails, year-round camping, two lakes, picnic pavilions, cabins, an outdoor swimming pool, and scenic vistas that offer panoramic views of the region's expansive forestlands that burst with colorful leaf displays in autumn.

The park's centerpiece is Abe Martin Lodge, Depression-era construction named after cartoonist Kin Hubbard's character. For nearly 25 years, Hubbard's nationally syndicated cartoon spread Abe Martin's wry country wisdom around the nation, helping to publicize Brown County as the home of rustic philosophers. The lodge has undergone recent renovations and boasts a popular indoor aquatic center.

Drive through the park to the west entrance and turn north on IN 46 to Nashville, the epicenter of the Brown County tourist industry. Nashville is the county's governmental seat, largest town, and home to more than 300 shops, selling bric-a-brac and fine art from corn-husk brooms to handcrafted birdhouses to original oil paintings, candles, quilts, wrought iron, stained glass, toys and dolls, and enough saltwater taffy and fudge to fuel you far down the road. This and much, much more—it's all here for the dedicated shopper.

The 1874 redbrick courthouse at Main and Van Buren Streets has several "Liars' Benches," replicas of the one in the famous 1923 Frank Hohenberger photograph that captured a lineup of town storytellers swapping yarns. Catty-corner from the courthouse, the worn wooden floors of the Hob Nob Corner Restaurant have seen a lot of traffic since it was built in 1870. It's the county's oldest commercial structure. One block east of Van Buren, the Brown County Historical Society Museum Complex at Gould Street and Old School Way has, among other things, an 1840s log barn, an old log jail, a pioneer cabin, an early doctor's office, and an 1820s blacksmith shop. Interpreters help re-create the nineteenth-century lifestyle.

Drive north 5 miles on IN 135 to Beanblossom. The Beanblossom Overlook provides a stirring panorama of the hills. Just north of here, both the Illinoisan and Wisconsinan glaciers ground to a halt. The town is 1 mile farther. Beanblossom is renowned for the annual Beanblossom Bluegrass Festival made famous by bluegrass music pioneer Bill Monroe. Thousands make the pilgrimage yearly to Bill Monroe's Music Park and Campground to hear the plangent chords and high plaintive notes of bluegrass music performed onstage or in parking lot jam sessions. It is the longest-running bluegrass festival in the world.

Turn west on IN 45. Helmsburg, 2.5 miles west, was once a bustling railroad town. It's the hometown of 1950s singer Bobby Helms, famous for such hit records as "Fraulein," "Jingle Bell Rock," and "My Special Angel." Trevlac, 2.7

miles farther west, also thrived during the railroad's heyday. Col. Cecil Calvert founded the town and named it after himself, but the spelling was reversed when a post office was established in 1907 and the US Postal Service pointed out there already was an Indiana town named Calvert. One mile south is the little railroad burg of Needmore, site of the colorful hippie Needmore Commune in the 1960s and 1970s. The South Shore Road in Needmore leads in 1.7 miles to Lake Lemon, a 1,650-acre lake created in the 1950s to be a water and recreation resource for nearby Bloomington. Riddle Point Park has a public beach, playground, and picnic area, while Lake Lemon serves as the home for Indiana University's rowing teams and the Bloomington Yacht Club.

Return to Needmore and take a right turn on IN 45, then an immediate left turn on Plum Creek Road. Quirky surviving examples of houses that reflect the 1960s-era wood butchers' art are still scattered along the road.

Drive 2.5 miles to Lanam Ridge Road and turn left. Drive 0.1 mile and turn right on Owl Creek Road. The road down to the valley is a green tunnel of trees past vintage log cabins and prosperous new homes. In 2.2 miles turn right onto Helmsburg Road. The road leads through a green valley and then climbs upward. Nashville is 2.3 miles farther. The road leads directly to the courthouse square.

8

Sweet Owen

From Cataract to Bloomington

General description: The 32-mile drive runs from Lieber State Recreation Area through the rugged scenery of Owen and Monroe Counties to Bloomington.

Special attractions: Cataract Falls; McCormick's Creek State Park; the college town of Bloomington.

Location: South Central Indiana.

Drive route numbers and names: Cataract Road, US 231; IN 43 and 48.

Travel season: The roads are drivable in all but the worst of winter weather.

Camping: Lieber State Recreation Area (765) 276-0194 near Cloverdale; Cataract Falls State Recreation Area (765) 276-0194, McCormick's Creek State Park (812) 829-2235, and Owen-Putnam State Forest (812) 829-2462, all near Spencer; Blackhawk Campground and campgrounds at Cloverdale and Cloverdale RV Park.

Services: There are full services at Cloverdale, Spencer, and Bloomington, and gas and food at Cataract and near Whitehall at the junction of IN 43 and 48.

Nearby attractions: Cataract Falls and Lieber State Recreation Area; Cinema 67 Drive-In theater near Spencer; Owen-Putnam State Forest near Spencer; Tivoli Theater, Spencer; Owen Valley Winery, near Spencer; Gosport Tavern in Gosport; Indiana University in Bloomington.

The Drive

There is a soothing sound as the water falls over the shoals at Cataract Falls, the two-tiered waterfall downstream from **Cagles Mill Lake** at Lieber State Recreation Area. The lake was built in 1952 as Indiana's first flood-control reservoir. Trees line burbling Mill Creek, and a red covered bridge dating to 1876 crosses the stream like a barely recalled memory.

The falls are the largest by volume in Indiana; the upper falls drop 45 feet over striated bands of limestone, and a little farther downstream the lower one falls 30 feet. The falls stand at the cusp of two dramatically different natural regions. To the north the glaciated prairies stretch in a fertile swath all the way to the Great Lakes. To the south, the rugged upland limestone belts rumple their way down to the Appalachians. The falls drop between them.

The tiny village of Cataract with its upright frame houses and old general store looks like something out of Norman Rockwell's New England. Cataract began in the 1820s when Isaac Teale erected a small mill. In 1842 Governor Jonathan Jennings's brother, Theodore, began the tiny town's mercantile boomlet when he erected a sawmill, flour and woolen mill, blacksmith shop, and general

Cataract to Bloomington

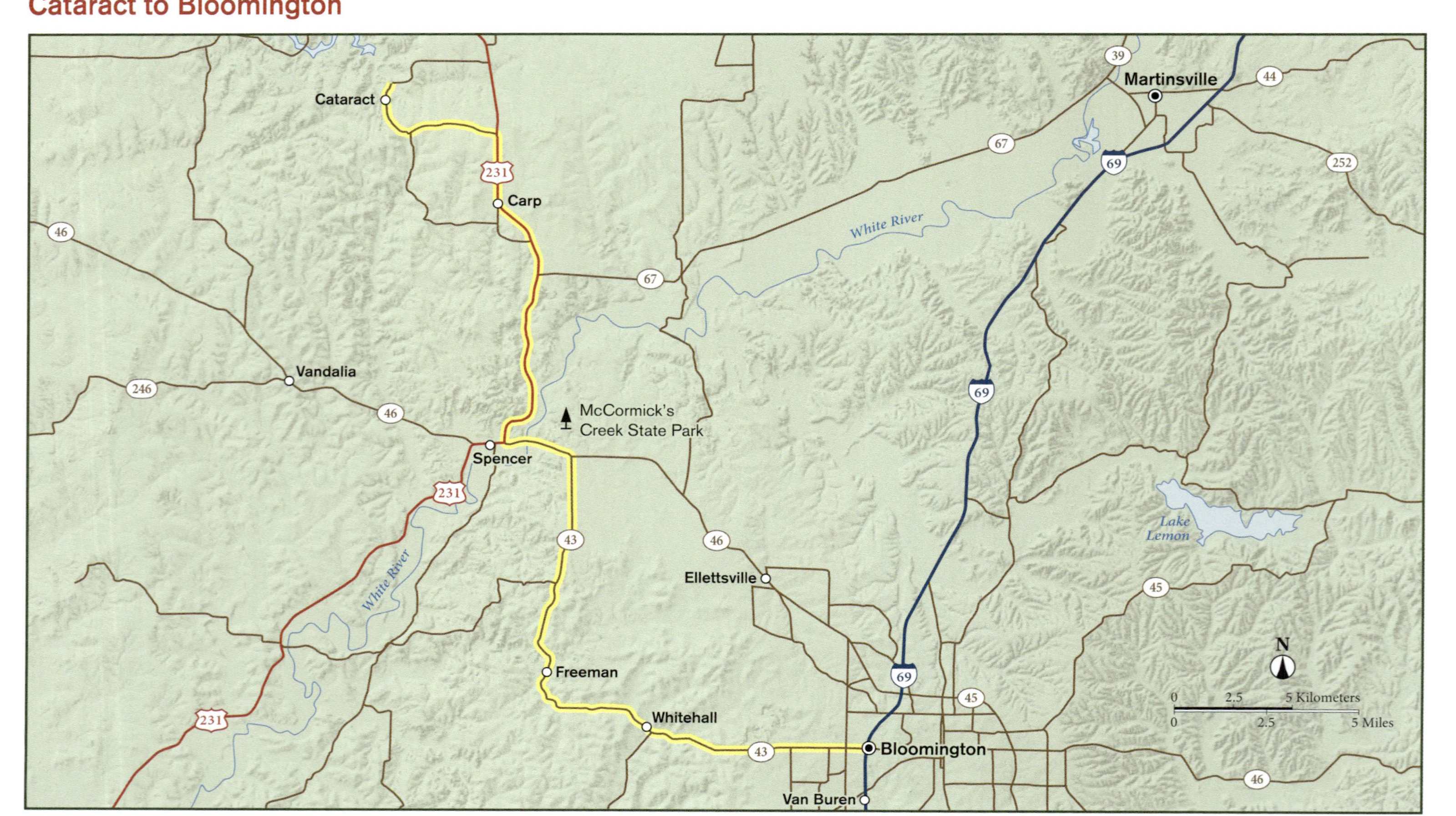

Two-tiered Cataract Falls is the largest waterfall by volume in Indiana. INDIANA DEPARTMENT OF NATURAL RESOURCES

store. For decades the town buzzed with lumbering and flour milling, selling to locales as far away as Louisville. At its peak in the last quarter of the nineteenth century, Cataract had three groceries, a hotel, and a drugstore. When the forests were depleted and the lumber mill closed, the other enterprises lost their customer base and the town devolved into the sleepy place you see today.

The Cataract General Store began in 1860 and is one of the oldest in the state. A pair of battered wooden doors swing open to an establishment lost in time. The shelves and walls are lined with a serendipitous collection of antiques and modern goods, potato chips beside the horse collar, old thread cases beside ones with new Case knives, wooden crank phones above the detergent. Soft drinks come out of a vintage Coca Cola case. Scythes and wooden rakes are there along with Ding Dongs and Twinkies. Outside, the owners converted an old outhouse into the Cataract Little Free Library and stocked it with an assortment of books.

Take South Cataract Road 1.4 miles and make a sharp left turn when the road intersects with CR 200 W. Continue on South Cataract Road another 2.6 miles to US 231 and turn south through the tiny town of Carp. A few miles south, the road begins to descend into the Hoosier uplands where the limestone bones of the land become more pronounced.

Two miles south of Carp, you can take a side trip by turning east on IN 67 and driving 4 miles to Gosport. About 0.3 mile north of Gosport, there are two highway markers denoting the 10 O'Clock Line, the 1809 treaty boundary negotiated by William Henry Harrison and Chief Little Turtle that brought almost 3 million acres into US government control at a cost of about 3 cents an acre. The town of Gosport began in 1829 as a flatboat shipping port on the White River. For many years an odd hybrid bridge crossed the White River between Owen and Monroe County; half of the bridge was steel girders and half was a wooden covered bridge, with each county following its own style.

While the town still retains a historic air, fires and thoughtless demolition have robbed it of many of its landmarks. Still, a 7-square-block area in the center of town was designated a National Historic District in 2013. A notable standout in the district is the Dr. Horace G. Good House, completed in two phases between 1850 and 1880. One landmark that remains is the curious Chivalry Trough, a 4 × 8–foot spring-fed concrete bath. In previous days the town's grooms grimly awaited the traditional late-night dunking in the trough on their wedding eves. The trough is hidden in the weeds near the remains of the Brewer Flour Mill. Take Main west to Fifth Street, turn north, and proceed to East North Street, then turn back east and the mill and trough are about 4 blocks farther.

Return west on IN 67 to US 231/IN 67 and turn south to Spencer. Founded in 1820, the town was incorporated in 1866, and the coming of the railroad two years later gave the town a boost.

Owen County itself was organized in 1818 and is still among the state's most rural in character.

The present courthouse in Spencer dates to 1911 and features a copper dome that houses a Seth Thomas clock with faces on four sides. The *Spirit of the American Doughboy* statue on the courthouse lawn is by Spencer native Ernest Viquesney, a renowned early-twentieth-century sculptor.

The Allison-Robinson House at Franklin and Montgomery Streets was built between 1855 and 1860. It originally was located across the street but was moved to its current location in 1990. Despite the move, the house still earned a spot on the National Register of Historic Places three years later. Continue north on Montgomery Street to Hillside Avenue. The street is a gracious residential street with several sprawling turn-of-the-century homes.

Return to the junction of IN 67 and IN 46 and proceed east across the White River 1.8 miles to McCormick's Creek State Park. The park is the state's oldest, dating to 1916, chosen for its extraordinary natural beauty and unique features. Tongues of a glacier crept across the present White River and climbed the bluffs in and around the park. A badly eroded ridge that represents an ancient glacial moraine tops the bluff there. Ancient lake beds formed by the runoff are a few miles east near Ellettsville, creating a formation known as flatwoods. Within the park, a 1-mile-long 100-foot-high canyon is a dramatic remnant of glacial melt.

The park is the site of an early limestone quarry that furnished the stone for the state capitol. There are numerous recreational facilities, the Canyon Inn, and more than a dozen family cabins offer cozy lodging.

The turnoff for IN 43 is just east of the park entrance. Proceed south on IN 43. The road goes through another flat glaciated area for about 3.4 miles to the site of the old Owen County Poor Farm, which also served as the Owen County Asylum.

The road quickly begins a serpentine twist through deep ravined woods. It is the land of the upland South yeoman farmers, many descendants of nineteenth-century North Carolina mountain people who settled the hills in the 1840s. Not many decades before that, there were still hunter-gatherers wresting their livings from the forests. Ginseng gathering—"sang"— is still a lucrative local sideline, and spring mushroom hunting is a fevered pastime.

South of the county farm 1.5 miles, turn west on County Road 525 South (Sherfield Road) for 1.4 miles to The Nature Conservancy's nature preserve, Green's Bluff. The area is a refuge for eastern hemlock that thrives in the cool, moist environment of Raccoon Creek's sandstone bluffs. Other rare plants include species of ferns, goldenseal, and spleenwort.

Return to IN 43 and proceed 0.5 mile to Crisp, a tiny ridgetop hamlet with a restored one-room schoolhouse that is still used for local gatherings.

The road snakes out of Crisp, down to Freeman, and into the Raccoon Creek valley. It is still a traditional valley despite the new homes mixed in with vernacular double-pen structures. The Little Flock Primitive Baptist Church 0.1 mile north of IN 43 on Little Flock Road looks like it belongs in the hills of Elmer Gantry's rural South.

IN 43 continues into Whitehall, a modest hamlet strung along the roadside.

The Monroe County line is 0.2 mile from Whitehall, and there are gas and groceries available at the junction of IN 48. IN 48 parallels Richland Creek in another bucolic valley. The two-story Queen Anne Victorian home on the left is the Beaumont House, a five-room bed-and-breakfast built in 1869.

The large structure on the right at Garrison Chapel Road is the Mother of the Redeemer Retreat Center. What began in 1993 as a prayer gathering in the basement of the farm owners' home gradually expanded with a chapel, two-story guesthouse, and dining hall.

The road bounds over two humpy hills, and the industrial underbelly of Bloomington appears. The local airport, industrial parks, new subdivisions, and strip malls form the gateway to the city. (Bloomington is covered in Drive 9.)

9

Culture to Culture

Bloomington to Columbus

General description: The 60-mile drive is through the rumpled hills of Monroe, Brown, and Bartholomew Counties between the culturally diverse college town of Bloomington and the architectural wonder of Columbus.

Special attractions: In Bloomington: Courthouse Square, Indiana University campus, Tibetan Cultural Center. In Columbus: modernist and vintage architecture.

Location: South Central Indiana.

Drive route numbers and names: IN 46.

Travel season: The roads traverse a hilly region and can be treacherous in snowy weather, but they are drivable most of the year. Fall weekends bring out foliage fans in amazing numbers, clogging the roads coming into Nashville.

Camping: Brown County State Park (812) 988-6406 in Nashville; Yellowwood State Forest (812) 988-7945; numerous private campgrounds near Nashville; Woods-N-Waters Campground (812) 342-1619 in Columbus; Hoosier National Forest, Bedford Office (877) 444-6777.

Services: There are full services in Bloomington, Nashville, and Columbus, and numerous opportunities for gas and food enroute.

Nearby attractions: Lake Monroe, Hoosier National Forest, and Deam Wilderness Area south of Bloomington; Griffy Lake, north of Bloomington; Heartwork Brewing, Metal Works Brewing, Upland Brewing, and Cardinal Spirits in Bloomington; Oliver Winery and Butler Winery near Bloomington; Zaharakos Ice Cream in Columbus; Mill Race Park in Columbus; numerous architectural highlights in Columbus.

The Drive

The tour begins on the courthouse square in Bloomington, home of Indiana University (IU). The 1908 courthouse and the surrounding square reflect Bloomington's polyglot population and quirky mix of lifestyles and esthetics. Around the square, ethnic clothing stores sit next to abstract companies and local attorneys. Shoppers peruse fine designer jewelry made of ancient fossils, Peruvian folk art, and cutting-edge computer games, before toddling off for a cappuccino or a loaf of European bread. The cafes and restaurants of the downtown area offer fare from Moroccan to Afghani, Japanese to Hoosier.

Given the diversity, it's not that surprising that Bloomington is considered a Little Tibet. In a town better known for basketball, songwriters John Mellencamp and Hoagy Carmichael, bicycling, and the Kinsey Institute for Sex Research, this link to the traditional culture of the high Himalayas seems incongruous. But an

Bloomington to Columbus

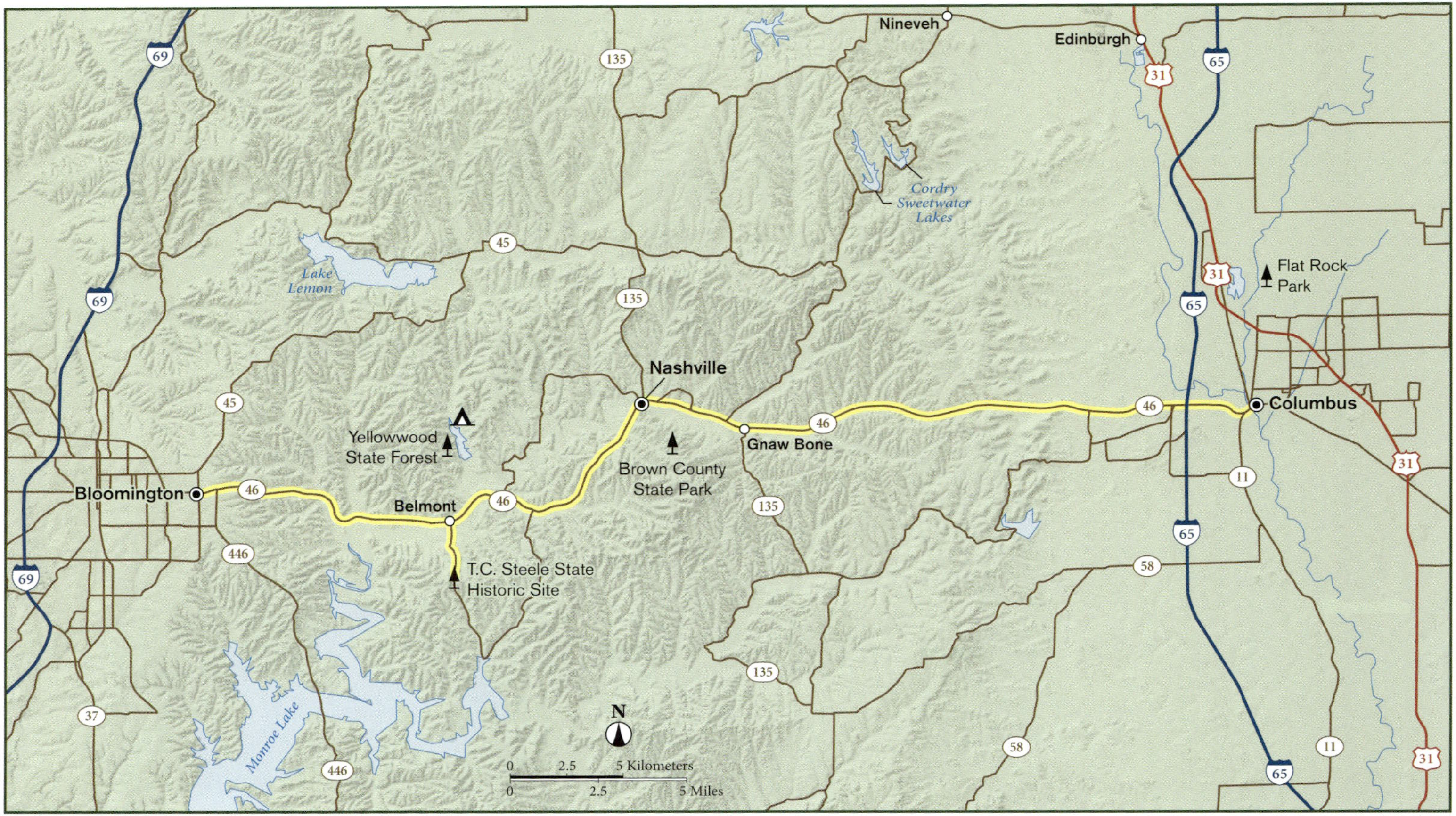

enormous Buddhist stupa, a massive spire-topped cylindrical shrine, glints gold and white on the town's outskirts, surrounded by fluttering prayer flags. It is the focus of the Tibetan Mongolian Buddhist Cultural Center located at 3655 Snoddy Rd., on the southeast side of town. IU professor emeritus Thubten J. Norbu established the center in 1979 to introduce people to the culture and history of his native Tibet. His younger brother, the 14th Dalai Lama, has visited the 90-acre site numerous times.

Bloomington has two Tibetan restaurants. Cars with "Free Tibet" bumper stickers announce Tibet supporters. Shaven-headed monks dressed in maroon are a common sight in town, leading meditation groups, giving concerts of their remarkable chanting, and visiting their countrymen.

Since their founding early in the nineteenth century, Bloomington and Indiana University have been connected whole and part. The town's first settlers moved into what President James Madison named "Seminary Township," designated for the location of a state university. It was located on the highest ground in the region to protect the townsfolk from ravaging floods and the malaria of the more fertile lowlands.

A nascent university began in 1820 but teetered along for 60 years, barely alive. The town itself, strangled by the endemic water shortage, also limped along. Given the water problem, it's not surprising that it was a fire in 1883 that finally

Sample Gates are a welcome entry point to Indiana University's oldest campus buildings.
Visit Bloomington

got the place going. After the university's science building burned to the ground along with President David Starr Jordan's scientific collections (Jordan later served as president of Stanford University), he convinced the trustees to rebuild in the countryside east of Bloomington, and it has been there since.

The limestone industry fortuitously boomed at the same time, and a world-famous limestone campus is the result. The shady campus with the tiny Campus River running through it, ennobled with Gothic and contemporary architecture, has long been ranked one of the nation's most beautiful universities.

Proceed east on Kirkwood (Fifth Street) to the campus at Indiana Avenue. The Sample Gates are the entrance to the earliest part of the campus. The Old Crescent surrounding Dunn's Woods in the southwest corner of campus contains nine buildings constructed between 1884 and 1908.

Northeast of the Beck Chapel on Seventh Street, the Fine Arts Plaza surrounding the Showalter "Birth of Venus" Fountain is dedicated to culture and the arts. The IU Auditorium was erected during the Great Depression, partially funded and built under the auspices of the WPA. Inside, the Hall of Murals is decorated with Regionalist Thomas Hart Benton's bodice-busting depictions of Indiana's economic and social evolution. Benton painted the murals for Chicago's 1933–34 Century of Progress International Exhibition. The state installed them in the auditorium in 1940.

Designed by architect I. M. Pei, the wedge-shaped **Eskenazi Museum of Art** is an evolution (or devolution, depending on the critic) of the East Wing of the National Gallery. It houses IU's outstanding collections of Mediterranean, Asian, African, Oceana, and American art, as well as a collection of twentieth-century Western European art. The Lilly Library across the plaza is one of the country's great repositories of rare books, including an original Gutenberg Bible.

Return to Jordan Avenue and continue north to 17th Street to Assembly Hall, a 17,222-seat basketball arena that has been the home of IU men's and women's teams since 1971. Farther north on North Fee Lane, Bill Armstrong Stadium is home to the Little 500 yearly bicycle race that inspired the cult-classic movie *Breaking Away*, as well as one of the nation's finest soccer facilities, home to Indiana's perennial powerhouse teams.

Take IN 46 out of Bloomington as it twists through the rough terrain of Brown County to the east. Turn south at T. C. Steele Road in Belmont. The T. C. Steele State Historic Site is 1.5 miles farther. The limestone arches, surrounded by acres of daffodils in spring, lead to the former home of Indiana's most beloved painter and the founder of the Brown County Art Colony. In 1945 his widow donated the 211 acres, the house, the 900-volume library, and 300 paintings to the state. The two studios and the Trailside Museum are open for visitors, as well as several walking trails that inspired Steele's Impressionist canvases.

Return to IN 46 East. Yellowwood State Forest is directly north, accessed by Jackson Creek Road 0.6 mile east of Belmont. The 23,764-acre forest is land that the federal government bought during the Depression when the hill people fled the rugged, unfriendly hills and the eroded fields stood idle. The government paid an average of $9.19 an acre. CCC workers reforested the land, and in 1956 the federal government turned over the woodlands to the state. There are three lakes, three state-dedicated nature preserves, numerous trails, primitive campsites, and the newly renovated Lodge at Yellowwood cabin.

Continue east on IN 46 as the road climbs precipitously, offering a stirring panorama at the top of the surrounding Norman Upland. The west entrance to Brown County State Park is just beyond.

The park opened in 1929, and with nearly 16,000 acres it is the state's largest. Runoff from the Illinois-period glacier formed the streambeds of Beanblossom and Salt Creeks and the ravined hills between them. The park has extensive recreational facilities including two lakes, a swimming pool, horseback and hiking trails, mountain bike trails, a nature center, and the Abe Martin Lodge with meeting space and an indoor aquatic center.

Because of the difficult terrain, settlers came late to Brown County. Once they learned farming was a bad deal, they turned to timber, salt, and gold for economic development, although no significant gold reserves were ever found.

Since the 1930s, tourism has formed the backbone of Brown County's economy. Each year, millions converge on the county's little towns and hamlets to partake in a bit of nostalgic visitation. On fall weekends it's said that the fastest way to get into Nashville on either IN 46 or IN 135 is to walk on the hoods of cars that are lined up for miles trying to get into the tourist town. (See Drive 7 for information on Nashville.)

The north entrance to Brown County State Park is 1.7 miles east of Nashville, followed 2 miles farther by Gnaw Bone, a flea market haven. There are no stoplights in the unincorporated town with an odd name of unexplained origin. According to local lore, one early settler, when asked the whereabouts of another, replied, "I seed him a-settin' on a log above the sawmill a-gnawin' on a bone," and the name stuck. Most likely the original settlers' French name of Narbonne was Hoosiered. The **Gnaw Bone Country Store and Bakery** at 4883 IN 46 is in a renovated building of a previous store that featured a horse-powered sorghum mill—a single horse harnessed to a pole that drove the press, crushing the sorghum as the horse walked in circles around the mill.

Brown County Winery and Bear Wallow Distillery are two must-stops for those who appreciate adult beverages.

Bartholomew County is the home of Columbus, an internationally renowned architectural mecca. Driving past silos and barns and near-iconic rows of deep green corn, you'll spot the twin red arches rising incongruously from the prairie at the west edge of Columbus. It's the first sign you are entering an unusual town. By the time you see the Empire-style county courthouse, all belfries and widow's walks and looming redbrick rectitude, you'll know this isn't your standard Indiana town.

Columbus people like to say they're different—different by design. And they are. Since the 1940s, Columbus has engaged in a remarkable experiment in modern living, hiring the top international architects to design their public buildings and meld them into the fabric of their nineteenth-century town of 50,500. There are more than fifty buildings representing an honor roll of modern architects, including César Pelli, both Saarinens (Eero and Eilel), Harry Weese, Kevin Roche, I. M. Pei, Robert Venturi, Deborah Berke, and Richard Meier. The American Institute of Architects named Columbus the sixth-most architecturally significant city in the United States, behind only New York, Chicago, Los Angeles, Boston, and Washington, D.C. It has become a cultural tourism shrine.

Downtown, the visitor center at Fifth and Franklin Streets is an ideal spot to pick up maps, literature, and information. Nearby at 531 Fifth St., the austere geometric First Christian Church—designed by Finland's foremost architect, Eilel Saarinen—is a striking counterpoint to the common Gothic and Georgian churches of the Midwest. The piazza in front of the church centers on Henry

Even bridges are architectural treats in Columbus.

Moore's bronze sculpture *Large Arch*, a 20-foot-high primal paean to Stonehenge, I. M. Pei's town library, and the Commons, a glass-boxed downtown shopping center designed by Cesar Pelli, where kids sit under surrealist Jean Tinguely's enormous *Chaos I* sculpture with its scavenged gears and levers.

The last work by architect Eero Saarinen (of St. Louis Arch fame) is the North Christian Church, which stands on the north edge of town along IN 46 East at 850 Tipton Lane. Hexagonal walls leap from the bermed earth with one dynamic pulse into a needle-thin spire that etches the sky—a bold, modern, timeless design.

Columbus is an architectural petri dish, where the idea that good architecture improves the human condition is still being tested—with an almost naive faith. Robert Venturi designed one of the fire stations, Robert A. M. Stern the hospital. Pritzker Prize winner Kevin Roche, who created the Metropolitan Museum of Art's master plan, designed the sleek post office at 450 Jackson on the tidy Victorian main street, across from Zaharakos Confectionery, where ice cream is still sold at the rococo 1890s onyx soda fountain bought at the 1890s Columbian Exposition.

The folks still love their old buildings here despite all the modernist architecture. In fact, many buildings and some districts are on the National Register of Historic Places. Small wonder that the first postmodernist architect, Harry Weese, found Columbus an ideal place to explore the value of folk architecture, blending it into his buildings and the Columbus neighborhoods in the 1950s.

10

Autumn Loop I

An autumn ride through southern Indiana near Bedford to Paoli and back

General description: The 80-mile loop courses through the southern Indiana hills from Bedford through Shoals, West Baden, Paoli, and back to Bedford.

Special attractions: Spring Mill State Park, Bluespring Caverns Park, Paoli Square, French Lick Springs Hotel, West Baden Springs Hotel.

Location: South Central Indiana.

Drive route numbers and names: US 150; IN 37 and 450; and CR 500.

Travel season: The roads are drivable in all but the worst of winter weather.

Camping: Spring Mill State Park (812) 849-3534 near Mitchell; Bluespring Caverns Park (812) 279-9471 near Bedford; Hoosier National Forest, Bedford Office (877) 444-6777; Patoka Lake (812) 338-5589; Patoka Pines RV Campground (812) 203-2725 and Painter Creek Campground (812) -936-7545), both at French Lick; Patoka Lake.

Services: There are full services at Bedford, Shoals, French Lick–West Baden, and Paoli. Food and gas are available in Orleans and several places enroute.

Nearby attractions: Bluespring Caverns Park near Bedford; Green Hills Cemetery in Bedford; Williams Covered Bridge in Williams; Jug Rock and Bluffs of Beaver Bend near Paoli; Patoka Lake and Pioneer Mothers Memorial Forest near Paoli; Mitchell Opera House in Mitchell; Carousel Winery in Mitchell; Gus Grissom Memorial Museum at Spring Mill State Park; Patoka Lake Winery, Old Homestead Distilling, and Patoka Lake Brewing in Birdseye; French Lick Winery and Spirits of French Lick Distillery in West Baden.

The Drive

The loop begins in Bedford, center of the Indiana limestone industry. About 340 million years ago, the ground we call Indiana was down by the equator covered by a shallow ocean. It was a comparatively calm sea where trillions of tiny animals—crinoids and gastropods and other slithery sea creatures—lived out their lives. As they came to their natural ends, their carcasses piled atop one another for eons on end, until shoals of the bodies lie on the ocean floor. Where the sea bottom and currents coalesced in optimal ways, the shoals rose to great heights.

As time moved on, so did the continent, migrating north to place Indiana where it is today. The vast shoals, now compressed into rock by the weight of water and earth and endless time, awaited the next great geologic moment. A million years ago, give or take a few millennia, the great glaciers ground down from the north. While the glaciers stopped short of scouring southern Indiana, the

Bedford to Paoli and Back

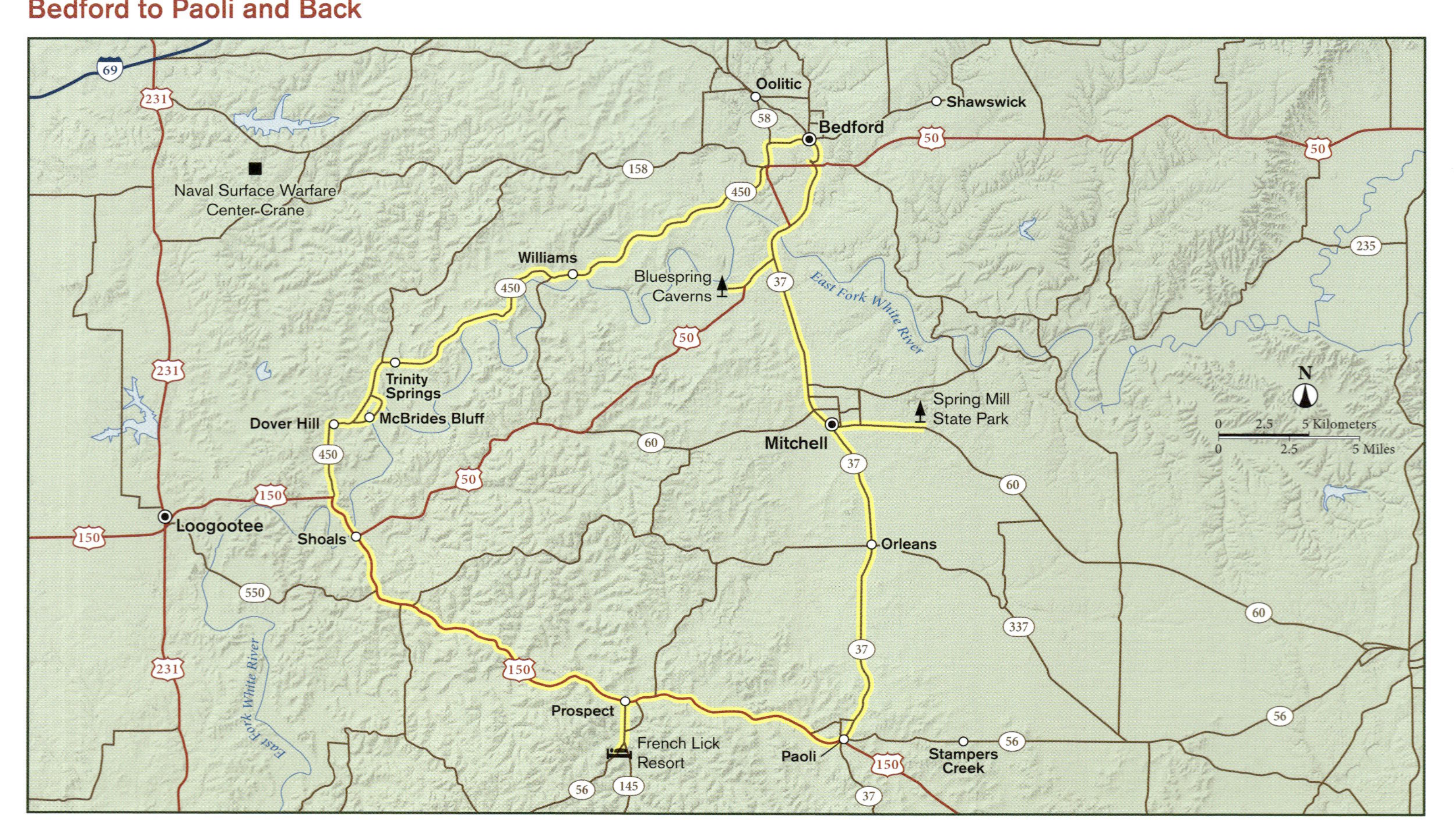

meltwater from the mile-high glaciers eroded most of the rock shoals. Only a slender band of the ancient reefs wiggling through southern Indiana escaped erosion, leaving outcrops of pristine limestone—the best in an area only 30 miles long by 2 miles wide—of barely 28,000 acres. And Bedford is in the middle of that band.

Dozens of stone companies have worked the limestone belt since the beginning of the limestone industry in the nineteenth century, and their product has been used far and wide. Thirty-five of fifty state capitols in the United States are constructed with Indiana limestone. So are the Empire State Building, the Pentagon, the Biltmore Estate, the National Cathedral, and many others.

The influence of the limestone culture can be seen around Bedford's downtown square. The Lawrence County Courthouse is a neoclassic design that dates to 1930, though it has the aesthetics of a building half a century older. The square retains several exceptional examples of the stonecutters' art.

At 18th and L Streets, the Green Hill Cemetery is a veritable gallery of stone-carving art, a rich repository of formal and folk monuments. In the southwest corner of the cemetery, a full-sized craftsman stands to memorialize the Journeymen Stonecutters Association. Nearby, the gravestone of carver Louis Baker is an extraordinary sculpture done by his co-workers, depicting his workbench as it appeared the day he died of typhoid fever in 1917. Other impressive and uniquely carved limestone markers can be found throughout the cemetery. More than thirty markers depict tree stumps, none more moving than the one for 7-year-old Evalou Gaussin, adorned with her hat and high-button shoes, lilies, ivy, roses, a crucifix, and wreath as symbols of innocence and her brief life.

Take 16th Street west for 0.2 mile from the intersection with US 50/IN 37 to IN 450 and turn south. It is a twisty ride along the East Fork of the White River. Williams is 5 miles southwest. The small town boasts one of the state's longest covered bridges—376 feet long. The 100-year-old structure uses a Howe Truss design first patented in 1840. It was closed to vehicular traffic in 2010 but not before earning a spot on the National Register of Historic Places. The town dam was built in 1912 for one of the state's first hydroelectric power plants, but like the bridge, that too is out of service. The river as it flows through Williams was a prime mussel-gathering site used in Japanese cultured-pearl production, but the state banned collection of freshwater mussels in 1991 to protect their depleted populations.

Continue southwest 8 miles to Trinity Springs, a now-defunct mineral springs resort. At its turn-of-the-century peak, Trinity Springs had seven hotels and a bustle of activity surrounding three mineral springs at the north end of the village.

Proceed another 2 miles down IN 450 to Tommy George Road (IN 106) and turn east, then south on IN 17 to McBride's Bluff along the White River. The area to the south allegedly holds a fortune in Indian treasure. According to legend,

Choctaw Indians captured early settler Absalom Fields and took him, blindfolded, to their cave hideout along the river. There they showed him a mound of silver molded into brick sand, then returned him to his home. The Indians left the area soon after. Fields spent the balance of his days trying to retrace his steps to find the fortune. Twice since then, bars of silver that fit the description have been found in the fields, or so the tale goes.

Backtrack to IN 450 and turn left. Dover Hill is 1.5 miles farther, a disappearing little hamlet strung along the road. It was the Martin County seat from 1848 to 1857. Proceed 3.5 miles to US 150 and turn left toward Shoals.

Shoals, originally named Memphis, is the seventh town to be Martin County's governmental seat, wresting the honor in 1877 (See Drive 1 for more information on Shoals.)

Proceed 13 miles south on US 150 to IN 56 in Prospect and turn south to West Baden and French Lick. The two communities share the Springs Valley, noted since pioneer days for the sulfurous smells. Since early in the days of human habitation, the valley was noted for its salt springs.

Indians hunted the abundant game drawn to the salt licks, including the bison herds that pounded down Indiana's first highway, or "trace," as they migrated from the Illinois prairies to near present-day Louisville, Kentucky. The first Europeans followed suit, using the buffalo trace to travel between the two areas of early settlement on the Wabash and the Ohio Rivers. In the eighteenth century, French fur trappers and Jesuit priests visited the area.

Given the importance of salt in food preservation, the young state of Indiana carefully reserved all saline springs in the state for common use, including "French Lick," as the area was known. Following the failure of state-sponsored salt wells due to the weakness of the saline waters, Dr. William A. Bowles bought the French Lick springs and started the first hotel in the valley in 1840.

The venture prospered due to the advantageous location midway on the state's main highway and the increasing consumption of medicinal mineral water. In 1855 Dr. John A. Lane opened a competing hotel a mile to the north, initially calling it the Mile Lick Hotel. Later, the name was changed to the West Baden Springs Hotel to capitalize on the cachet of the renowned European baths at Wiesbaden, Germany.

When the Monon Railroad finished a 17.7-mile branch line from Orleans, the hotel's clientele traveled in the newest steam-driven trains to take to the healing waters, and the valley boomed.

With its magnificent dome spanning 200 feet across, the West Baden Springs Hotel was one of the world's top watering holes. The mineral water resorts offered their wealthy clientele the latest in physical therapies and mental rejuvenation. Sprudel water, as the spa's water was known, was reputed to cure more than fifty

The magnificent 200-foot dome spans the fully restored West Baden Springs Hotel.

ailments and diseases including sprains, cancer, sterility, rheumatism and asthma, constipation, diabetes, gout, insomnia, and urinary afflictions.

The resort offered an array of activities for guests: An opera house brought in Broadway stars and a sparkling lineup of seasonal shows, plus there were bowling lanes, billiards, an enclosed natatorium, a shooting range, and handball courts. A 300-foot-long, two-story turreted causeway linked the hotel to a gambling casino, one of dozens in the valley.

The immense hotel shut its doors during the Great Depression, and it served as a Jesuit College and private business college for decades. After a sad decline, the structure went through a remarkable restoration and is again open for business. The neighboring French Lick Springs Resort is another Roaring Twenties spa. It has remained open and offers a full resort experience including a casino, championship golf courses, and tennis courts.

Return to US 150 and turn east. Proceed 8 miles through a rustic valley. Paoli Peaks ski resort is south of the highway on the high hills overlooking the valley. Its unique snowmaking machines continue to spew out snow for the slopes in all but the warmest of winters.

Paoli has the quintessential town square with its Greek Revival courthouse. Built from 1848 to 1850, the brick and stone structure has outside iron staircases to save interior room for the workings of the law. North Carolina Quakers settled the town in 1811, part of the Great Quaker Migration out of the slaveholding South. This part of Orange County was strongly abolitionist, with a fugitive-slave community known as Lick Creek, 3 miles south of town.

The Mineral Springs Hotel on the south side of the square is yet another resort. The hotel opened in 1896 after drillers hit a sulfur spring on the banks of nearby Lick Creek. It never gained the notoriety of the French Lick and West Baden resorts but operated until 1958.

Just south of Paoli on IN 37 is the Pioneer Mothers Memorial Forest, an 88-acre site managed by the US Forest Service as part of the Hoosier National Forest. It is a rare remnant of old-growth forest in Indiana.

Return north from Pioneer Mothers on IN 37 and continue north from Paoli. The road passes through the Mitchell Plain, a region of porous karst topography and thousands of sinkholes. In 4 miles the road crosses the Lost River, a unique sinking stream that rises and falls across its 22-mile watershed, sometimes above ground, sometimes below.

Proceed north another 3 miles to Orleans, the first town in Orange County, founded two months after Andrew Jackson's victory at the Battle of New Orleans, hence the name. The square, with its gazebo, is called Seminary Square after an academy that stood on the square from the 1870s to 1963. In 1966 hundreds of flowering dogwoods were planted in the town's yards, parks, and street sides, and now it is known as the Dogwood Capital of Indiana.

Proceed north 4.2 miles to IN 60 and turn east to **Spring Mill State Park**, where the past is preserved in a pioneer village. The village's roots date to 1814

A massive water-powered gristmill is the centerpiece of a restored pioneer village at Spring Mill State Park.

when an adrift Canadian seaman built a mill in the deep valley. It hung on as a small mill village until the arrival of the Ohio and Mississippi Railroad in the 1850s spurred the growth of nearby Mitchell. The county bought the derelict mill in 1916 and convinced the state to turn it into a state park. Today, with a host of different recreational options including caves, swimming, trail riding, and boating, the park is one of the most popular in the state. The restored village serves as a reminder of pioneer days, and the nearby Donaldson's Woods Nature Preserve is an 80-acre stand of virgin forest. Vintage Spring Mill Inn offers rustic charm and Hoosier homestyle cooking.

The park also has the Grissom Memorial, dedicated to Gus Grissom, Lawrence County's first astronaut and America's second man in space. On display at the museum are objects from his personal and professional life, one of his space suits, and "Molly Brown," the *Gemini 3* spacecraft he flew along with John Young for three orbits of earth. Two other American astronauts also called the small rural county their birthplace: Charlie Walker and Ken Bowersox.

Nearby Mitchell has a wide Victorian main street that has blossomed with antique shops and malls. Return to IN 37 and proceed north toward Bedford.

Before reaching **Bedford**, turn west at the intersection with US 50 and go 5 miles to Bluesprings Caverns, one of five show caves in Indiana. The cavern is 0.5 mile from the highway via a well-marked road. The cave was formed by a spring cutting through the soft limestone bedrock and forming an underground channel that fed the White River. The cave was hidden until the 1940s when a large farm pond disappeared overnight after heavy rain, revealing the entrance to the cave. The cave has more than 21 miles of recorded passages, making it one of the longest in Indiana. The featured activity is an hour-long boat ride on the subterranean river.

11

Autumn Loop II

Bloomington through eastern Greene County

General description: The drive is through the rugged hills of eastern Greene County on back roads through hill villages to a remarkable 1906 viaduct that leaps across the Richland Valley.

Special attractions: Indiana Railroad trestle at Tulip; scenic countryside.

Location: South Central Indiana.

Drive route numbers and names: IN 48 and 43;Tulip Road and E. Tulip Road, E. Bland Road, N. Shingle Mill Road, E. Calvertsville Road, E. McVille Road.

Travel season: The roads are drivable in all but the worst of winter weather.

Camping: Lake Monroe (812) 837-9546; Lake Monroe Village Resort (812) 824-2267).

Services: There are full services in Bloomington, and gas and food at the junction of IN 48 and 43.

Nearby attractions: Hendricksville Diner; McCormick's Creek State Park near Spencer north of the loop.

The Drive

The loop begins at the junction of I-69 (also IN 37) and IN 48 in Bloomington. (Bloomington is covered in Drive 9.) Proceed west on IN 48. Mother of the Redeemer Retreat Center is 4.3 miles west, a Catholic pilgrimage site relating to a purported vision of the Virgin Mary in the early 1990s. A two-story guesthouse is the centerpiece of the complex, which includes a conference room, dining hall, and chapel. A trail leads to a chapel and the pilgrimage site at the top of the hill.

The road follows Richland Creek Valley. After traveling 1.2 miles west, bear left on IN 43 South and follow a snaky road along a rim of the valley. The Greene County line is 0.5 mile farther. Greene County is the state's fourth largest in land area, stretching from the rich coalfields in the western part of the county to the chaotic hills and small ridgetop pastureland farther east. The White River bisects the sprawling county and roughly divides the rugged forestland from the rolling farmland and coalfields of the western half.

The **Hendricksville Diner**, 2.5 miles farther, is a local hangout (cash only). The sign reads "You've got to be tough to eat here," but it relates more to one's ability to handle heavy down-home cooking.

The town of Hendricksville is 0.2 mile past the diner. The sleepy appearance belies the bustle that was once here. The big business was the Hendricksville pottery shop. Five potters spun out utilitarian ware for over half a century, the wheels powered by a water wheel that also powered the local gristmill. A two-story

Bloomington through eastern Greene County

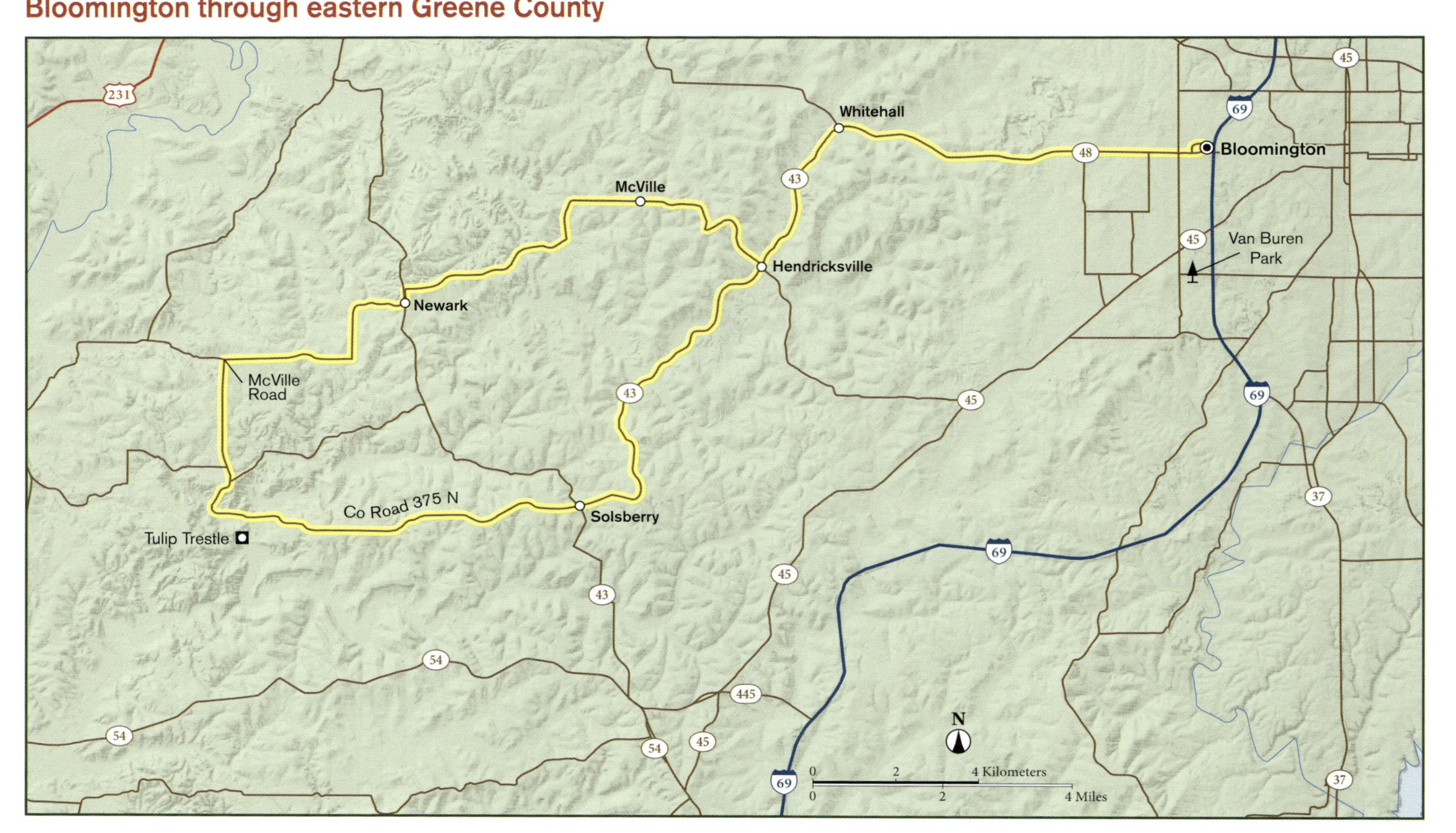

general store served the area for many years until the pull of Bloomington merchants shut it down in the 1970s.

After Hendricksville the road ramps up and down past modest little houses perched on the ridge sides. The Union Church was an early place of worship for the settlers and retains a devout and determined congregation. A mile farther the road opens into one of the rare broad open valleys tucked in the hills, before climbing a steep hill. There is a sharp right turn at the top of the hill with broad hilltop pastures around. To the left, a large old cemetery shares the field with several giant hay rolls parked beside it.

The village of Solsberry is 2 miles beyond. Solsberry dates to 1846 when the town's namesake, Solomon Wilkerson, laid out sixteen lots on top of the watershed between Beech and Richland Creeks. The conflict over slavery wracked the town's early years. An antislavery Wesleyan Methodist church was burned to the ground in the 1850s by slavery proponents, and the congregation was forced to meet in homes until long after the Civil War.

The village and surrounding hill farms subsisted on cattle, grain, and timbering until the Illinois Central came through town in 1906. With a railroad siding, the town prospered. A grain mill was built beside the tracks. Lumberyards stored the fine hardwoods for shipment to the burgeoning city markets. Buyers roamed the hills buying cattle to ship from the stock pens beside the tracks.

The Yoho General Store has served the Solsberry community for nearly 100 years.

The **Sculpture Trails Outdoor Museum** features more than sixty large-scale sculptures along 3 miles of hiking trails. The Old Tobacco Barn at the museum's entrance offers art workshops and craft shows. The Yoho General Store at the center of Solsberry has been serving breakfast, lunch, and dinner to customers for nearly 100 years.

Take Tulip Road to the left of the general store, proceeding west past the post office. The road passes over the railroad on a bridge 1 mile farther. The railroad cut down below is evidence of the travails the railroad workers had trying to lay track through the hill country.

Tulip Road twists and turns over the next few miles. A lovely ravined glade at the junction of CR 580 East offers a glimpse into the sylvan beauty of the forested hill.

The road makes an abrupt turn at the intersection with North Verde Valley Road. Stay left on Tulip Road and continue down the hill into the Richland Creek valley.

Look to the left for the remarkable Indiana Railroad's Tulip Trestle, known locally as the Viaduct. Built in 1906 by Italian laborers, the 2,295-foot-long trestle rises 157 feet over the stream. The eighteen daddy-longlegs supporting steel columns rest on steel-reinforced concrete foundations that are 8 feet wide at the base. More than 167,000 board-feet of pine was used for the decking. Even with the steel workers making 30 cents an hour, and laborers half that, the viaduct cost an estimated $250,000 to build. The trestle was the longest in the country and third longest in the world when completed and is still in use today.

A local group—Tulip Trestle Community Restoration—was formed in 2015 to upgrade and maintain an observation deck, which is accessed off Tulip Road on North Viaduct Road.

Return from the observation deck to Tulip Road and turn left. Drive 0.7 mile to the intersection with East Bland Road. Turn right on East Bland and drive 0.5 mile to North Shingle Mill Road. Turn left and drive 4.8 miles along forest glades choked with springtime mayapples and spreads of trout lilies to E. Calvertville Road. Continue for 5.5 miles to Newark.

Newark (pronounced New Ark) was named after Newark, Ohio, at its founding in 1859. At one time, there were three general stores, a post office, two blacksmith shops, a flour mill, a slaughterhouse, a stave bunger, a wagon factory, a cabinet shop, a doctor, an undertaker, two churches, and three cemeteries. The

Nearly 2,300 feet long, the Tulip Trestle was the longest in America when built in 1906.

churches remain, but the decrepit buildings are evidence that the good times are behind them.

Turn left, then right on East McVille Road after a half mile and continue for 6.5 miles to McVille.

The tall green water tower and a red barn announce the former town. McVille was originally named McHaleyville in 1836 after founder John McHaley. Little has been left of the town for many decades.

Stay straight on East McVille Road and twist along a ridgetop 2.6 miles down into the Richland Creek valley at Hendricksville. Liberty Church of Christ dates to 1850. The current 1985 church replaces one built in 1868. Turn left on IN 43 and drive 2.8 miles back to the IN 48 junction and bear right back to Bloomington, which is another 8 miles.

CENTRAL INDIANA

12

Early Indiana

New Trenton through the Whitewater River Valley

General description: The 65-mile tour loops through the region of some of Indiana's earliest regions of settlement in the valleys of the state's swiftest and steepest stream.

Special attractions: In Brookville: historic architecture and canoe rentals. In Metamora: Whitewater Canal State Historic Site. In Oldenburg: historic architecture.

Location: Southeastern Indiana.

Drive route numbers and names: US 52 and IN 121, 229, 46, and 101 (St. Marys Road).

Travel season: The roads are drivable in all but the worst of winter weather. Canal Days in Metamora bring many thousands to the old canal town, making visits a crowded festival event.

Camping: Brookville Lake (765) 647-2657; Whitewater Memorial State Park (765) 458-5565; Franklin County Parks 4-H Grounds (765) 647-4422, Garr Hill Campground (765) 647-22154, both in Brookville; Kolb Campground (765) 265-8225 and Whitewater Valley Gateway Park (765) 647-2541, both in Metamora.

Services: There are full services in Brookville, Metamora, Connersville, and Batesville. Gas and food are available in Cambridge City, Knightstown, and other small towns enroute.

Nearby attractions: Whitewater Memorial State Park; Brookville Lake; Backroads Winery in Laurel; Creek Bottom Brewery in Oldenburg; Farm Hill Winery in Brookville; Metamora Gem Mine; Haunted and Historic Tours in Metamora; Greenacres Michaela Farm at Oldenburg; Richmond.

The Drive

The drive begins at the south end of US 52 near New Trenton, the gateway to the scenic Whitewater Valley. While Native Americans long inhabited the valley, leaving their pre-Columbian mounds on heights above the river and its tributaries, New Trenton is one of the earliest European American towns. The first pioneers arrived in 1803, platting the town in 1816.

The Whitewater River is the state's steepest and swiftest, dropping from the highest point in the state in two forks that rush southward in valleys that parallel one another until they join at Brookville. The river continues south in a shallow rock-filled stream to the Miami River near Cincinnati. Big-shouldered hills hulk over much of the narrow valley.

When the state of Indiana embarked on the Mammoth Internal Improvement Program of turnpike, railroad, and canal building in 1836, the Whitewater Canal was the first project, since the valley had a quarter of the state's citizens

Bloomington through Eastern Greene County

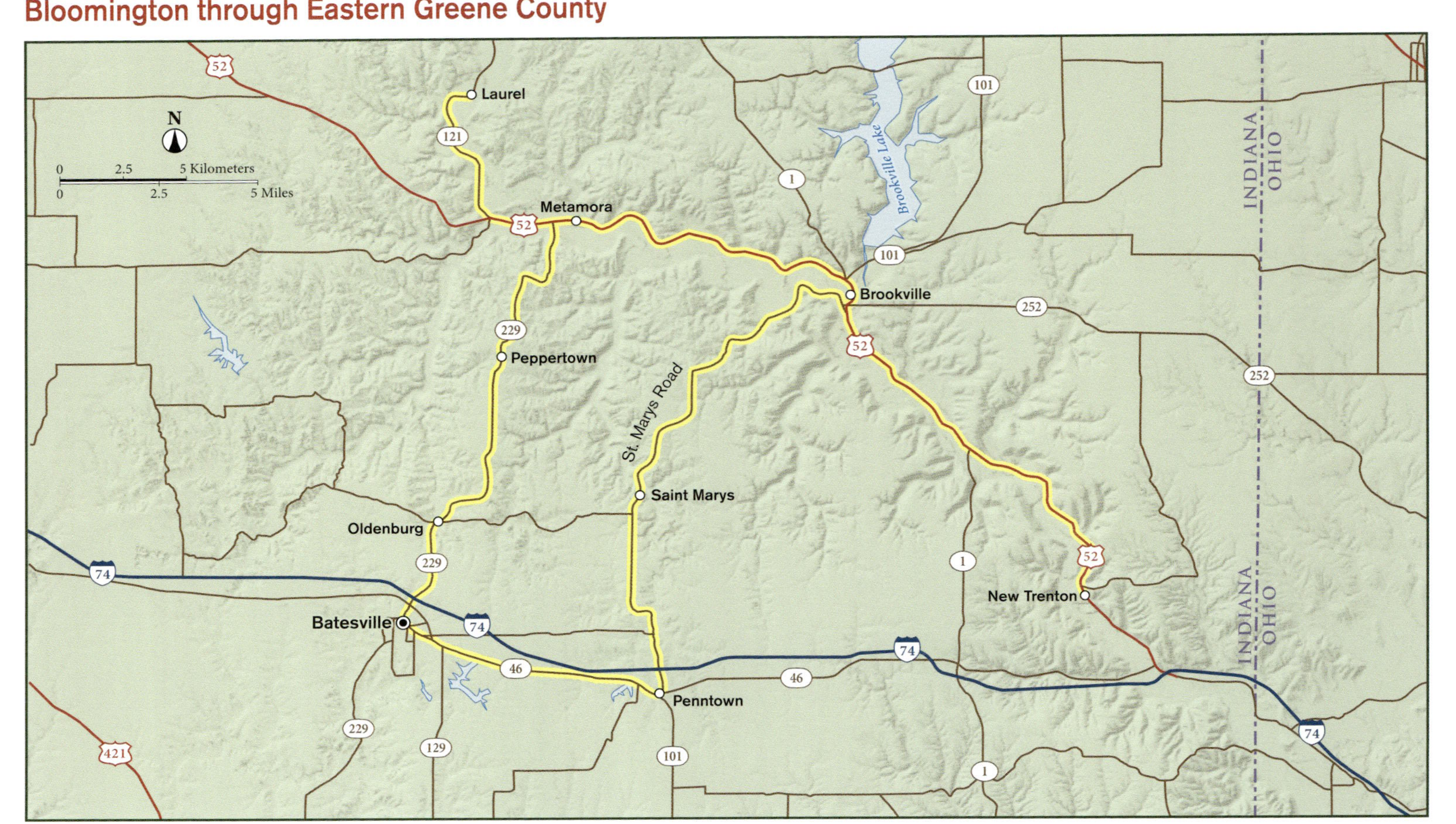

and the most political clout. Indiana finished 20 miles of the canal, until the vast expansion's voodoo economics did the state in, and bankruptcy was declared. A private corporation finished the balance of the canal up to Cambridge City on the National Road in 1846, and Hagerstown a few miles north dug its own channel to join it in Cambridge City.

Floods roaring down the steep valley in 1847 and 1848 washed out major sections of the channel, as well as aqueducts and locks, causing $200,000 in damage. But the ultimate problem was the arrival of the railroad that offered dependable all-season transport of goods and passengers. Eventually the canal company collapsed, and the railroads took over the towpath for their roadbed. US 52 parallels the river and the path of the Whitewater Canal for 31 miles northwest.

New Trenton's two taverns, the Rockafellar and the Manwarring, were popular stops for the canal workers. Thomas Manwarring double-tasked at his tavern, dispensing hard liquor through the week and preaching to the assembled pioneers on Sunday from the steps of the tavern, which was built in 1810. The two-story brick tavern at the intersection of US 52 and Broadway Street now houses an antique store.

Cedar Grove is 5 miles north on US 52. Little Cedar Grove Baptist Church is the oldest church in Indiana still on its original foundation. It is constructed of hand-hewn timbers with a brick exterior. Rows of slots in the second-story exterior speak of its early history. The parishioners used the slots as rifle ports in pioneering days.

Brookville, the county seat for picturesque Franklin County, sits on a bluff at the junction of the east and west forks of the Whitewater River. It was founded in 1808 and became the county seat in 1811. The location of the federal land office fueled the town's growth as settlers flocked into the territory following the signing of Indian treaties. When the land office moved north to Indianapolis in 1825, town luminaries, including several future governors, went with it. The site is at 766 Main St. Nearby, between Sixth and Seventh Streets on the west side of Main Street, a plaque notes the site of an early Indian trading post.

For the most part, Brookville has basked gently in the valley air for the last half century, with enough money to maintain its canal-days' structures, giving the town today an ambient nineteenth-century feel.

The Whitewater Valley emerged as one of Indiana's art colonies at the turn of the century. While the "Richmond School" became dominant, Brookville was the home of several celebrated artists, including some who later came to fame in Brown County. T. C. Steele, Indiana's preeminent Impressionist, owned the Hermitage on Eighth Street with J. Ottis Adams. Fellow artists William Forsyth and Otto Stark were frequent visitors.

The site of Brookville College, established in 1852, is at 10th and Franklin, a block east of Main Street. It originally was organized as a female academy, and several of the state's notable women were graduates.

The Governor Ray House at 210 East 10th was the home of James Brown Ray, Indiana's governor from 1825 to 1831. The ornate Palladium-style window almost cost him the election, as opponents said it proved he was too highfalutin to be governor of the state. Ray was elected as a proponent of the Mammoth Internal Improvement Act but broke with the group over the Wabash and Erie Canal. Ray correctly foresaw the advantages of railroads, though the fight destroyed his political career. Not a shy fellow, he is said to have always signed hotel registers, "J. Brown Ray, Governor of Indiana and Commander-in-Chief of the Army and Navy thereof."

The Hermitage, Brookville College, Governor Ray House, and more than 650 other structures comprise the Brookville Historic District on the National Register of Historic Places, most of them built before 1900.

Proceed 8 miles west on US 52 to Metamora, an old canal town. In its heyday in the 1840s, several gristmills and factories were located here. When the canal company lapsed and the railroad took over the towpath, the town grittily hung on. But the discontinuation of passenger service in the 1930s and the relocation of US 52 outside of town sent it into a decline.

Metamora, an 1840s canal town, is preserved as part of Whitewater Canal State Historic Site. Indiana Department of Natural Resources

The state jump-started the town in the 1940s with the establishment of the Whitewater Canal State Historic Site, which rebuilt 14 miles of canal from Metamora to the dam at Laurel and took over the Metamora Grist and Roller Mill. The 14-ton, 44-foot-long *Ben Franklin* plies the waterway, drawn by horses down the old towpath. The Duck Creek Aqueduct is a rare surviving example of what was once common on the canals—a long water-filled covered bridge that allowed the canal boats to pass over the streams they encountered. The 90-foot-long bridge, originally built in 1846, levitates 16 feet over Duck Creek and is the only remaining wooden aqueduct in the country.

Several vintage structures remain in the little tourist town. The Banes House a block east of the mill is a Federal-style house built in the 1840s. Across the street, the three-story building is the 1853 Odd Fellows Lodge. Farther east, the Martindale House dates to 1838, built by a shipping agent for the canal boats and open today as a restaurant and tavern with limited hours. Go west 3 miles to IN 121 North and turn right, driving 3.7 miles along the river valley to Laurel, another canal town with a feeder dam and an enormous turning basin that can be seen beside the new bridge over the Whitewater. It is the only one of seven feeder dams built for the Whitewater Canal that is still in existence. The canal that arrived in 1843 was the latecomer to the town's transportation. The Whetzel Trace began at Laurel and blazed across the country to the White River Bluffs near Waverly in Morgan County in 1819. It was an important east–west trail for the settlers. A pre-Columbian Indian mound at the western edge of town indicates even earlier pioneers.

A building boom erupted when the canal arrived in 1843. Remnants can still be seen, including the Federal-style Whitehall Tavern that sits above the old turning basin at Baltimore and Franklin Streets. The 1850 Laurel Hotel at Franklin and Pearl Streets is the only east-facing building in town.

Return south to US 52 and drive east for 1.7 miles to IN 229 South. Turn south on IN 229. The road is a roller coaster through sycamores and old hemlock. Cupp's Chapel, 2 miles later, is a simple board-and-batten country church ennobled by a Greek Revival cornice. Peppertown is 4.4 miles south of US 52. The redbrick St. Nicholas Lutheran Church anchors the town despite being closed since 1981. Peppertown was founded in 1851 when August Pepper began a store and tavern in his limestone house on Beacon Road. The lane has other 1830s and 1840s examples of primitive rubblestone masonry.

Five miles south of Peppertown, the many spires of Oldenburg rise from a bucolic landscape. German immigrants flooded into surrounding southeastern Franklin County in a great migration in 1832 and 1833, fleeing the economic chaos of post–Napoleonic War Europe. The emigrants, known as auswanderers, platted Oldenburg in 1837. The devout settlers built so many massive churches that the town became known as the "Village of Spires."

The huge barn on the left coming into town is known as the Sisters' Cow Barn, built in 1875 as an adjunct to Michaela Farm, which the Sisters of Saint Francis operated until selling it in 2018 to Greenacres Foundation of Cincinnati. The Franciscan monastery opened here in1894 and operates today as a retreat center. The town is a Teutonic throwback, with many of the old rubblestone houses still standing and the street signs in German.

The enormous, brooding Holy Family Church was built in 1861, the third church erected by the indefatigable Father Franz Joseph Rudolf, the pastor of Oldenburg from 1844 to 1866. The Franciscan convent and monastery surrounded the massive brick structure until the monastery was razed in 1984. The Franciscan nuns began educating girls from surrounding communities and established **Oldenburg Academy** as a boarding school for elementary and high school students in 1852. The elementary school was eliminated in 1941, the high school resident program ended in 1999, and boys were admitted for the first time in 2000.

The elaborate tinwork of the **Pearl Street Pub**, built as the Hohman Saloon and later the King's Tavern, on Pearl Street is a fine example of Prussian-born tinsmith Casper Gaupel, who worked in town in the 1860s. The Oldenburg Flower Shop at Hauptstrasse and Fernending (Main and Pearl) Streets was the old Hackman's General Store. It has Gaupel's ornate tin fancies in the eaves and cornices.

The stone Town Hall between the tavern and Schweineschwanz Gasse (Pigtail Alley) was built in 1878 as a fire station. Next door, the 1845 Huegel Tavern has

Holy Family Church helps Oldenburg earn the title "Village of Spires." Sisters of St. Francis

a well-carved sun and moon above the lintel. The Waechter-Schmidt-Hoelker House on Wasser Strasse (Water Street) has a remarkable carved and curlicued balcony that cantilevers from the brick house. Wasser Strasse has the earliest houses in town, clapboard structures that include medieval European wattle-and-daub construction. The house and blacksmith shop at IN 229 and Wasser Strasse are both of this type, though the shop dates to 1880 and the house to 1836, a testimony to the enduring customs of the town.

Batesville is 2.5 miles south on IN 229. It's a Johnny-come-lately town for the area, laid out in 1852 when the railroad arrived. The dense hardwood forests attracted German craftsmen and timber buyers, primarily from the industrial boomtown of Cincinnati. The Hillenbrand family was one of the leaders of the town, as they are now, the scions of the family industries that include casket, hospital equipment, insurance, and furniture companies.

The Sherman Inn at Main and George Streets dates from the town's founding and has been a favorite stop since. It originally was named **Brinkmann House**, but the owner changed the name in 1865 in honor of Civil War General William Tecumseh Sherman. The hotel escaped one of the town's periodic infernos in 1872 by the piling of salt bags on the roof. Today it is decorated in a faux Bavarian-Viennese style, but the food is still renowned.

Weberding's Carving Shop is a throwback to the days of artisanal carving, still producing elaborate wood statues and industrial models by hand. It is located 1 mile east on IN 46. They welcome visitors.

Proceed east on IN 46 to IN 101 North. Proceeding north on IN 101 over I-74, the road becomes St. Marys Road. Bear left at the Y, 1 mile farther north, where a small hand-painted sign points the way to St. Marys. The road that leads to Brookville begins in a ravined woodland and opens into a land of hills and dales as lovely as the Yorkshire hills. Prosperous farm buildings peek from tidy fields.

The prim Victorian Gothic steeple of St. Marys of the Rock church emerges from the green hills and forests. It is another mid-nineteenth-century German village with fine masonry rubblestone and brick homes. Most of the town's structures were built from 1850 to 1870. Built in 1844, the church closed in 2013 after it merged with Holy Family parish in **Oldenburg**.

Oak Forest, 2 miles north, has the **Oratory of Saints Philomena and Cecilia** with a white striped steeple like St. Marys. Log cabins and upright brick homes intersperse as the road drops down to a sycamore-lined stream. A historic marker notes the boundary lines of the 1795 Treaty of Greenville, Ohio, and the 1805 Treaty of Grouseland.

Running along the valley, the road leads across the Whitewater onto Brookville's West Sixth Street which intersects US 52.

13

The Old National Road

Richmond to Indianapolis

General description: The 70-mile drive courses along the route of the first road from the eastern seaboard into the heartland of the United States.

Special attractions: In Richmond: *Madonna of the Trail* statue at Glen Miller Park, Hayes Arboretum. In Centerville: Federal-era buildings and Antique Alley. In Cambridge City: Whitewater Canal architecture. In Knightstown: Knightstown Academy and Hoosier Gym. In Greenfield: James Whitcomb Riley Birthplace. In Indianapolis: Irvington, James Whitcomb Riley Home.

Location: Eastern and central Indiana.

Drive route numbers and names: US 40.

Travel season: The highway is fine for travel in all seasons barring bad weather. For the most part, US 40 parallels the truck-clogged I-70. Driving time on the National Road from the state line to the eastern edge of Indianapolis is almost the same and much less nerve-racking.

Camping: Deer Ridge Camping Resort (765) 939-0888, Grandpa's Farm Campground (765) 962-7907, and KOA Holiday Campground (765) 962-7907, all in Richmond; Doc-O-Lake (765) 478-4709 in Milton; KOA Holiday (317) 894-1397, S&H Campground (317) 326-3208 in Greenfield.

Services: There are full services, hotels, restaurants, shopping, movies, and more in Richmond, Greenfield, and Indianapolis. Gas and food are available in Cambridge City, Knightstown, and other small towns enroute.

Nearby attractions: Whitewater Memorial State Park; Brookville Lake; Metamora Canal State Historic Site; Martindale State Fishing Area in Jacksonburg; Whitewater Valley Railroad in Connersville; The Hoosier Gym in Knightstown; Indiana Basketball Hall of Fame in New Castle; Wilbur Wright Fish and Wildlife Area north of New Castle; and numerous Indianapolis attractions.

The Drive

The National Road was authorized by an act of Congress in 1806 to stimulate settlement of public lands in the West, as the heartland was known in the early days of the Republic. Leaders dating back to George Washington saw the need to connect the populous East with the lands newly opened to settlement.

Crews moving westward from the terminus at Cumberland, Maryland, surveyed and graveled to the Ohio River at Wheeling, West Virginia, by 1818 and reached Columbus, Ohio, in 1835. When the federal government turned over the road to the states in 1839, Indiana, still smarting from the canal bust, leased the Hoosier section to a private company that paved it with thick planks, making one of the best wagon roads in the world—until the planks rotted, that is.

Richmond to Indianapolis

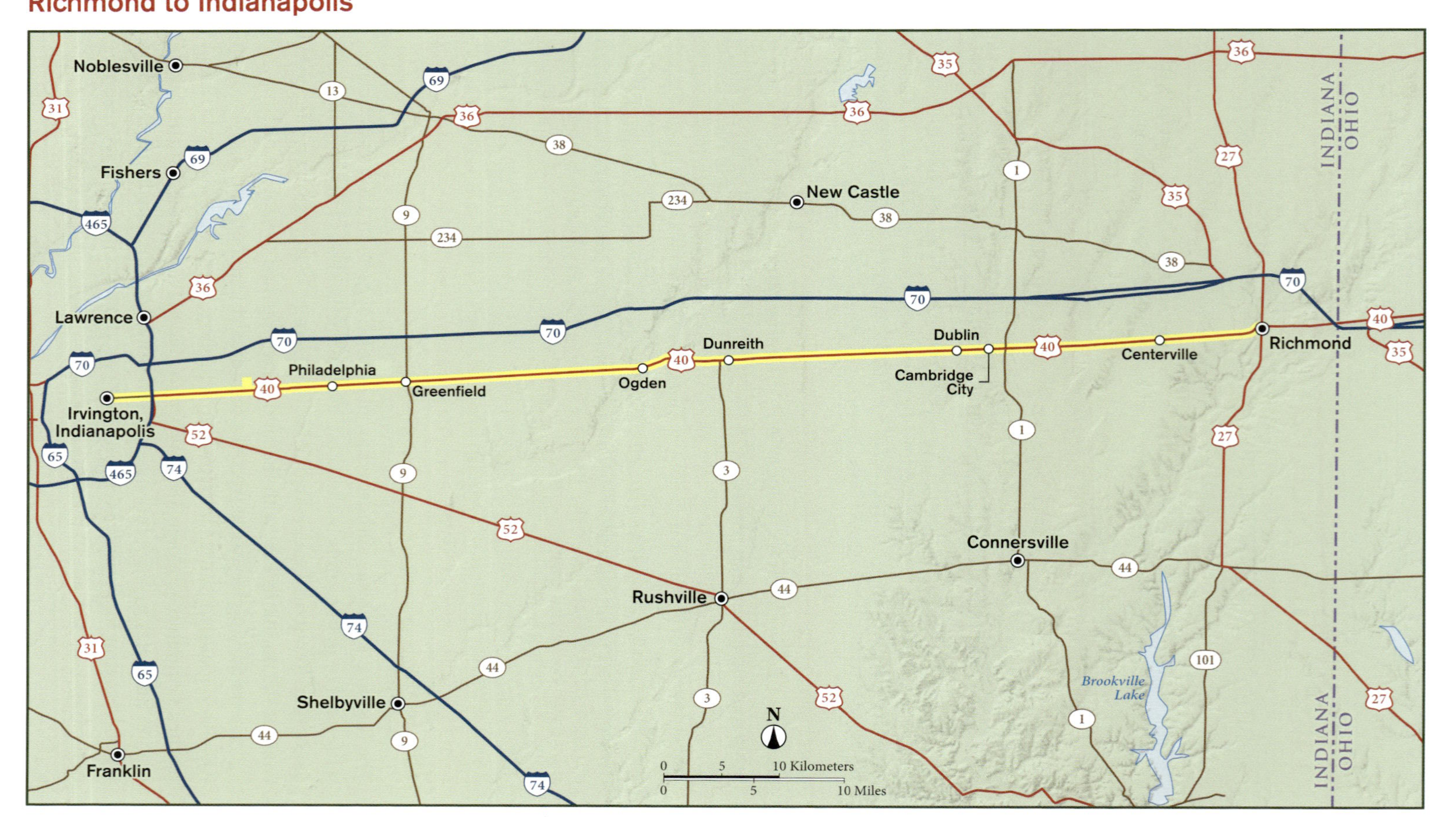

By 1850 Irish laborers and local farmers paved the Indiana road in the most modern means available, macadamization. The process, invented by a Scottish engineer, consisted of layers of stone starting with 7-inch rocks laid a foot below the surface and graded up with smaller stones mixed with soil and crowned for drainage.

Down the road through the 1840s and '50s, stagecoaches thundered to the inns that dotted the road every 5 miles or so. Mail coaches announced their imminent arrival with blasts of their trumpets; postmasters raced out to throw the bag. Looking like an odd land-bound craft, settlers' and pikemen's canvas-covered Conestoga wagons sailed across the prairie, pulled by solid teams of six horses. Whole towns in the East pulled up stakes and moved West, drawn by the lure of cheap land and a new life, passing through the little pike towns of Indiana that grew prosperous on the trade.

The drive begins at the Old National Road Welcome Center east of Richmond. (Richmond is covered in depth in Drive 15.) Fifteen interpretive markers describe key points between **Richmond** and **Terre Haute** on the west side of the state.

The two-lane covered National Bridge across the Whitewater Gorge was considered one of the engineering marvels of the age—the finest span from Maryland to St. Louis. Building commenced in 1833 and finished in 1835. It was an elegant entrance into Richmond until it closed in 1893. Three replacement bridges across the **Whitewater River** were built over the years, the most recent opening in 2000.

The *Madonna of the Trail* statue in Richmond at the entrance to Glen Miller Park at 22nd and East Main Streets is a 10-foot-high, 5-ton statue of a pioneer woman striding forward. Looking stolidly off into the future, she holds one babe to her breast while her young son clutches at the hem of her dress. One of the four plaques on the base notes that Indiana's first tollgate was located nearby.

Gray Gables, a large, gray-painted stucco structure on the south side of the road 2 miles from the edge of Richmond, was a National Road tavern and inn and later a private home for the county's mentally ill citizens. Two derelict two-story I-houses just past the Gray Gables are reputed to have been Underground Railroad stops.

Centerville is 5 miles west of downtown Richmond. The town was platted in 1814 and became a major town on the National Road. As many as 200 wagons a day passed through the town in the pre–Civil War heyday of the National Road.

Centerville is an architectural restatement of Eastern sensibilities. Brick row houses with shared sidewalls walled off the back spaces from egress, so the old tidewater habit of arched passageways was added. Today five of the original eleven remain. The Lantz House Inn Bed and Breakfast at 214 West Main is an excellent example—the arch leading into what was a nineteenth-century version of a well-equipped truck stop: a wagon-making and blacksmith business that could repair any wagon or horse ill you might have or sell you a new one. The space above was the local Oddfellows lodge.

The Mansion House Inn, 214 East Main St., is an 1840 Greek Revival former stagecoach stop. Today it is the home of Historic Centerville Inc.

The old Sheriff's House at East Main and First Streets bears the mark of Centerville's last hurrah as the county seat. When two men from Centerville heard the news that the court records were to be moved to Richmond, they fired a cannon load of iron scraps from an archway across the way from the mouth of locally celebrated Black Betty. It scared off the jailer, but the state militiamen restored order and conveyed the ledgers to Richmond. The scars of the last battle can still be seen in the brickwork above the door.

Today, the town center feels much as it did when the Republic was young and Indiana was still the West. More than one hundred buildings are on the National Register of Historic Places. The two-story Federal-style home at 214 West Main St. was the home of Israel Abram, Jewish pioneer and merchant. The first floor was a wagon shop, and the Masonic Lodge met in the room above. The Morton Home at the southeast corner of West Main and Willow Grove was the onetime home of Civil War Governor Oliver P. Morton.

Antique dealers discovered the town in the 1960s, and now Centerville is known as the beginning of "Antique Alley of Indiana"—a 33-mile stretch of US 40 where more than 1,200 antique dealers offer their wares.

Pennville and East Germantown, 6 and 7.6 miles west, respectively, have sprinklings of early architecture, some uninhabited, most down-at-the-heels.

The old Whitewater Canal town of Cambridge City differs from other Wayne County towns both in ethnic makeup (it has few Quakers and is mainly German) and age. The town was incorporated in 1841 to take advantage of the coming Whitewater Canal, which arrived in 1846. The old Vinton House Inn at 22 West Main St. was a stagecoach and canal boat stop beginning in the late 1840s. One sidewall was angled for a canal-side location. It's now an antique shop.

At 520 East Church St. in Cambridge City, the Lackey-Overbeck House is the oldest and perhaps most illustrious house in town. The Federal-style house was built in the late 1830s and was the home—from 1911 to 1955—to the six Overbeck Sisters, who produced the highly collectable Arts and Crafts Overbeck Pottery. The kiln was just west of the house. The Museum of Overbeck Art Pottery at 33 West Main St. preserves the memory of Cambridge City's most famous artists and has examples of their wares.

The Huddleston Farmhouse Inn Museum is a period restoration of the National Road enterprise built in the road's heyday. Unlike most inns of the day that readily served "strong waters to relieve the inhabitants," the temperate Quaker Huddlestons didn't serve liquor.

While the road declined with the advent of the railroad, the Huddlestons continued to prosper with their rich farmland and business dealings. Accordingly, the next generations of Huddlestons spiffed up the austere three-story Federal structure with the Victorian trappings of the day, which include the louvered Italianate cupolas on the barn. Indiana Landmarks, a preservation organization, now operates the house as a museum and community center.

Dublin is just down the road. While the name may relate to Ireland, locals say the origin is more likely attributed to the teamsters' habit of adding another team of horses at this point—"doublin"—because the next stretch of road was exceptionally rough. Another theory is that a local tavern had two entrances, hence "double-in." In the boom years, twelve stagecoach lines operated over the pike.

At Dublin, US 40 becomes a four-lane highway. Dunreith is 12 miles west. The original name of Coffin's Station, named after town founder Emery Dunreith Coffin, thankfully gave way to Dunreith in 1865.

North 2.2 miles on IN 3 is Spiceland, home of the former **Quaker Spiceland Academy**, which began in 1827 and was a renowned educational institution. The eminent American historian Charles A. Beard was a graduate of the academy. Return to US 40.

A two-lane remnant of the original National Road provides an alternate route from Dunreith to Knightstown. Turn south on Water Street in Dunreith and follow the contours of the land through woods and fields as nineteenth-century travelers did. Marked as Old National Road, the two-lane road passes through **Ogden**, platted in 1820 as **Middletown**. It was renamed Ogden to honor one of the National Road's engineers after it was discovered another Middletown already existed in Henry County.

Knightstown was named for Jonathan Knight, the government engineer responsible for this section of the National Road. Within its 1-square-mile footprint, **Knightstown** boasts 536 buildings in its historic district. The most visible, for two reasons, is the Elias Hinshaw House. For starters, it's right on US 40 (16 West Main St.). Then there's the four-story central tower that rises above the two-story Italian villa–style home built by Knightstown founder Waitsell Cary and later bought by Hinshaw.

Eight blocks north of Main Street on Penn Street is **Hoosier Gym**, famous for being the setting of the 1986 basketball movie *Hoosiers*. Built in 1921 with $14,400 in local donations, the bandbox gym was the home court for Knightstown High School until 1966. Mostly idle until the movie filming, the gym escaped the wrecking ball in 1988 and now entertains eighty basketball games each year.

Hoosier Gym in Knightstown gained fame from the movie Hoosiers.

Behind the gym is the former **Knightstown Academy**. The three-story, Second Empire–style school was built in 1876 and served as a luminary private school for many years. The city converted it into a public school when the private school folded, but it has since been turned into apartments. The 40-foot-high twin towers have immense models of a globe and a telescope at their peaks, symbolizing education and science.

Return to US 40 and drive west 0.5 mile to 517 West Main, the former home of John J. Lehmanowsky, a Polish Jew who converted to Christianity as a young man. He served as a colonel in Napoleon's Imperial Guard and saw action in Spain, Russia, and at Waterloo. Imprisoned after Waterloo, he was condemned to death but escaped to America and settled in Knightstown as pastor of the Lutheran church.

Charlottesville, 4.3 miles west, is on Rush County's northern line. It is another fertile, well-watered agricultural county, with more than 90% of the county under cultivation. Turn south in little Charlottesville on Carthage Road and drive 2 miles to County Road 1000 North. Turn left and drive 1.7 miles to CR 725 West. A long lane 0.3 mile farther leads to Beech Grove Church, which served a congregation of free African Americans who migrated to the area in the 1830s at the behest of local Quakers. The congregation voted in 1832 to merge their affiliations and join the African Methodist Church (AME). The Indiana AME was organized here in 1840. The present white clapboard structure was erected in 1860 to replace an 1838 log church. Yearly homecomings have taken place since 1914.

Return to US 40 and continue west. Cleveland, 1 mile farther west of Charlottesville, is more farm country with healthy-looking cattle and horses with glistening coats. Prosperous farms line the road.

The Hoosier Poet Motel used to be the harbinger of Greenfield, birthplace of famous Hoosier poet James Whitcomb Riley. The motel was an example of roadside architecture that stretched back to the 1950s when motels like it lined the highways coast-to-coast. Alas, the Hoosier Poet Motel no longer functions as a motel and was last being used for storage by a local business.

Greenfield still has plenty of connections to its most famous resident. The James Whitcomb Riley Home and Museum at 250 West Main St. resonates the cozy family life that suffuses so much of Riley's poetry. Built in 1849–50 by Riley's father, Reuben, the home is a two-story clapboard house with Italianate styling. The interior, with period Victoriana and warm walnut trim, exudes a homey charm. A statue of Riley seated on a bench is in front of the home, now owned by the city. Since 1937 the house has been a National Historic Site. The James Whitcomb Riley Memorial Park was dedicated in 1925.

The Hancock County Courthouse statue of Riley presents him in academic robes, representing the honorary doctorate he received from Indiana University in 1907. The courthouse itself was built from 1896 to 1898 in a Romanesque Revival style. It is the centerpiece of the town's historic district, which includes seventy-one other buildings.

The Hancock County Historical Society occupies two buildings on North Apple Street—the Old Log Jail built in 1828 and the 1876 Old Chapel in the Park, a white-frame building that was a United Methodist church.

Philadelphia is 3.6 miles west, formerly an important stage stop for National Road travelers. It was also the former home of Mary Alice (Smith) Gray, the childhood playmate of Riley and the model for his famous poem "Little Orphan Annie." To see her house, proceed west 0.8 mile from Philadelphia on US 40 to Spring Lake Road (a.k.a. CR 250S) and turn south 0.8 mile. The white-frame house is on the right.

Modern America rapidly replaced heritage landscapes as the exurban bulge of Indianapolis reached out into the prairie. Cumberland, named after the eastern terminus of the National Road, is primarily a modest bedroom community of Indianapolis. The mammoth Washington Square Mall is soon after, the first of the capital city's necklace of suburban shopping malls.

Proceeding west into Indianapolis on Washington Avenue (US 40) is a trip backward in time from the postmodern shopping malls. The tiny turn-of-the-century neighborhood of Irvington is a quiet residential place dotted with low-scale tile-roofed shopping arcades. In 1987 the entire community of some 2,300 structures was put on the National Register of Historic Places. The styles range from Second Empire, Classical, and Queen Anne to Arts and Crafts and Prairie Style. Walking tour maps can be purchased from the Irvington Landmarks Foundation at 312 S. Downey St.

The campus of Butler University was on Downey Street from 1825 to 1928, along with the nationally renowned College of Missions, which trained Protestant missionaries to carry the gospel into far-flung lands. For many years, it was the only place in the country where languages like Tibetan were taught.

Return to Washington Street and drive west through a gauntlet of ramshackle pawn shops, used-car lots, car repair places, small ethnic cafes, rough-looking bars, and vintage commercial buildings. A pair of cowled stone gnomes clutch books beside the front doors of the Indianapolis Public Library on the north side of Washington and Rural Streets.

After passing under I-65, turn north at North College Avenue to Lockerbie Street and turn west again to the center of Lockerbie Square and back into the mid-nineteenth century. Lockerbie Square was settled in 1830, and in the 1860s the more substantial homes of the well-to-do began to be interspersed with the cottages of local artisans.

The area owes its survival to James Whitcomb Riley's last home, which is located at 528 Lockerbie St. He moved into the home of his friends, the Holsteins, in 1893 and spent the last 23 years of his life there. Following his death in 1916 (and the subsequent deaths of the Holsteins), a group of his influential friends arranged to purchase the home and turn it into a museum, and it has been a tourist destination since. All the furnishings and art that accompanied Riley in his last years are still there, along with his top hat, piano, and the painting of his beloved dog, Lockerbie. The house was placed on the National Register of Historic Places in 1963 and it formed the anchor of Lockerbie Square.

Beginning in the 1960s, the neighborhood underwent a startling renaissance from a low-end rental area with moldering and collapsing houses to one of the most prestigious residential areas in Indianapolis.

14

The Old National Road II

Indianapolis to Terre Haute

General description: The western leg of the National Road begins among downtown Indianapolis attractions and courses through a few small towns to complete its Indiana section in Terre Haute.

Special attractions: Indiana State Capitol, Eiteljorg Museum of American Indians and Western Art, Indiana State Museum, NCAA Hall of Champions, White River State Park, Indianapolis Zoo, Oasis Diner in Plainfield, CANDLES Holocaust Museum and Education Center in Terre Haute.

Location: Western Indiana.

Drive route numbers and names: US 40.

Travel season: The road is drivable in all but the worst of winter weather.

Camping: Lazy L Lake Campground (812) 533-1562, Prairie Creek Park (812) 898-2270, Fowler Park (812) 462-3413, Hawthorn Park (812) 462-3225, Camp Wabashi (812) 299-1058, and Terre Haute Campground (812) 917-5671, all in Terre Haute. Quarry Lake Campground (765) 386-7332 near Stilesville.

Services: There are full services, hotels, restaurants, shopping, movies, etc., in Indianapolis, Plainfield, Brazil, and Terre Haute.

Nearby attractions: Indiana Medical History Museum in Indianapolis; Deer Creek Fish & Wildlife Area in Putnamville; Chafariz dos Contos Fountain in Brazil; Rose-Hulman Institute of Technology and Wabashiki Fish and Wildlife Area in Terre Haute; Larry Bird and Eugene V. Debs Museums in Terre Haute.

The Drive

Start the western leg of the **National Road at Lockerbie Square** by turning south on North East Street and going 7 blocks to East Washington Street (a.k.a. the National Road).

Turn right. The **Indianapolis Arts Garden** quickly comes into view. The seven-story glass-and-steel structure hangs over the intersection with Meridian Street and is the location of more than 300 events annually.

Meridian Street is the main thoroughfare running north and south through Indianapolis. Turn right at Meridian and go 1 block north to **Monument Circle**, where the Soldiers & Sailors Monument towers over the circular street. It was the site of the governor's mansion from 1827 to 1857 before being razed and converted to a city park in 1862. A quarter century later the state legislature approved funding to build a monument honoring Hoosier soldiers who served in the Civil War and other conflicts, from the Revolutionary War to the Spanish-American War.

Indianapolis to Terre Haute

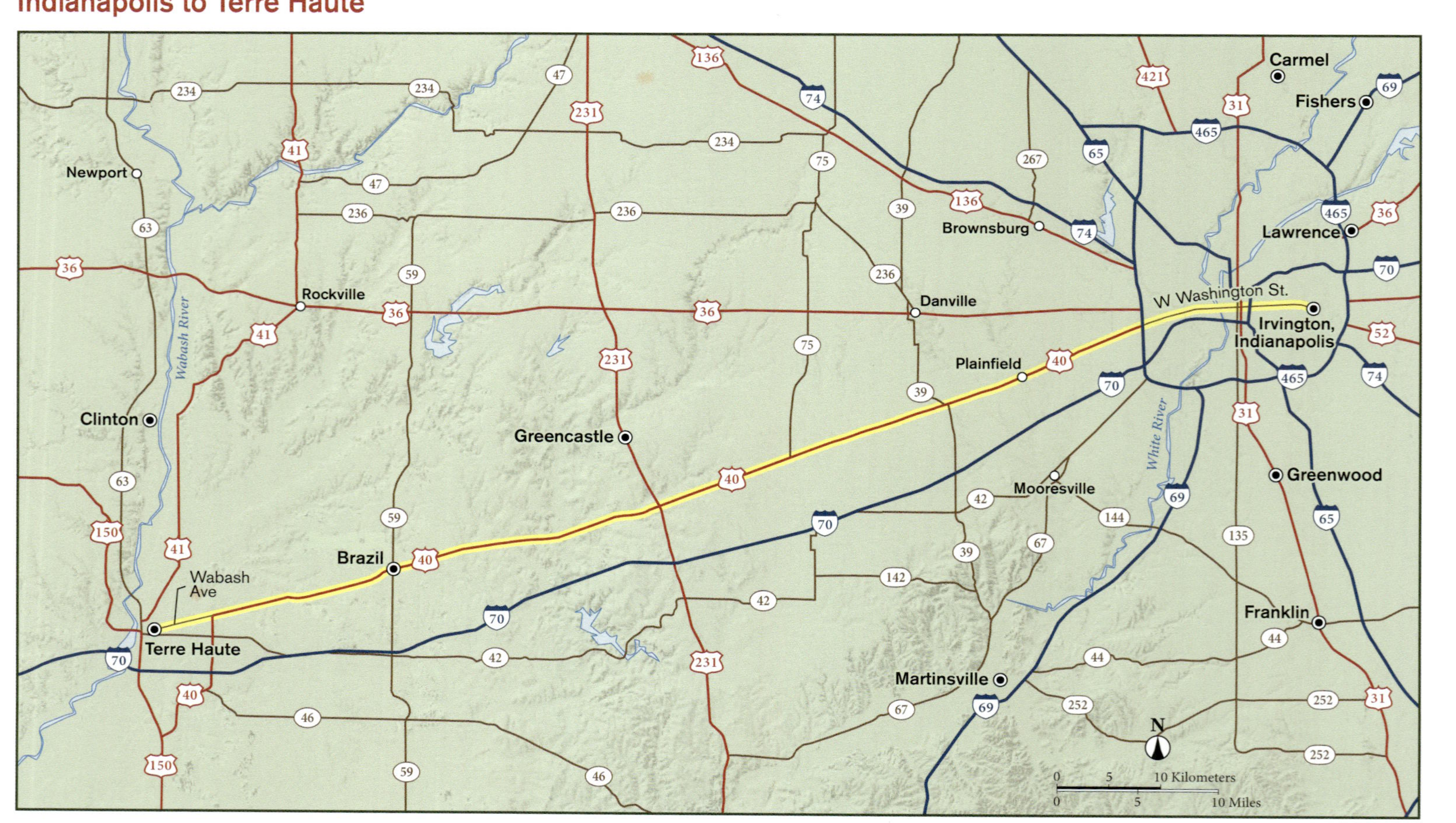

The 286-foot-tall monument—topped by a 38-foot statue of Victory—was designed by German architect Bruno Schmitz and took 13 years to build. The obelisk is constructed of Indiana limestone and has an observation deck 231 feet aboveground that can be reached by elevator or 331 steps. Since 1962, the monument has been adorned with lights and garlands stretching from street level to the top, earning it the title "the world's largest Christmas tree."

Soldiers and Sailors Monument honors military personnel from the Revolutionary War to present-day conflicts. Visit Indy/Scott Crone

After circling the monument, return south on Meridian to West Washington Street and turn right. In a matter of a few blocks, pass the state capitol, government offices, the **Eiteljorg Museum of American Indians and Western Art**, the **Indiana State Museum**, IMAX Theater, **Victory Field**, the NCAA Hall of Champions, **White River State Park**, and the **Indianapolis Zoo** before crossing over the White River.

It's a long slog from there through Indianapolis residential areas with one noteworthy location: the Indiana Medical History Museum at 3270 Kirkbride Way, a few blocks north of West Washington Street via North Tibbs Avenue. The museum is on the grounds of the former Central State Hospital, originally known as the Indiana Hospital of the Insane. The hospital's pathology department opened in 1896 and closed in the 1960s before being reborn as a museum in 1969. Tours and special events are offered on the history of science and medicine, forensic science, and mental health care.

Turn right after returning to West Washington Street and continue for 12 miles to Plainfield's historic downtown district. The area encompasses 174 buildings featuring a mix of architectural styles, from Greek Revival to Queen Anne to American Craftsman.

At the west end of the district is the **Oasis Diner**, a stainless-steel restaurant built in New Jersey and transported to Plainfield in 1954. After several ownership changes, the diner closed in 2008 but gained a new life two years later after Indiana Landmarks put the restaurant on its Most Endangered list. New owners were found, and the aging diner was restored and moved 4 miles to its current location for a 2014 reopening. It is the only such diner on Indiana's portion of the National Road.

After leaving Plainfield, the National Road takes on a mostly rural appearance the rest of the way to Terre Haute except for a few small towns, the largest being Brazil.

First up is **Stilesville**, 10 miles west of Plainfield. The town was settled in 1827, and the National Road was built through here in 1830. Never a big town, Stilesville's population falls short of 300 people, making the outsized cemetery a point of interest. Town founder Jeremiah Stiles created the cemetery when his wife died. A pioneer group traveling through Stilesville stopped for food and rest, but several ended up with food poisoning and fourteen died.

Continue west from Stilesville for 1.5 miles to Rising Hall, currently a bed-and-breakfast and special-event center on the south side of the road. The Italianate home was built in 1872 by Melville McHaffie for $2,500 and features eight interior stairways, hence the name Rising Hall. McHaffie had a hand in the Civil War by providing the most mules to the Union Army, an act that earned him special commendation from President Abraham Lincoln. The legendary horse Dan Patch reportedly trained here during the early 1900s and went on to never lose a race while setting fourteen world speed records.

Oasis Diner in Plainfield is the only one of its kind on Indiana's portion of the National Road.

About halfway between Stilesville and Brazil is **Putnamville**, pioneered in 1830 by James Townsend and a handful of emancipated slaves.

Putnamville Correctional Facility, which began as the Indiana State Farm, is located here. The medium security penal farm was known as much for raising food products for other prisons as it was for alleged mistreatment of prisoners in the early 1900s, which prompted a newspaper editor to call it "The Black Hole of Indiana." The original facility covered 3,500 acres, but in 2010 nearly 2,000 acres were transferred to the Department of Natural Resources for the development of Deer Creek Fish & Wildlife Area.

In **Brazil**, which was founded in 1844 and named for the South American country, the National Road is labeled National Avenue and runs through the center of town. In 1956 the country gave its namesake the Chafariz dos Contos Fountain (translated the Fountain of Tales). Located 9 blocks south of the National Road on IN 59, it's a replica of a fountain in Ouro Preto, Brazil, dating to 1745.

A 2018 study tabbed Brazil as the poorest city in Indiana, with nearly 32% of the population below the poverty line. But more than a century earlier, it was a boomtown thanks largely to nearby coal and clay deposits. Prior to the arrival of the National Road in 1920, Brazil boasted thirteen coal mines, eleven clay factories, four banks, an opera house, six newspapers, nine hotels and restaurants, eleven meat markets, more than a dozen attorneys and doctors, and forty-three saloons.

The three-story limestone **Clay County Courthouse** at 609 E. National Ave. is the centerpiece of Brazil's downtown district. Built in 1919, it is one of many buildings in Brazil on the National Register of Historic Places. The Clay County Historical Society is housed in Brazil's former post office at 100 E. National Ave.

A must-stop before leaving Brazil is Lynn's Pharmacy at 22 W. National Ave. Although it's a modern pharmacy, owner Lynn Hostettler has given it an old-fashioned appearance with black-and-white checkered tile flooring, a tin ceiling, antique furniture, and a soda parlor that seats forty to fifty customers. The 12-foot-wide stainless-steel and oak-trimmed soda fountain was retrieved from a northern Indiana parlor that closed in 1969.

The ending point of the National Road in Indiana is Terre Haute, 10 miles west of Brazil. Two landmarks on the route into Terre Haute are Twigg Rest Park and the campus of **Rose-Hulman Institute of Technology**. The park opened in 1935 as one of the first rest stops on the Indiana section of the National Road. Terre Haute acquired and restored the site in the 1980s. Rose-Hulman has been turning out engineers, mathematicians, and other scientists for more than 150 years.

Just past Rose-Hulman's baseball and softball fields is the **Old National Road Filling Station**. Built in 1931 by a whiskey distiller, it was marked for demolition when the Indiana National Road Association rescued it and moved the stone cottage to its current location, where it serves as a concession stand for the college's athletic events.

After running mostly as a straight line from Indianapolis, US 40 takes a sharp left turn and continues south to merge with I-70, then goes west for another 15 miles to the Indiana-Illinois state line.

An alternative is to stay straight onto Wabash Avenue to take in several attractions, including the **Vigo County Historical Museum** (929 Wabash Ave.), **Terre Haute Children's Museum** (727 Wabash Ave.), and the Larry Bird Museum (800 Wabash Ave.). All three are on the south boundary of Indiana State University, where Bird was a basketball star before going on to a legendary career with the Boston Celtics in the National Basketball Association.

Deeper into the ISU campus is the Eugene V. Debs Museum. Debs, who dropped out of school at age 14, became a union activist and leader of the Socialist Party of America, running five times as a presidential candidate in the early 1900s, the last time while serving a 10-year sentence on sedition charges in violation of the Espionage Act of 1917.

Return south to Wabash Avenue, turn right, and continue to US 41, where the massive Vigo County Courthouse towers over the city. Built of Indiana limestone in the late 1800s for $443,000, the courthouse is 282 feet tall and topped with a clock tower and dome that houses a 2-ton bell.

Ten blocks south on US 41 is the **CANDLES Holocaust Museum and Education Center**. The acronym in the title stands for Children of Auschwitz Nazi Deadly Lab Experiment Survivors. Eva Mozes Kor, herself a Holocaust survivor, opened the facility in 1995. An arsonist firebombed the building in 2003. Undaunted by the damage done, the museum was repaired in time to reopen in 2005.

15

Underground Railroad

Quaker Heritage and the Underground Railroad

General description: The 55-mile drive explores Richmond and Fountain City with their Quaker traditions and a loop through Wayne County and a bit of Randolph.

Special attractions: In Richmond: Earlham College, Samuel Charles Home, Wayne County Historical Museum, Gennett Records Site, Old Richmond and Starr Historic Districts. In Fountain City: the Levi and Catharine Coffin State Historic Site.

Location: Eastern Indiana.

Drive route numbers and names: US 40, 27, and 36; IN 227, 35, and 1; Arba Pike; County Roads 600 South, 800 East, and 850 East.

Travel season: The roads are drivable in all but the worst of winter weather.

Camping: Deer Ridge Camping Resort (765) 939-0888, Grandpa's Farm Campground (765) 962-7907, and KOA Holiday Campground (765) 962-7907, all in Richmond.

Services: There are full services, hotels, restaurants, shopping, movies, etc., in Richmond. Gas and food are available in Fountain City, Hagerstown, and Cambridge City.

Nearby attractions: Whitewater Memorial State Park; Brookville Lake; Nettle Creek Valley Museum in Hagerstown; Fountain Acres Amish Store in Fountain City.

The Drive

The Great Quaker Migration into Wayne County began in 1806 when North Carolina Quakers settled in former Native American hunting and fishing grounds at the Whitewater River Gorge. They were the first of a vast flow of southern Quakers who escaped the South's "peculiar institution" of slavery to help pioneer the free state of Indiana.

By 1821 the Whitewater Friends Meeting had grown to become the Indiana Yearly Meeting with jurisdiction that stretched to the Pacific, encompassing more than 14,000 Quakers. Richmond and Wayne County became the country's second-largest concentration of Quakers behind only Philadelphia—a distinction the area still holds.

The large aggregate of Quakers naturally made Wayne County a hotbed of abolitionism in the decades before the Civil War, though the region was by no means unanimous in the tactics to be used. There were several wings of the antislavery movement, which ranged from gradualists who argued slavery could be eliminated over time to lessen the economic blow to the South, to antislavery groups who argued for immediate manumission without compensation to the slave owners.

Quakers and the Underground Railroad

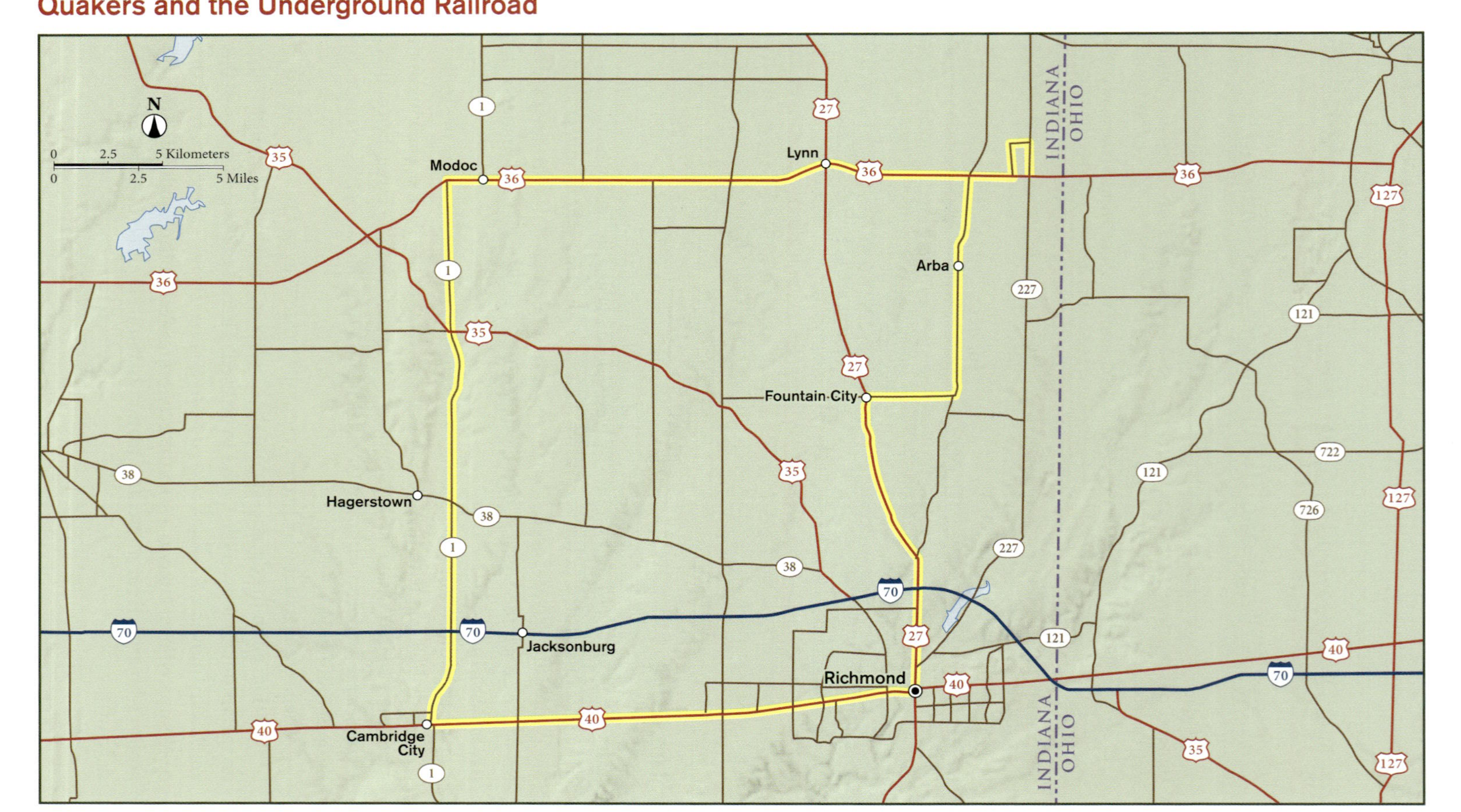

The Quakers entered their feelings in the national debate in 1842 when slave-owning Henry Clay addressed a crowd of 20,000 at the corner of Seventh and A Streets in Richmond. A local farmer, Hiram Mendenhall, gave Clay a petition signed by 2,000 Richmond Quakers asking him to free his slaves. Clay snorted that his fifty slaves were worth $15,000 and asked his hecklers if he were to free them would they raise the money for recompense. He concluded by suggesting that the petitioner should go home and mind his own business. The local Quakers have long suggested that resulting national uproar cost Clay his presidential contest with Polk, though historians have had to dissuade them of the idea.

The Underground Railroad, the shadowy organization that helped spirit fugitive slaves from the South to freedom in Canada, was the extreme wing of the Abolitionist movement. There were several main routes north to Canada. A major route from the Upper South slave states of Kentucky and Tennessee drove north through Ohio and Indiana. Slaves moved at night, always keeping the North Star as their guide. Once they negotiated the Ohio River, often with the help of freemen who lived in the northern border towns, the fugitives were helped northward by a network of Underground Railroaders.

The various fugitive slave laws that culminated in the particularly onerous Fugitive Slave Law of 1850 made cooperation with the Underground Railroad strictly illegal and subject to severe punishment and confiscation. In Wayne County the antislavery controversy and other sectarian fights tore the Quaker community apart. From the late 1820s, there were competing meetinghouses in town, each certain of their beliefs. In Fountain City (known as Newport then), the leaders of the Underground Railroad, including Levi Coffin, who was termed the president of the railroad, were expelled from the New Garden Meeting, the oldest Quaker meeting, for what was perceived as illegal and extremist activities.

The drive begins in Richmond, home of Earlham College, which was founded in 1847. The college is in the 1000 block of West National Road (US 40). It is the third-largest Quaker college after Friends House in London and Haverford College in Philadelphia. There are currently about 600 students with a particular concentration in peace studies and the sciences. The Joseph Moore Museum of Natural History on the south side of the campus holds a packrat's dream of diverse items, from a 15,000-year-old mastodon skeleton to an Egyptian mummy to a live snake collection.

Nearby at 1150 North A St., the Wayne County Historical Museum holds the other mummy in town, as well as airplanes, jazz recording exhibits, pioneering roller skates, exotic bikes, and fine early autos. It's a giant curiosity case of Wayne County's early entrepreneurial activities and the collections of the resulting nabobs. A thirteenth-century Buddha head graces the front lawn, serenely meditating on the passing Richmond scene. It is housed in the 1865 Hicksite Meeting Houses, one of the sectarian congregations that sprang up before the Civil War.

The Starr Historic District, which surrounds the museum, is on the National Register of Historic Places. It stretches from North A to North E Streets, and from North 10th to North 16th. It has long been the home of the local elite. The Andrew F. Scott Home was built in 1858, an Italianate structure at 126 North 10th that was an annex to the county museum until being sold into private hands in 2004 after it became a financial drain on the museum. High Tower at 326 North 10th St. was the home of Elizabeth Starr, wife of an early Richmond promoter. Her son, James, established the Starr Piano Company and lived in the house. The district also includes two houses once owned by the Wright Brothers, Orville and Wilbur.

The Starr Piano Company was long-lived, but one of Richmond's smaller enterprises remains one of its claims to fame. Gennett Records began in 1916 and by 1922 was producing 3 million records annually. From 1916 to 1934 the Richmond studio made jazz history, recording luminaries like Jelly Roll Morton, King Oliver's Creole Jazz Band with a young Louis Armstrong, the New Orleans Rhythm Kings, Duke Ellington, Hoagy Carmichael, Lawrence Welk, and Tommy Dorsey with Bix Beiderbecke and his Jazz Wolverines.

When trains rumbled by on the nearby tracks, recording would have to cease, though a few early recordings have the tremor of passing boxcars. A fragment of the last of the Starr's thirty-one buildings, which still has the Gennett sign painted on it, can be seen by going south on South First Street at the east end of East Main

Gennett Records in Richmond made jazz history with the likes of Duke Ellington and Louis Armstrong.

Street Bridge. The Richmond Parks & Recreation Department manages the building as rentable event space.

The Whitewater Valley Gorge Park is at the bottom of an Ice Age canyon where the Whitewater River has cut through the ancient limestone and shale. The gorge runs for 3.5 miles through Richmond and ranges from 200 to 300 feet across and 50 to 80 feet deep. It is renowned as a fossil hunters' haven, a great source of trilobites, brachiopods, and corals. The rubble piles in the park are free game for collectors. The gorge was originally the site of early industrial Richmond, and remains of a woolen mill, an electric power dam, and the Starr-Gennett building are in the valley.

Another early neighborhood, the Old Richmond Historic District, between South A and South East Streets and South 11th Street and the railroad, is a mixed commercial, residential, and industrial neighborhood. The upright homes and buildings speak of the German immigrants who migrated to Richmond in the 1840s and 1850s. Their stern rectitude and lack of ostentation fit well with the Quakers' simple aesthetics and lifestyle.

The Gaar House Museum at 2411 Pleasant View Rd. reflects another aesthetic entirely. It is an opulent, mansard-roofed mansion built in 1872 with a remarkable collection of elaborate turn-of-the-century furnishings. The tiles on the roof modestly spell out "A. Gaar," the proprietor's name. The Gaars were steam-thresher tycoons who were benefactors of Richmond. The house, with many of its original furnishings, is now a museum.

The Pennsylvania Railroad Depot on North E Street between 9th and 10th Streets is one of Daniel Burnham's (famous for his Washington, D.C., Union Station design) masterpieces, a 1902 Roman Renaissance fancy. The two-story, red-brick classical columns are particularly rare. The once bustling depot drew such famous travelers as Louis Armstrong, Gene Autry, Jack Benny, Buffalo Bill Cody, Joe DiMaggio, Robert Frost, Eleanor Roosevelt, Babe Ruth, and the Marx Brothers. It's now home to small businesses, restaurants, and assorted shops. The Richmond Art Association dates to 1898 when a local group organized to encourage popular appreciation in art. The McGuire Memorial Hall was opened in 1941 as an addition to Richmond High School, 350 Whitewater Blvd., in the hopes it will kindle a love of art in the malleable students. Since then, the association and the museum have been stalwarts in art appreciation for a wide swath of Indiana and neighboring Ohio. The curvilinear tiled space has four galleries filled with diverse art, with particular strengths in Indiana Impressionists and Overbeck art pottery.

East of downtown, Glen Miller Park is a 194-acre urban grove with picnic grounds and recreational facilities as well as an award-winning rose garden. Farther east, the E. G. Hill Memorial Rose Garden is a blooming wonder, with more than one hundred rose varieties.

The Samuel Charles Home directly behind the garden was built in 1813 of gray stone and stucco by a North Carolina Quaker. Reportedly the parlor's flagstone fireplace had a removable section that led to hidden cellar steps where fugitive slaves could hide.

Proceed from Richmond on US 27 North, 8.5 miles to Fountain City. It was originally named New Garden in 1818 and later Newport before being renamed Fountain City in 1878. The tidy brick church just south of Fountain City on New Garden Road is one of the earliest in the county and is still used for worship.

During the national upheaval over slavery prior to the Civil War, the small town was called the "Grand Central Station of the Underground Railroad," with local storekeeper Levi Coffin its president. As many as 2,000 fleeing slaves made their way from Cincinnati, Madison, and Jeffersonville through Fountain City on their way farther north, most finding refuge in Coffin's small home at the corner of Mill Street and US 27.

Coffin moved to Fountain City in 1826 from North Carolina and founded a general store and mill. He said he "knew the horrors of slavery first-hand." Almost immediately he embarked on his life work of shepherding ex-slaves to safety farther north. He built a taut two-story, redbrick house in 1839 and made sure it was designed to assist him in his work.

Levi and Catharine Coffin's house was dubbed the "Grand Central Station of the Underground Railroad." INDIANA DEPARTMENT OF NATURAL RESOURCES

From the time it was erected, fugitives were hidden in the house, one, two, three at a time, sometimes more. Once a farm wagon pulled in front of the house in the dark of night, and Coffin's wife Catharine opened the door. "How many?" she asked. "All of Kentucky," the driver answered, as seventeen weary refugees filed in.

Five years after Coffin built his home, he started a Free Labor store, dedicated to selling only goods made with non-slave hands. In the 1840s it was difficult to purchase Southern goods such as cotton and sugar without it being worked with slaves. In 1847, at the behest of abolitionists, Coffin moved to Cincinnati to run a wholesale version of a Free Labor store, to supply other retailers with Free Labor material. During the Civil War, he became the general agent for the Western Freedmen, who raised funds for freed slaves. It is often said that the protagonists of Harriet Beecher Stowe's *Uncle Tom's Cabin* were based on the Coffin couple.

The **Coffin House** passed through a variety of owners but was purchased by the state and is now a state historic site. The house is furnished with period furniture true to the austere style of the Quakers. The attic hiding spot is open for those who want to crawl into the warren and experience a few moments of a fugitive slave on the run.

The next stop northward for the fugitive was most often Cabin Creek, a community of African American freemen in Randolph County. While the Underground Railroad is often celebrated as an organization of right-thinking white folk, it was often the African Americans who bore the greatest risk and took the most dangerous jobs of the Railroad.

Cabin Creek has long since moldered into the earth, though the noble memory lives on.

Return from the Levi and Catharine Coffin Historic Site on US 27 to Fountain City Pike. Turn left (east) and drive 2.5 miles to Arba Pike, then drive north to the Wayne-Randolph County line. Arba Pike was the early trail known as the Quaker Trace that settlers established by running along the east fork of the Whitewater in 1817 to the Miami trading post at Fort Kekionga at today's Fort Wayne.

A mile east on the county line road is the state's highest point at 1,257 feet—**Hoosier Hill**—even though it is only about 30 feet higher than the surrounding area.

Just over the county line on Arba Road, Arba was the first settlement in Randolph County. For many years it was the largest town in the county. North of Arba on Arba Pike, bear right 0.6 mile past the new Quaker meetinghouse. Spartanburg is 3.5 miles north. Proceed north 1.2 miles to County Road 600 South and turn east (right). The remains of the brick, two-story Union Literary Institute are 2 miles farther, southeast of the intersection of CR 850 East. It was a Quaker school established in 1845 to provide elementary and secondary education to both white and African American students. The Union Literary Institute Preservation Society acquired the site in 2010 and is working on a restoration plan.

Return west 0.5 mile to CR 800 East (IN 227) and turn left. Drive 2 miles south to US 36 and go west 6 miles to Lynn, which suffered a horrendous tornado in 1986 that damaged 284 buildings and destroyed 24 houses. Amazingly enough, there were no casualties. Continue west to Modoc and turn south on IN 1. Hagerstown is 9.5 miles south.

German Baptists, or Dunkards, arrived in the area around 1820, joining New Jersey migrants who had come in 1815. In 1836 an influx of settlers coming down the National Road caused a name change from Elizabethtown to Hagerstown after Hagerstown, Maryland, the jumping-off point for the National Road.

Hagerstown was a brief boomtown when the Whitewater Canal terminated there in 1847. Within six years it was kaput and it has been a small sleepy burb since, except when crowds surge into the buffet at Willie and Red's Restaurant, formerly Welliver's Smorgasbord, or hit Abbott's Candy Shop, which has been making caramel and chocolate treats since 1890. The Nettle Creek Valley Museum at 96 Main St. is dedicated to the town's past, housed in an 1880s public hall graced with 1913 frescos painted by local artist Charles Newcomb.

Drive 6.8 miles south on IN 1 to Cambridge City and proceed 12 miles back to Richmond on US 40. See Drive 13 for information on US 40 and Cambridge City.

16

Mansions to Barns

Hamilton County

General description: The 55-mile drive explores Hamilton County from the pioneer past to the rustic farm towns to the upscale neighborhoods near Geist Reservoir.

Special attractions: Conner Prairie Living History Museum in Fishers; Courthouse Square in Noblesville; Morse Reservoir in Cicero; Geist Reservoir near Indianapolis.

Location: Central Indiana.

Drive route numbers and names: US 32 and 31. Various city and county roads.

Travel season: The roads are drivable in all but the worst of winter weather, but otherwise it is smooth sailing across the prairie.

Camping: White River Campground (317) 770-4430 at Cicero; River Bend Campground (317) 773-3333, Sleepy Bear Campground (317) 691-2339, and Mud Creek Campground (317) 420-1090, all at Noblesville.

Services: There are full services in Fishers and Noblesville: hotels, restaurants, shopping, movies, etc. Gas and food are available in Westfield, Cicero, and Atlanta.

Nearby attractions: Nickel Plate Express historic train excursions in Forest Park; Koteewi Park in Strawtown; Ruoff Music Center in Noblesville; Grand Park sports complex in Westfield; Monon Trail; White River; Four Finger Distillery and West Fork Whiskey Co. in Westfield; King Jugg Brewing Company, MashCraft, Sun King in Fishers; Northbrook Brewing Co. in Arcadia.

The Drive

The tour begins at Conner Prairie, a re-created 1836 pioneer settlement located at 13400 Allisonville Rd. in Fishers. In many ways Conner Prairie mirrors Hamilton County from its beginnings on the frontier, through the booming days of settlement and farming, to its decline and then rejuvenation as part of the industrial heartland.

William Conner arrived on the frontier in 1800, migrating from Ohio. He served as a trader and as a liaison between the European settlers and the Delaware Indians who lived along the White River.

He later married Mekinges, daughter of a prominent Lenape chief, and had six children with her. One of his duties as liaison was to translate during the 1818 Treaty of St. Mary's, which required the Lenape to move west of the Mississippi. Accordingly, Mekinges and their children went west with their kinsmen, while Conner stayed behind.

He quickly remarried, to Elizabeth Chapman, a young white woman, and produced another large brood. After his remarriage he built a large brick home to

Mansions to Barns, Hamilton County

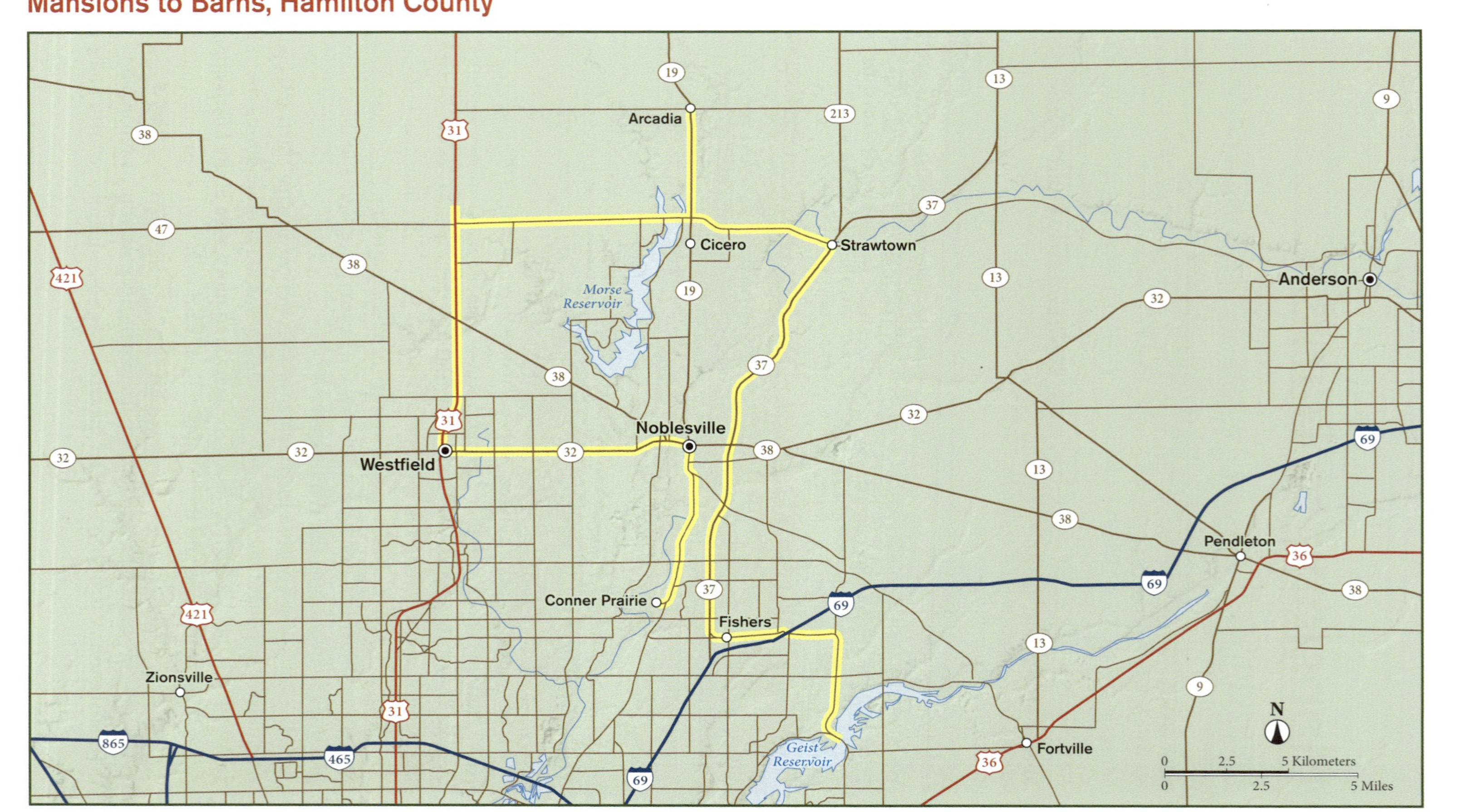

replace his cabin. Following the removal of the Lenape, Conner took his place as a patriarch of the frontier.

Conner successfully developed towns, stores, and mills, and invested in canals and railroads. He served as state representative for three non-consecutive terms between 1829 and 1837. Like most successful country boys, he headed for the city when he made his fortune—in this case Noblesville, where he died in 1855.

The Conner House and farm slowly declined, until the place was bought by industrialist Eli Lilly in 1934. After some restoration Lilly opened the house to visitation and turned the surrounding 1,000-plus acres into a model farm.

Lilly created a charitable trust in 1964 that transferred the farm to Earlham College as trustee. The college operated it as a museum and living history farm until 2003 when a dispute between Earlham and the Conner Prairie board resulted in the museum becoming an independent operation. Today a variety of buildings from across Indiana are clustered together on the farm to re-create an 1836 settler village. Costumed interpreters bring history to life with vivid portrayals of pioneer people. The 65,000-square-foot Museum Experience Center contains six immersive areas, galleries, cafes, a library, gift shop, and administrative offices. Earlham's Quaker heritage is incorporated into Conner Prairie via a Quaker cabin and a stirring living history depiction of the life of a fugitive slave on the Underground Railroad.

Conner Prairie re-creates Hamilton County's pioneering era of the 1830s. Conner Prairie

Noblesville is 4 miles north on Allisonville Road. William Conner and Josiah Polk platted the town in 1823 as the county seat. The county slumbered as a farming region for many years, but beginning in the 1970s, the county became a bedroom community of Indianapolis with the population jumping more than 300% in a few decades.

Turn west on Conner Street to the courthouse square. The courthouse is a Second Empire structure dating to 1878. The lurid murder trial of Ku Klux Klan Grand Dragon and state kingpin D. C. Stephenson was held in the courthouse in 1925. The jury convicted Stephenson and gave him a life sentence. The Hamilton County Jail southwest of the courthouse is where Stephenson was jailed during the trial. The wedding-cake sheriff's residence is now a historical museum.

The Victorian square has experienced a revival as an upscale shopping and dining destination. There are fine restaurants and antique shops and malls scattered in with the attorneys and hardware store.

Return to IN 32 and drive 5 miles west across the prairie to Westfield, where new suburban developments along the road supplant the collapsing barns. From its beginnings in 1836 as a Quaker settlement, Westfield was active in the Underground Railroad. North on Westfield Boulevard (Union Street) 0.3 mile, the Union Bible Seminary was a Quaker academy dating to 1861. In the twentieth century it became a fundamentalist school for the training of Christian missionaries and is now known as **Union Bible College**.

Turn right (north) on US 31 and drive 7 miles across the flat land, past sprawling corporate headquarters and office buildings, to 236th Street and turn east. Cicero and Morse Reservoir are 6.2 miles east of US 31. A cemetery at the edge of town has an exceptional carved limestone gravestone. The marker, rendered as a lifelike dead tree with severed limbs, is meant to represent a person dead before their time, cut off in the prime of life.

Cicero is a nineteenth-century brick and limestone railroad town, named after **Cicero Creek**, a tributary of the White River. Seventh Day Adventists settled the town, and their Indiana Academy founded in 1902 is still a major employer in town. The other major attraction in Cicero is Morse Reservoir, a water source for Indianapolis and a holiday getaway for Hoosiers. Lakefront lots have become another choice location for Indianapolis McMansions.

Turn north on IN 19 and drive across the swells and swales of the Tipton Till prairie land. Arcadia, another railroad town, is 2.9 miles north. In its heyday it was a glassblowing town, fueled by central Indiana's gas boom at the turn of the century. The town's motto is "Where small-town America still exists."

Return to IN 19 South and drive south 2.4 miles to Cicero. Take East Jackston Street east, which becomes 234th Street. Proceed 2.5 miles to Strawtown on the White River, site of the village of Chief Straw of the Delaware tribe. Strawtown offers a fine view of the White River. The 800-acre Koteewi Park pays homage to Native Americans who once called the area home. Park features include an aerial adventure trail, archery range, a natural history center, and biking, hiking, and equestrian trails.

Four of Indiana's ten-largest cities are on the banks of the White River. The entire watershed of the river drains more than a third of Indiana before joining the Wabash.

Proceed 12 miles south on IN 37 through Noblesville to 126th Street in Fishers. Go east on 126th to Brook School Road. Turn south on Brook School Road to Fall Creek Road. Turn west on Fall Creek Road to peruse the many affluent homes that surround Geist Reservoir—faux Tudors mingled with Louis XV hunting-lodge reproductions next to curiously overdeveloped Frank Lloyd Wright–inspired mansions.

Because of the growth in upscale suburbs and the availability of farmland, Hamilton County has become known as a premier golfing destination. There are fifteen golf courses in the county and three golf schools. The county boasts championship courses designed by some of America's best golf-course designers, including Pete Dye and Robert Trent Jones Jr.

17

Crossing the Hoosier Prairie

Greencastle to Lafayette

General description: The 60-mile drive explores the Indiana prairie through the college towns of Greencastle, Crawfordsville, and **West Lafayette**.

Special attractions: In Greencastle and Putnam County: DePauw University and covered bridges. In Crawfordsville and Montgomery County: Ben Hur Museum, Old Jail Museum, the Lane Place, and Linden Depot Museum. In Lafayette and Tippecanoe County: Purdue University, Fort Ouiatenon, Battle Ground Museum, and Prophetstown State Park.

Location: Western Indiana.

Drive route numbers and names: US 231 and 36; IN 234; multiple county roads.

Travel season: Except during bad winter weather, the roads are fine year-round. The covered-bridge section of the drive is particularly scenic in the fall leaf season.

Camping: Prophetstown State Park (765) 567-4919 and AOK Campground (765) 474-5030, both near Lafayette; Shades State Park (765) 435-2810.

Services: There are services in Greencastle, Crawfordsville, and Lafayette—hotels, restaurants, shopping, movies, etc. Gas and food are available in Cloverdale, Linden, and the US 74 interchange.

Nearby attractions: Fern Cliff Nature Preserve and DePauw Nature Park, both in Greencastle; Big Walnut Nature Preserve and Hall Woods Nature Preserve, both near Bainbridge; several historic covered bridges in Putnam County; Shades State Park is in the southeast corner of Montgomery County.

The Drive

Greencastle is Putnam County's seat of government, established in 1821. The courthouse square revolves around the 1905 limestone structure with a World War II V-1 German buzz bomb that terrorized London on the corner. Local citizens erected the war memorial on Memorial Day in 1947. It is one of only two buzz bomb missiles located in America, the other being in storage at the Smithsonian.

The courthouse square was also the site of pharmaceutical king Eli Lilly's first drugstore. At Washington and Indiana Streets, the Fleenor Building stands on the location of Lilly's 1861 apothecary. There is a plaque on the east side of the building. The store lasted but a short while before Lilly enlisted in the Union Army. After serving in several battles, he relocated to Indianapolis, where he commenced his career as an industrial giant.

Gangster John Dillinger visited the Central National Bank building at 26 West Washington in 1933, before it was converted to the retail and office space you see

Hoosier Prairie from Greencastle to Lafayette

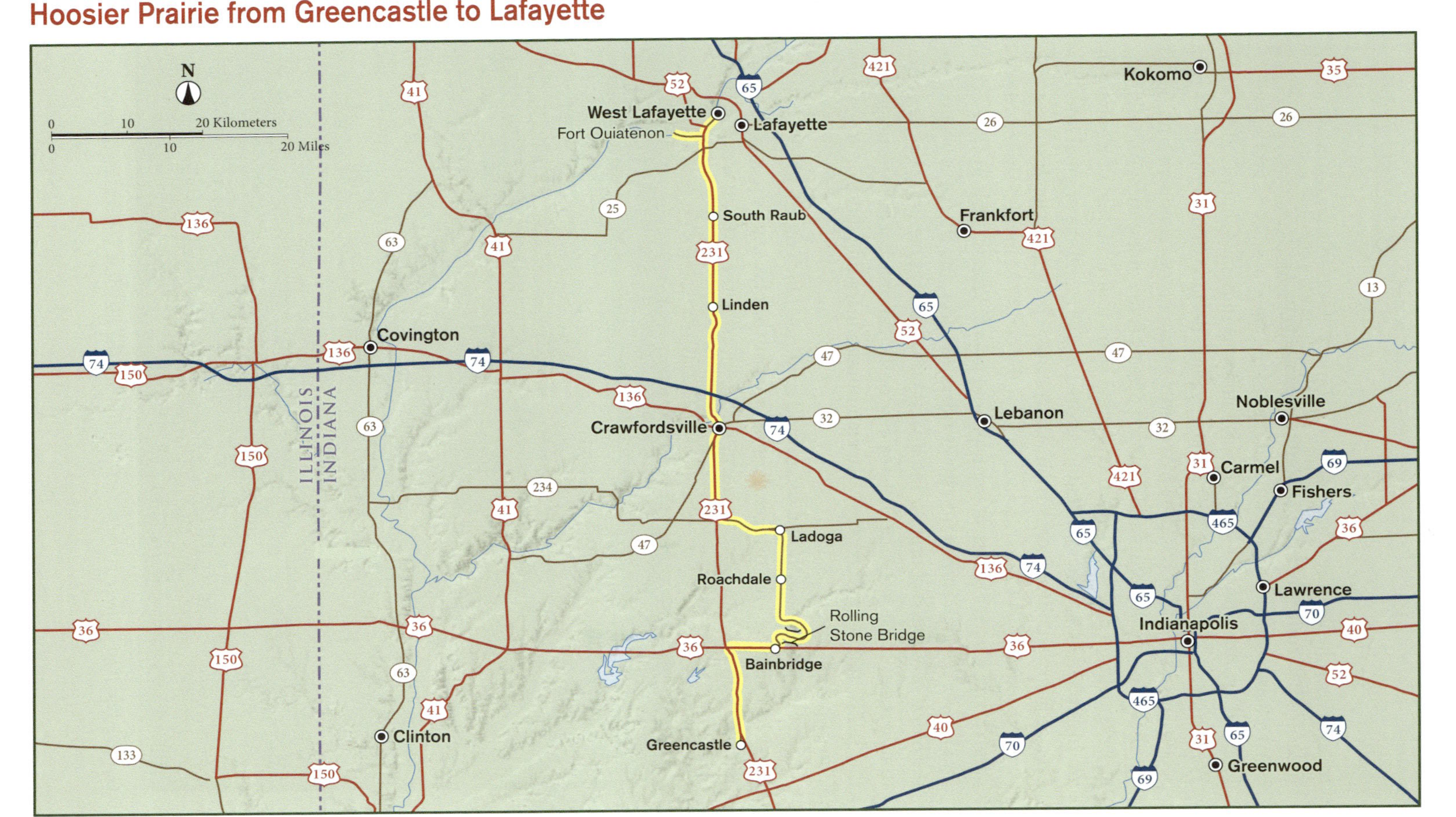

today. When he left, the bank was short about $75,000 (his biggest haul) as Dillinger scooted for his hideout in southern Parke County.

DePauw University is 6 blocks south of the square, a liberal arts school founded by Methodists in 1837. It was known as Indiana Asbury College until Washington C. DePauw, a New Albany tycoon, decided to underwrite the failing school in 1884. Their best-known alumnus is former vice president Dan Quayle.

East College at Locust and Simpson Streets is the oldest campus building, an 1871 belfried and turreted structure that soars four elaborate stories high in Gothic excess. It was magnificently restored in 1981, and the original interior with extraordinary woodwork and original furniture is lovingly maintained.

The Old Bethel Church stands behind the Gobin Memorial United Methodist Church and Charter House at Simpson and Locust Streets. Built in 1807 near the Ohio River at Charlestown for circuit riders' services, the church is believed to be the oldest Methodist church in Indiana. It was moved three times before coming to its current roost in 1953. The area east of the campus is a historic neighborhood that boasts many well-ordered Victorian homes, including those of several past college presidents.

Return to the courthouse square and continue north on US 231.

With nine covered bridges, Putnam County has the state's second-largest collection after Parke County. North of Greencastle, the road crosses Big Walnut

Gothic-style East College is the oldest building on the DePauw University campus.

Creek, which cuts diagonally across the county through the rumpled remnants of glacial melt. Most of the covered bridges are along this creek and Raccoon Creek.

The road traverses the melt line of the glaciers, where the flat land of the glacial scour meets the unglaciated woodlands. Proceed 8.9 miles to US 36, through the aptly named country hamlet of Brick Chapel with an imposing brick church on the knoll. Turn right (east) on US 36 and drive 3.9 miles to Bainbridge.

East of town, look for signs to the Oscar and Ruth Hall Woods Nature Preserve, a fine wildlife-viewing location, which is south of US 36 along Big Walnut Creek. The 94-acre preserve is a **National Natural Landmark**.

Return to the center of Bainbridge and head north on Washington Street, which becomes County Road 200 East. (The county has laid out a twisty path of covered bridges through the countryside that is well marked with signs. Should you become intrigued to investigate more than is laid out here, just make your way back west until you hit US 231 and proceed north on this route.)

Turn east on CR 800 North and snake through the woods 2 miles to Rolling Stone Bridge, then continue 1.4 miles to CR 525 E and turn left. Follow the combination of CR 525 E, 850 N, 500 E, and 900 N for another 1.8 miles to Pine Bluff Bridge. Big Walnut Natural Area, one of the state's loveliest, is along the country road. The gravelly roads weave in and out of the rugged valley, a land of farms, soaring hawks, and peering deer, with gaggles of wild turkeys at the roadside. After reintroduction in the 1970s, the wild turkeys have procreated with zest; it is not unusual to see flocks of a few dozen feeding beside rural roadsides.

After Pine Bluff Bridge, CR 900 continues for a half mile before curving left and becoming CR 950 N, which goes arrow-straight for another 1.4 miles to a T at CR 250 East. Turn north and drive 5 miles across a landscape of totemic silos and big skies through Roachdale to Ladoga across the Montgomery County line.

The town was laid out in 1836 on the former Shawnee hunting grounds along Big Raccoon Creek. The town was named after a birch-lined lake in Russia by a group of students who chose it from a geography book. The village was clustered around a four-story sawmill on the creek, and the local brickyard produced the material for several fine homes and buildings that are still standing.

In 1855 Baptists established the Ladoga Female Seminary, which operated until the Civil War. The building still stands on a hill in the center of town. The Central Indiana Normal School and Business Institute took over the building in 1876. The open-door institute offered education to students unable to afford it elsewhere.

In 1878 the school moved to Danville, Indiana. The old Normal School served as the public high school for more than 70 years and became an American Legion post in the 1970s.

Proceed 7.8 miles across the prairie on IN 234 to US 231. Parkersburg is 3.7 miles south, near the site of Chief Cornstalk's Snakefish village along Cornstalk Creek 3 miles east. From 1774 to 1820 the Eel River tribe of the Miami lived peaceably with the early settlers before being moved out to a reservation at Thorntown to the northeast.

Crawfordsville, another college town, is 11 miles north on US 231. Sometimes known as the "Athens of Indiana" because of its strong cultural interests and institutions, the town is famed as the home of Major General Lew Wallace, hero of the Mexican War and author of the wildly successful nineteenth-century novel *Ben Hur.*

On Pike Street, east of US 231, the General Lew Wallace Study and Museum stand surrounded by a brick wall, built by Wallace with the enormous profits from his book. The unique structure is an austere brick cube with a Greek-style portico, a Romanesque turret with an English-style fireplace, and an ornate Moorish central room that incorporates Wallace's interest in ancient architecture—Byzantine, Greek, Roman, Turkish, and Art Nouveau motifs and styles. Built in 1896, the structure houses 77 years of Wallace's memorabilia, which includes his military career in the Mexican and Civil Wars, vice presidency of the Lincoln assassination trials, governor of the New Mexico Territory, and US Minister to Turkey. There are oil paintings, objets d'art, military uniforms, gifts of the Sultan of Turkey, and Wallace's collection of over a thousand volumes.

Nearby, the Lane Place is a fine Greek-Revival antebellum house operated by the Montgomery County Historical Society. Built in 1845, it was the home of Henry Lane, congressman and confidant of Abraham Lincoln. The house is the centerpiece of Elston Grove, a neighborhood listed on the National Register of Historic Places. Examples of domestic architecture dating to the 1830s line the leafy streets, from Greek Revival and Tudor to Prairie Style and Arts and Crafts. The district is bounded at the north and south by Water Street and Wabash Avenue.

Wabash College, a four-year liberal arts college for men, is west of the library and Lane Place across US 231 on Wabash Avenue. Founded in 1832 as a high school, it became the Wabash Teachers Seminary and Manual Labor College a few years later. The name was shortened in 1839.

The northwest corner of the campus has three early buildings. The 1838 Caleb Mills House was the home of the college's first faculty member. Hovey Cottage was the 1837 home of one of the college's founders and first teachers, Presbyterian minister Edmund Hovey. The 1833 Forest Hall is the oldest structure on campus. The two-story frame building was the first classroom and dormitory building.

The architectural rigor of New England resonates throughout the campus. Several other Federal-style buildings line Wabash Avenue, and even the twentieth-century buildings are built in Georgian style. Center Hall anchors a landscaped mall in the center of campus. Built in several stages in the mid-nineteenth century, the hall contained numerous "recitation rooms," lecture halls, and a laboratory.

The whimsical Herron House at 406 West Wabash Ave. was the home of William Herron, a friend of Lew Wallace. The neo-Jacobean house was built in 1890.

The 1882 Old Jail Museum at 225 N. Washington St. features the remarkable rotary jail, a pie-shaped double-decker cell block that rotates to a single opening on each floor. The jail was one of seven built in the country and the only one still in operable condition.

The Montgomery County Courthouse at Main and Washington Streets was built in the neoclassical style in 1875. A 155-foot clocktower used to stand alongside the structure, but parsimonious commissioners had it removed in the 1940s.

Proceed north on US 231. Sugar Creek, one of the state's most scenic streams, courses by the highway. The road climbs from Sugar Creek's valley onto the tableland of the vast prairie. Enormous silos and inflatable grain storage structures hug the rail line. A giant dome of sky overhangs the empty vista. The only swells in the landscape are manmade—railroad overpasses and highway exit ramps.

The small railroad town of Linden is 10 miles north. The Linden Depot Museum sits beside the main line of the old Monon and Nickel Plate line. Today the CSX Railroad still thunders down the line between Indianapolis and Chicago. The 1909 depot is the oldest intact junction depot in the state, housing a museum with a collection that includes the gleaming red Nickel Plate Caboose No. 497 that rests on an adjacent track.

The Lindy Freeze on the highway is the place for ice cream and sodas. Just down the road, **Messer's Bar and Grill** serves up traditional bar fare.

New Richmond is 4.5 miles west of Linden on a well-marked road through a flat, pale landscape with utility lines punctuated by patient hawks. At the edge of town, a sign welcomes you to New Richmond, noting that it was chosen for the movie *Hoosiers*, which celebrated Indiana's basketball obsession. Set in the early 1950s, the film used New Richmond as the set, as it needed almost nothing changed to have a vintage look. Gene Hackman, Barbara Hershey, and Dennis Hopper starred in the basketball epic—the tale of small-town "Hickory" boys rising to the state championship.

A cheerful blue water tower overlooks the decaying grain elevator and empty railbed that stretches to the horizon. A faded sign painted on an old brick commercial building promises a fine selection of buggies and harnesses. The prairie fields lap up to the backyards where children play baseball beside the old maples.

Return to US 231 and turn north. The railroad town of South Raub, 7.8 miles to the north, has the **Throckmorton Purdue Ag Center** experimental farm, a harbinger that West Lafayette, home of the Purdue Boilermakers, is 6 miles north, across the Wabash River from its larger neighbor, Lafayette.

Lafayette sits at what was the head of the Wabash River's navigable water during the steamboat era. The town's founder, raffish Wabash River boatman William Digby, had the sense to purchase the land there. The fine central location convinced the county commissioners to choose the town as the seat of Tippecanoe County.

The current courthouse dates to 1885, a limestone wedding cake of Second Empire, Baroque, Gothic, Georgian, Beaux Arts, and neoclassical styles. The courthouse has one hundred columns. Four statues representing the four seasons surround the hollow, metal dome, which is topped by the Goddess of Liberty, who lost her sword and shield somewhere along the way. While the town prospered with increasing steamboat traffic (sixty arrived in 1832 alone), it got little respect. "Laugh-at" is the name the haughty Crawfordsville citizens preferred to use for the small market town. Lafayette boomed when the Wabash and Erie Canal arrived in 1843. From 1843 to 1850 the population jumped from 2,600 to 6,129. Manufacturing, beginning with pork-packing, added to the agricultural products of the region, increasingly transported by the railroads that arrived in 1852. Today the economic base is split between manufacturing and Purdue University.

The Fowler House at 909 South St. is an 1852 English Gothic mansion that was the home of the Tippecanoe County Historical Society for more than six decades. The 1852 Foundation acquired the home in 2015 and offers tours and other events, as well as a restaurant serving lunch and dinner.

The Purdue Block at 8 N. Second St. is the oldest surviving commercial structure, built in 1845 by John Purdue, the school's namesake. It is a Federal-style redbrick building that was the target of a $57 million redevelopment project. The Samuel Johnson House at 608 Ferry St. is the oldest house, built in 1844 for the first Episcopal pastor. The Perrin Historic District on Perrin Avenue between Main and 18th Streets is a nineteenth-century upper-middle-class neighborhood. The streets wind along the hilly landscape with a variety of Victorian styles still gracing the lanes.

European history in the area goes back to 1717 when the governor of New France assigned an ensign to fur trade among the Wea, part of the Miami tribe who camped at Wea Creek on the Wabash. It became Fort Ouiatenon, the first permanent European settlement in Indiana. By the late eighteenth century, the fort was no longer used.

The reconstructed blockhouses were built in the 1920s by a local physician and are the focal point for the annual autumn Feast of the Hunter's Moon, which re-creates the life of a French fur-trading fort with modern mountain men and period foods and crafts. The fort is southwest of West Lafayette, 3.8 miles from State Street.

Return to West Lafayette, formerly known as Chauncey. Turn west on State Street into the town. State legislators chose the village of Chauncey in 1869 as the site of the new state agricultural college after a rancorous four-year conflict. As was the common case among early educational institutions, leaders named the school after John Purdue and donated $150,000 to the college.

Today it is a world-class educational and research institution, with its agricultural and engineering schools particularly revered. The school nickname of Boilermaker comes from their early engineering focus. In general, Purdue is a red-brick campus, more noted for no-nonsense academic structures than architectural beauty. The Purdue Union, however, opened in 1924 and retains a neo-Gothic flavor with vintage woodwork and furnishings.

Amelia Earhart was part of the Purdue faculty when she took off in March 1937 from Purdue Airport, the world's first university airport, in her Lockheed Electra for her fateful round-the-world trip. The Purdue Research Foundation funded the plane's construction. From this early involvement with flight, the university has nurtured its aeronautical engineering schools and other technical programs relating to flight.

So many American astronauts have come from Purdue that it is known as the "Cradle of Astronauts." More than two dozen graduates of Purdue have been selected for space flight, Gus Grissom being the first. The first man on the moon, Neil Armstrong, was a Boilermaker, as was the last, Eugene Cernan.

Purdue University is proud of producing numerous U.S. astronauts, including the first man on the moon, Neil Armstrong.

18

Economic Meditation

Terre Haute to Williamsport

General description: The 65-mile drive follows the path of the fabled river and the 19th-century Wabash and Erie Canal, from the gritty industrial town of Terre Haute through the northern coal-mining town of Clinton to the old canal town of Williamsport.

Special attractions: In Terre Haute: Historical Museum of the Wabash Valley, Inland Aquatics, Farrington's Grove Historic District, Paul Dresser Home, Hippodrome Theatre, Indiana State University, Big Shoe's Barbecue and St. Mary-of-the-Woods. In Clinton: Immigrant Square, Four Seasons Fountain on the Wabash. In Dana: Ernie Pyle State Historic Site. In Williamsport: Williamsport Falls and historic architecture.

Location: Western Indiana.

Drive route numbers and names: US 36, 41, and 136; IN 63, 263, and 28.

Travel season: The roads are drivable in all but the worst of winter weather.

Camping: Horseshoe Lake Campground (765) 832-2487 near Clinton; Cayuga Park Campground (765) 492-4103 in Cayuga; Off the Trail Campground near Attica (765) 762-6189.

Services: There are services in Terre Haute: hotels, restaurants, shopping, movies, etc. Gas and food are available in Clinton, Dana, Williamsport, and Newport.

Nearby attractions: Portland Arch Nature Preserve, Shawnee Bottoms Nature Preserve, and Cates-Clawson Reserve, all near Covington; Fall Creek Gorge in Williamsport; TJ Haase Winery and Shaggy Ass Brewery in Clinton; Windy Ridge Winery & Distillery in Cayuga; Badlands Off-Road Park in Attica.

The Drive

The Wabash River curls across northern Indiana and swoops south down the western border, disgorging muddy and full into the Ohio at the southern toe of the state. It's a comfortable Midwestern river of willows and islands and muddy banks with stalking herons and scooting ducks.

The river looms large in the mind of Indiana. The Wabash drains 33,150 square miles, most of them Hoosier. More than four-fifths of Indiana's counties lie in its watershed, and it washes the banks of eleven county seats, forming an almost archetypal patterning in the state's consciousness.

Importantly, the Wabash River was Indiana's historical connection to the world outside the mid-continent. Through a few strategic portages, it connects the Great Lakes, the St. Lawrence River, and the Atlantic Ocean to the Mississippi River and the Gulf of Mexico. In the days of French *voyageurs* and unconquered

Terre Haute to Williamsport

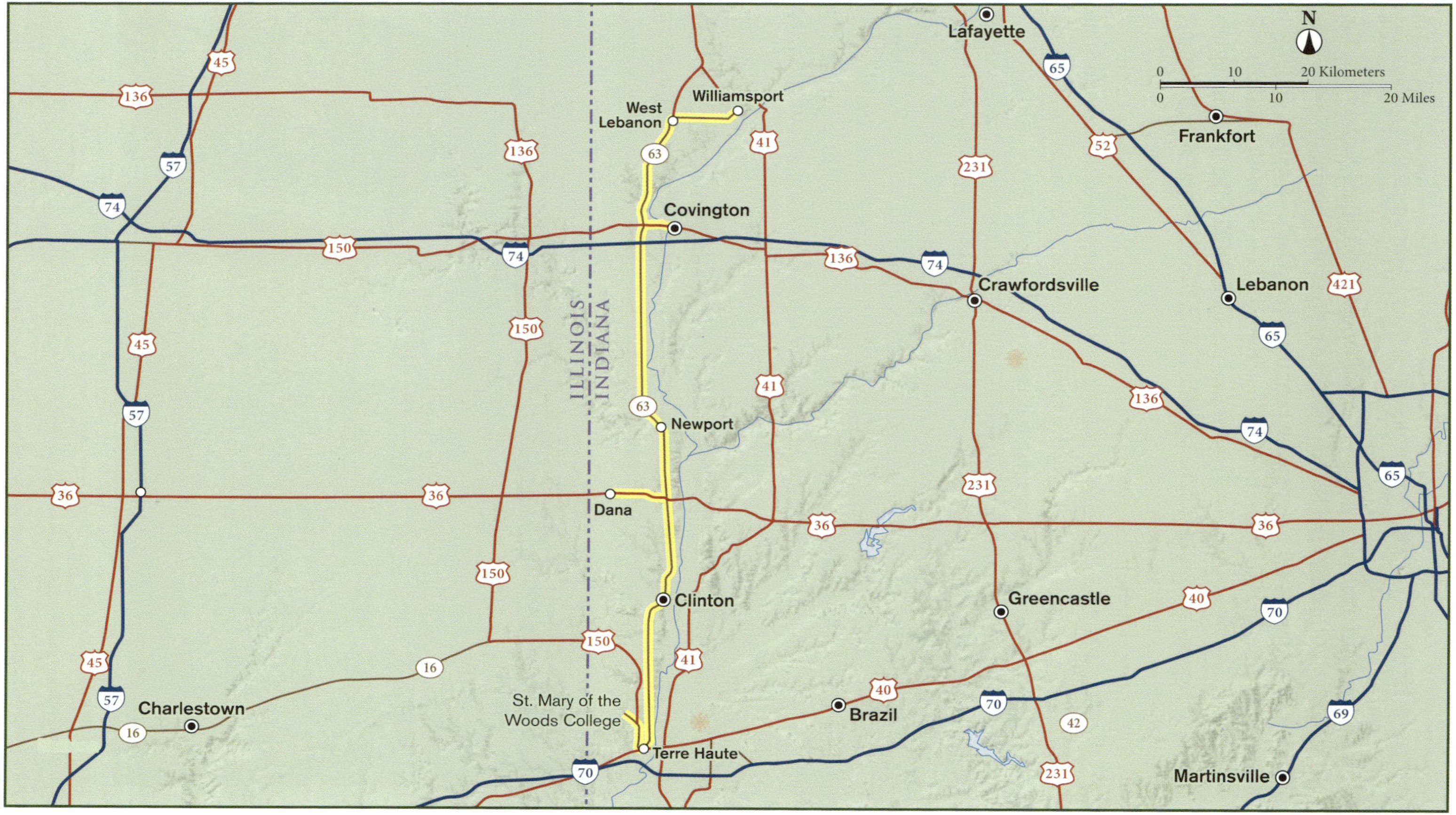

N
0 10 20 Kilometers
0 10 20 Miles

Lafayette
Williamsport
West Lebanon
Frankfort
Covington
Crawfordsville
Lebanon
ILLINOIS
INDIANA
Newport
Dana
Clinton
Greencastle
St. Mary of the Woods College
Terre Haute
Brazil
Charlestown
Martinsville

45 136 57 74 150 63 41 231 65 52 421 36 16 40 70 42 69

Indian tribes, the Wabash was the great canoeing thoroughfare between the fur markets of Montreal and the French administrations of Louisiana.

For a good part of the eighteenth century, Terre Haute (meaning "high land") was the dividing line between the French administration of Quebec and the colonial authority of New Orleans. Terre Haute prospered following its designation as the Vigo County seat in 1818. The current French Neo-baroque-style limestone courthouse was built in 1888.

The Memorial Hall, 219 Ohio St., across from the courthouse, is Terre Haute's oldest building, built from 1834 to 1836 as a branch of the Second State Bank. The impressive Greek Revival structure was later used as the local Grand Army of the Republic Memorial Hall. It is currently an attorney's office.

A confluence of transportation modes helped continue Terre Haute's development. The *Florence*, the first steamboat on the Wabash, churned to the banks in 1823. As the town was the northernmost navigable spot on the river, it became the entrepôt of the middle Wabash Valley. The National Road from Washington, D.C. (today's US 40) arrived in 1838. The Wabash and Erie Canal, America's longest artificial waterway, eventually stretching from Lake Erie at Toledo to the Ohio River at Evansville, reached Terre Haute in 1849, offering an outlet for the Wabash Valley products. The railroads arrived soon after, in 1852.

Initially, the agricultural bounty of the valley was the primary industry. Salted pork, hominy, and whiskey were the main exports of the region.

The pre–Civil War rise of ironworks, foundries, and rolling mills fueled by abundant Wabash Valley coal precipitated the town's almost congenital labor

Terre Haute has embraced basketball star Larry Bird for his time at Indiana State University.

management strife. By 1881 Terre Haute hosted a Midwestern labor conference that eventually created the American Federation of Labor from several craft unions.

Terre Haute's rough-and-tumble union scene spawned Eugene V. Debs, one of the luminaries of the American labor movement as well as the Socialist Party's perennial presidential candidate. His house is located at 451 N. Eighth St., an unpretentious two-story house as befits the champion of the working class. The structure is also the home of the Eugene V. Debs Foundation, a labor organization dedicated to Debs's ideals, as well as a library with his papers.

"The District" in Terre Haute ran north on Second and Third Streets and spread into the side streets, including Cherry Street, famous for its wide-open gambling parlors and elaborate bordellos. Born at the edge of the district in the mid-nineteenth century, Hoosier icons Theodore Dreiser and Paul Dresser watched the promenade from their windows and front porch, marking both for life. Theodore Dreiser's classics, *Sister Carrie* and *Jennie Gerhardt*, tell the stories of daughters of people forced into prostitution by economic necessity. His masterpiece, *An American Tragedy*, continued his theme of capitalism overwhelming the modest dreams of common men.

Life along the Wabash affected his brother Paul Dresser in another way. Dresser wrote "On the Banks of the Wabash, Far Away," by far the song most associated with Indiana. Dresser was sent at the age of 15 to St. Meinrad Catholic seminary to be trained as a priest. Evidently it didn't take, as he ran away and changed the spelling of his last name. He favored the high life and was a devotee of fancy bordellos and gambling casinos while penning dozens of hit songs. Dresser was considered the nation's most popular composer in his turn-of-the-century heyday.

The Paul Dresser home, a small two-story brick home, can be seen in Fairbanks Park along the Wabash. It was moved from the original location at 318 S. Second St. Take Fairbanks off US 41 to the park.

The Vigo County Historical Society has one of Dresser's pianos, as well as a collection of other historical memorabilia. The museum was once housed in the heart of Farrington's Grove Historic district, a haven of 1,100 homes and commercial structures dating from the mid-nineteenth century. In 2019 the historical society moved its collections to a restored former furniture factory building at 929 Wabash Ave.

The Indiana Theatre at Seventh and Ohio Streets is another example of Terre Haute's early twentieth-century florescence. The grandiose 1,660-seat cinema is an Andalusian fantasy, with Moorish ceilings, mosaic floors, and elaborate ceramic ornamentation.

A block away at Eighth and Ohio Streets is the former Hippodrome Theatre, built in 1915 in a German-Renaissance style with lion's heads balefully gazing from the gables. It was remodeled and renamed the Wabash Theatre in 1948. The Scottish Rite acquired the building in 1956 and used it as a museum and cathedral until it was sold in 2020. Two years later it was up for sale again.

The Sheldon Swope Art Museum at 25 S. Seventh St. features exceptional examples of 1930s and '40s-era regionalist painters such as Edward Hopper, Grant Wood, and Thomas Hart Benton. It is located in a 1901 Renaissance-revival building with an Art Deco interior.

At 820 Wabash St., the Terminal Arcade Building was built in a bombastically neoclassic Roman style as a terminal for the local interurban trolley company. The Hulman and Company Building at Ninth and Wabash Streets is a touch more sober: a redbrick Romanesque Revival building that housed the Hulman wholesale grocery business and their renowned Clabber Girl baking powder factory for more than a century before it was sold to a private developer in 2020. The Hulmans are best known for their longtime stewardship of the Indianapolis 500 racetrack.

Another Hoosier made his first crack at fame in Terre Haute. Basketball star Larry Bird, who led Indiana State to the 1979 NCAA championship game before losing to Magic Johnson and Michigan State, became the highest-paid rookie in NBA history when he joined the Boston Celtics for a stellar career. The Larry Bird Museum opened on Wabash Avenue in 2024 to honor his basketball exploits.

Proceed west on US 40 across the Wabash 1.8 miles to West Terre Haute. Originally a French town, West Terre Haute retained French speakers into the 1930s. At one time it was a prosperous coal-mining town, but it is now a modest suburb of Terre Haute.

Turn north on IN 150 and drive 4.8 miles to St. Mary-of-the-Woods College. It is the mother house of the Sisters of Providence, founded in 1840 to serve the German and French Catholic communities of the southern Indiana region. Although the number of women entering the convent has declined, St. Mary-of-the-Woods is still the home of 350 sisters. The Saint Mother Theodore Guerin Shrine features artifacts of early Catholic ministry in the region and a history of the Sisters of Providence.

Beginning late in the nineteenth century, St. Mary-of-the-Woods began offering degree programs for women and has pioneered new career paths for women, particularly non-traditional students. There are more than thirty specialized academic areas at what it is the oldest Catholic college in Indiana.

The college boasts some handsome turn-of-the-century buildings in Italian Renaissance style and a particularly charming Baroque Revival church. The Church of the Immaculate Conception was completed in 1886 and is lit by Bavarian stained-glass windows.

Return to West Terre Haute and turn left on US 150 to cross the Wabash River and reenter Terre Haute. Turn left on US 41, proceed north to IN 63, and continue north 11 miles through the Wabash bottoms, swooping over humpy hills as the river flows down a partially filled pre-glacial valley through a rich fertile land.

The gray-green stripper pits that dot the roadsides speak of the coal deposits that underlay the valley. Nearly 35 million tons of Indiana coal are extracted annually. While deep mining predominated in earlier production, most mining today is surface strip mining, done with monstrous draglines that munch the earth like fantastic creatures. The region is pocked with small mining communities that have fallen on hard times as the industry has consolidated, and labor-efficient mining techniques have supplanted the older backbreaking ways.

Turn northeast on East Hazel Bluff Road and continue into **Clinton**.

During the coal boom between the 1870s and 1920s, the town attracted more than twenty-five nationalities, including many Italians. The mines declined after the 1920s, but the Army ordnance plant north of Clinton stabilized employment beginning in World War II.

Clinton remains an Italian enclave, albeit distinctly of the Hoosier variety. There are several Italian restaurants in town, serving something that vaguely recalls the cuisine of the old country. The annual Labor Day Weekend Little Italy Festival is a town-wide celebration of Italian-ness. There are grape stomps and bocce games, polka dances, gondola rides on the Wabash, and more Italian street food than you can imagine. The locals dress in traditional Italian costumes and the grape-arbored Museo del Vino opens for wine tastings under the vines.

The Immigrant Park at Ninth and Clinton Streets is a small, wrought iron–fenced park with a fine statue of a young immigrant carrying a suitcase, waving goodbye with a confident look on his face. The statue (which stands on a pile of faux coal) and bull's head fountain were cast in Torino, Italy. A riverside classical "Four Seasons" fountain, surrounded by grape vines, terraces, and a promenade at Elm and Water, also reflects Clinton's Italian pride.

Return to IN 63 and proceed north through a panorama of broad, open fields. Turn west on US 36 and drive 4.8 miles to Dana.

It's a vast prairie vista under a blue dome of sky. Iconic silos and enormous feed mills mirror the fertility of the soil. Trains thunder across the landscape like slender messages. They rumble through Dana's redbrick downtown, past a modest white clapboard house with lace curtains and a few touches of classical trim, the home where journalist Ernie Pyle was born before going off to find his fame as a World War II correspondent.

When World War II swept millions of Americans into its maelstrom, Pyle trotted along with them, from the European theater to the war in the Pacific, chronicling the war as the dog soldier saw it. Pyle was shot and killed by a Japanese machine gunner on Ie Shima near Okinawa in April 1945.

Dana honors its native son, World War II war correspondent Ernie Pyle.

The state of Indiana moved Pyle's birthplace from its original rural setting to the railroad side at Maple and Briarwood Streets in Dana and made it a state historic site. The state transferred ownership in 2010 to the Friends of Ernie Pyle, a nonprofit that operates the site as the **Ernie Pyle World War II Museum**. There are two Quonset huts that house the visitor center, with its multimedia World War II stories and scenes.

Two miles north of Dana on IN 71 on West County Road 200 S is the seven-story **Hazelwood Round Barn**. Originally built as a three-story barn, it was modified by a previous owner in the 1940s as a labor-saving scientific chicken coop with a capacity for 84,000 chickens. Chicks went in the top floor and emerged from the bottom as fryers.

Return via IN 71 to US 36 on the south side of Dana. Turn left (east) to reconnect with IN 63 North. The earth alternately swells and then relaxes again into prairie. Newport is 6.9 miles north, county seat of Vermillion County, called the "shoestring county" because it is 37 miles long but averages only 7 miles in width. The Beaux Arts limestone Vermillion County courthouse was built in 1925.

Newport was the site of a 1909 automobile hill climb. The 140-foot-high, 1,800-foot-long climb at the edge of town was a daunting challenge for the early cars, and the event drew big crowds until its demise in 1915. The hill climb for vintage cars was revived in 1963 and it remains a popular October event.

The courthouse square is pure Americana with Gidget's Deli Market and a military mural on the side of the local American Legion. Across the way, a small frame building houses the Newport Chemical Stockpile Outreach Office, a chilling reminder of America's Cold War history.

The Newport Chemical Stockpile southwest of town was established in 1941 by the Department of Defense for warfare chemical production on 22,000 acres of land. The plant produced the explosives TNT and RDX as well as heavy water production for the Manhattan Project, which culminated in the atomic bomb. The plant also produced the lethal chemical nerve agent VX, which can kill a human in 15 minutes with less than a pinpoint drop. In 1968 VX production was halted, though the facility continued to store the entire US VX stockpile until a decade-long project to neutralize and destroy the 1,200-ton VX supply was completed in 2008. The former depot is now an industrial park.

Continue north on IN 63. The Cayuga Power Plant is a 1,062-megawatt generating facility, once ranked second in the nation for sulfur dioxide emissions. Two units were retrofitted in 2008 with new technology that reduced the SO_2 emissions by 95%. As the road crosses Little Vermillion River, it is near the site of Harrison's Crossing, where William Henry Harrison and his army forded the river enroute to his battle with the Indian confederacy at the 1811 Battle of Tippecanoe.

At the **Warren County** line 6 miles past Newport, the rich fields and plump white barns of the prairie give way to abrupt hills. Waterman, 2.8 miles to the east on IN 234, was known as Lodi during the heyday of the Wabash and Erie Canal. Lodi was a major port with locks and dam. The town still appears on some maps as Lodi.

Forty feet wide and 4 feet deep, the canal snaked along the Wabash and Maumee Rivers back to Lake Erie. Packets and freight boats coursed across the prairie and through the forest to the sounds of boatmen's horns and cries of "ste-a-dy ste-a-dy." Passengers traveled in relative luxury in the packets, with stylishly dressed canal men in slouch hats and top boots as their squires. The line boats hauling freight presented a more raffish scene—the boats like floating packing crates and the boatmen renowned for their "brigandish guise."

In the peak years the canal bustled with commerce: 7 million pounds of bacon, 2 million bushels of corn, 1 million of wheat, thousands of perches of peaches and stone, hoop poles (staves used to bind barrels), glass, ale, tobacco, and clocks floated down the stream.

But within a quarter century, the big ditch became a bog of silted channels, leaking banks, and weary locks. The canal had its greatest impact on the Wabash Valley in northern Indiana, where the dependable transportation link back to the Great Lakes transformed communities like Huntington, Logansport, and Wabash. The upper valley's population increased 500% from 1830 to the canal's decline.

US 136 is 13.9 miles north on IN 63. Turn east 3.3 miles to Covington.

Covington, another canal town, is the seat of Fountain County. The courthouse dates to 1937, and murals inside depict the history of the county. Major General Lew Wallace, hero of the Mexican War and author of *Ben Hur*, grew up in Covington and started his law practice there.

The **Sewell-Freese House** at 602 East Washington is on the National Register of Historic Places. William C. B. Sewell built the home in 1867 for his bride. The Italianate-style house is known locally as the "House with the Lions" for a pair of cast-iron lions guarding the sidewalk that are replicas of ones at the Yalta Palace in Russia.

Return west on US 136 to IN 263 and drive north 10.1 miles to West Lebanon, which dates to 1869, when the Wabash Railroad passed through town. Proceed 5.2 miles east on IN 28 to Williamsport.

Williamsport is an early town on the Wabash, site of a horse ferry across the river. The settlers were from Maryland, Ohio, and Pennsylvania, and with the aggregate of historic architecture, the town retains an air of the eastern seaboard.

The Warren County Historical Society Museum is on Monroe Street by the railroad tracks in an antique building, featuring the history of the county. Farther down Monroe, the Gothic Presbyterian Church is a picturesque example of the style. The Tower House at 303 Lincoln is a Tuscan-style 1854 mansion built by a local merchant. The High House at 404 East Monroe is an 1850s sandstone tavern built in the Federal style.

The highest waterfall in Indiana, Williamsport Falls, drops 90 feet in the middle of the small town—a thin silver torrent falling into a fern-strewn and lichened grotto. The Fall Branch that forms the falls is a scenic walking stream above the falls.

19

Parke County

Covered Bridge Capital

General description: The 50-mile drive loops through the rural beauty of Parke County, home of the largest collection of covered bridges in the nation. Located on the edge of the last great glacier advance, the county is a rumpled quilt of diverse topography.

Special attractions: Mansfield Roller Mill and Covered Bridge in Mansfield; Billie Creek Village, historic downtown square and historical museum in Rockville; Reeder Park canal boat turning basin in Montezuma; Raccoon Lake State Recreation Area; 31 covered bridges.

Location: Western Indiana.

Drive route numbers and names: US 41 and 36; IN 59; and multiple county roads.

Travel season: The drive is over roads of various types, from US highways to gravel roads. All are in good condition, but inclement weather may make back roads tedious. Heavy snow can make some of the roads difficult. The county's roads become more crowded during its annual festivals, though it remains an attractive destination.

Camping: Shades State Park (765) 435-2810, Turkey Run State Park (765) 597-2635, Raccoon Lake State Recreation Area (765) 344-1884, Rockville Lake Park (765) 569-6541, all near Rockville; Cherokee Village Campground (765) 597-2029 near Bloomingdale.

Services: There are services in Rockville: hotels, restaurants, shopping, movies, etc. Gas and food are available in Montezuma and Rosedale. Smaller villages such as Mecca and Mansfield have food, particularly during festivals.

Nearby attractions: Turkey Run and Shades State Parks; Chelsea's General Store & Pickin' Post in Rockville; Collom's General Store in Bridgeton; Cross at a Walk Britton Winery in Rockville; G&M Variety Store in Rockville; Indiana State Sanatorium paranormal investigations and tours; Lake Waveland Park in Waveland; Mecca One-Room Schoolhouse in Mecca; Montezuma Railroad Bridge in Montezuma.

The Drive

While Parke County may be a rural place, it is an internationally famous one. Millions travel annually to Parke County to visit the unique collection of covered bridges—many more than a century old—that span the countless streams and creeks winding through the scenic countryside. Of the fifty-two and one-half covered bridges the county once owned (they shared one bridge with neighboring Vermillion County), thirty-one still stand tidy and resplendent.

Rockville is the county seat, where the ornate Second Empire–style Parke County courthouse anchors a vintage Victorian square with brick-faced Italianate

An historic covered bridge and mill are highlights of Bridgeton.

BRIDGETON MILL

commercial buildings housing a variety of establishments. The G&M Variety Store, craft stores, and antique shops share the square with lawyers' offices and abstract companies. The Soda Shop sits resolutely on the corner with its Art Deco signage. The marquee of the 1920s Ritz Theater is still lit up, offering almost up-to-date Hollywood fare to the small-town crowd. The town remains the county seat of yore, the bustling center of an agricultural county that bills itself as the "Covered Bridge Capital of the World."

The 1883 Rockville Train Depot east of the courthouse on Ohio Street (Route 36) is the local tourist information center, with precise maps of this up-and-down county. Should the route laid out in this chapter whet your appetite for more, the local driving map shows five color-coded driving routes.

The covered bridge route begins on Howard Avenue, northwest of the courthouse square off Market Street. Proceed north on Strawberry Road through corn and bean field vistas 4.5 miles to the shambling town of Coloma, an old Quaker community.

The 1896 Melcher Bridge is 2.8 miles farther west on Strawberry Road, built by Joseph J. Daniels to span Leatherwood Creek. Covered bridges were designed to shield the floor timbers from the elements as well as preventing horses from shying as they crossed the running water. Note the entrance to the bridges resembles a barn opening, increasing the horses' sense of order. Daniels favored a square-cut top opening, while his bridge-building rival J. A. Britton used an arched opening. There are some bridges in the county where one end is arched and the other squared-off, the result of one builder getting the original contract and the other the repair contract, each marking his work with his signature style.

Past the Melcher Bridge 1 mile, turn north on CR 600 West. The West Union Bridge, built by Daniels in 1876, is the longest bridge in Parke County at 315 feet long. The bridge crosses Sugar Creek on hand-cut sandstone piers. The sign warning to cross the bridge at a walk is a remnant of horse and buggy days when the canter of a horse could set up damaging vibrations.

The West Union Bridge and all but one Parke County bridge are supported by Burr arches, the internal frame that carries the structure's weight. The Burr arch was patented in the 1820s by Theodore Burr, a cousin of Aaron Burr. The arch and the internal framing member were made of poplar because of its resistance to moisture and insects. The builders used steam to bend the timbers into the required arch shape and white oak for the flooring because of its strength.

In the days when all the work was done by hand, it took six months to a year to build a bridge. All the beams were hand-hewn with a broad ax and adze and fastened with wooden pegs. The only metal in the bridges were nuts and bolts connecting the largest timbers.

Covered Bridges

Just to the right of the bridge, there was a Wabash and Erie Canal feeder ditch and turning basin, where the canal boats could anchor or turn around. The first canal boats reached Parke County in 1839, though financial problems and the rise of railroads sent the canal into a sharp decline within a few decades. The hamlet of West Union was one of the early settlements on the canal.

Montezuma, located 6 miles south of the **West Union Bridge** on US 36 via CR 600 West, was a major canal town. Remnants of the canal can be seen as trails along the road into the town. Founded in 1823 on the site of an Indian village, Montezuma boomed during the canal days. Reeder Park on Water Street is the site of Benson's Basin, an enormous turnaround anchorage for canal boats whose shape can still be seen. The traces of the canal can be seen along Canal and Pond Streets.

A sanitorium that opened in Montezuma in 1906 touted the health benefits of sulfur water drawn from a well south of the canal basin. The forty-room building burned in the 1930s.

The old wooden Brady Boarding House frequented by the Irish workers stood on Water Street before it was razed in 1972. Mrs. Brady charged 25 cents for a night's lodging but was said never to turn away a penniless sojourner, saying, "He might come back and pay me sometime."

Railroads made it to Parke County not long after the canal. By 1860 locomotives were chuffing across the landscape, changing the human culture in its wake. Montezuma was one of the towns that precipitously declined when the trains arrived. Later railroad towns like Bloomingdale withered when the railroads pulled up their tracks and left grassy mounds running off to the empty horizon.

Proceed south on US 36 for 2.5 miles to the 1883 Sim Smith Bridge. It was built over Leatherwood Creek by J. A. Britton. The bridge is reputed to be haunted—the sound of a cantering ghost horse being heard for many years.

Maintenance of the covered bridges is done with a variety of resources. The Indiana State Covered Bridge Repair Fund appropriates $2,500 a year per bridge. While the intent is good, the money doesn't go far. Luckily, many private individuals pitch in to help the county, providing money and time for upkeep of the structures. The Parke County Adopt-a-Bridge organization raised almost $14,000 from 1995 to 1997 and helped put a new cedar roof on the Thorpe Ford Bridge near Rosedale. The Wabash Heritage River Corridor Commission also provides funds for bridge maintenance.

Continue east onto CR W 40N for 0.5 mile to Arabia Road. Turn right (south) and cross the **Phillips Bridge**, the shortest covered bridge in the county at 43 feet. Proceed 0.3 mile south to the picturesque Arabia cemetery, with some fine headstones, including one for Civil War soldier Joseph Crew with a carved militiaman standing at rest with his rifle.

Arabia Road segues into CR 420 after 1 mile. Turn right and go another 2.5 miles to Mecca, a booming railroad town at one time. The fine seams of clay were Mecca's key to success, providing the raw material for three clay plants at one time. The Mecca Bridge is the site of the annual Covered Bridge Festival Dance, and the Mecca schoolhouse next to it was an oft-used meeting spot until it was damaged by fire in 2022. Both the bridge and the schoolhouse are on the National Register of Historic Places.

Follow Coxville Road south out of town for 6.8 miles to CR 325 W in Coxville. Turn left to cross the **Roseville Covered Bridge**, built in 1910 over **Big Raccoon Creek**, one of the area's best canoeing streams. The bridge crosses over to Chauncy Rose's (of Rose Hulman fame) sand mines. The distinctive green color of the original Coca-Cola bottle made in Terre Haute is due to the characteristics of Parke County sand. The Harry Evans Bridge is 0.8 mile north on CR 325 W.

On the south edge of Coxville sat the Longhorn Tavern, which had ties to longtime movie cowboy Tex Terry. He was the black-hatted bad guy of a hundred Hollywood westerns of the Tom Mix and Gene Autry era before retiring back to his home county and building the Longhorn Tavern in 1979. For decades the region's schoolchildren thrilled to his arrival for convocations in his vast car decorated with steer horns and six shooters. The tavern changed ownership in the 1980s and was reincarnated as the Rock Run Café and Bakery before being destroyed by fire in 2016.

Rosedale, 2 miles farther south, was an old coal mining town. The heyday of the mines was the first half of the twentieth century, when more than 13 million tons were wrested from the ground. It was a dawn-to-dusk mining existence, for $1.50 a day. At its peak, the town had a population of almost 1,500. A December 2023 fire destroyed another nearby eatery—**Rosedale's Rod and Gun Steakhouse**, which opened in 1921 as the Spring Brook Rod and Gun Club. It was a favorite hangout of notorious bank robber John Dillinger and other gangsters.

Proceed east from Rosedale on Center Street to Rosedale Road and turn south. Go 4.9 miles to High Banks Road and turn north, continuing to Bridgeton Road and another north turn that leads into Bridgeton. It is 8 miles from Rosedale to Bridgeton.

Bridgeton was founded in 1818 on the banks of the Big Raccoon Creek. The village was the site of the first timber bridge in the county in 1849, which collapsed in 1857, and another which fell into the creek a decade later. The third one, built by J. J. Daniels in 1868, lasted a touch longer but was closed to vehicular traffic in 1968. It fell victim to arson in 2005 but was reconstructed a year later using Daniels's original design.

Daniels constructed the double-arch, 247-foot-long bridge with the hand techniques of the day. As in many covered bridges, the flooring is cambered to give with the weight of traffic and spring back to shape.

Built in 1870, the current Bridgeton Mill is the fourth on the site. It was converted from water to electric power in 1957. Today the mill is the last family-owned operating gristmill in the county, grinding out corn meal and flour for the festival-day hordes that descend on the otherwise soporific hamlet. The village hosts a Civil War Days reenactment, a Mountain Man Rendezvous, Bridgeton Milling Days, the Covered Bridge Festival, and Bridgeton Country Christmas.

The Masonic Lodge beside the mill is one of the oldest in the state and the oldest in Bridgeton. It is a moon lodge, which meets the first Saturday after the full moon. During the summer, sounds from the swimming hole across the creek from the mill are reminiscent of a James Whitcomb Riley poem.

Proceed east from **Bridgeton** on Hawkins Road to Mansfield Road, then go another 4 miles to the village of Mansfield, which hosts the annual Covered Bridge Festival and swamps the town with thousands of vendors and vast throngs of fairgoers. Irish settlers who arrived in the early 1800s first named the village New Dublin.

Mansfield's covered bridge spans Big Raccoon Creek, which also supplies water to the Mansfield Roller Mill, a state historic site managed by the DNR Division of State Parks. The mill is a pristine example of an 1880s flour mill, when mills shifted from stone gristmill to roller grinding. The mill's roots reach to 1821, when James Kelsey and Francis Dickson laid out a sandstone foundation beside Big Raccoon Creek. The current mill was built by Jacob Rohm in 1880 and modernized in 1893 to the newfangled roller process, producing mass-marketed flour and meal. Because of the efficiencies gained by the roller process, the mill could be run with only three men.

By 1929 the mill couldn't compete with industrial flour mills and was converted into a local feed mill. From 1933 to 1967 the mill was maintained with the machinery intact. It passed through several hands who added some ersatz touches such as the non-functioning water wheel (the mill was run by two water turbines located under the mill). In 1990 the mill was listed on the National Register of Historic Places and gifted to the state in 1995 as a historic site.

Proceed 6 miles north on IN 59 to US 36 West in Bellmore. Billie Creek Village, 5.5 miles west, is a re-created turn-of-the-century village with vintage buildings and three covered bridges—Billie Creek, Beeson, and Leatherwood Station, each one on the National Register of Historic Places. The village dates to the mid-1960s when local movers and shakers decided to develop the county as a year-round tourist destination. Several antique buildings from Rockville and the surrounding county were moved to the site to initiate a "living museum," with old-time craftspeople and products. The village ran into financial issues and has changed ownership twice in the past decade or so.

The Billie Creek General Store was originally built between 1850 and 1860 in the Quaker town of Annapolis in northern Parke County. When the B&O Railroad chose to go through the town of Bloomingdale 0.5 mile south, the store followed, and it rested there until 1968 when it again migrated. Since then, it has anchored Billie Creek Village and boasts the crafts of Wabash Valley crafters as well as pioneer toys and geegaws for all ages. It also has the bridge-building tools of master builder J. A. Britton.

The village has a demonstration maple sugar camp, tapping 300 trees in the early spring. In the summer the herb garden is a riot of more than fifty pioneer herb plants. A 1913 one-room schoolhouse portrays the educational ways of rural Indiana. A burr mill spins corn into meal as it did at its original home near Alamo, Indiana, before a tornado flung it into a hundred pieces, necessitating a particularly tedious restoration.

Two churches grace the village, a charming 1886 clapboard Catholic church with a "living heart"–entwined frieze board and the 1859 Union Baptist Church. A governor's house, livery stable, print shop, commons gazebo, and sundry craftsmen's building all add to the verisimilitude.

Festivals and special events happen virtually every month. During the Covered Bridge Festival, the village is awash with people enjoying the fun. The Civil War Days in early May host Indiana's largest re-enactment.

Proceed west to Rockville and turn north on North Erie Street across from the Depot tourism information office. Erie Street will become Marshall Road. Seven miles north, the small town of Marshall sits primly on the plain. In the middle of town, a lighted World War I victory arch still leaps over the main street, one of only two victory arches left in the state.

The Poplar Grove Cemetery at the north edge of town is a well-cared-for place. The lawns are immaculate, and the lanes are plowed on any day with a hint of snow. The cemetery board is recompensed, certainly an unusual occurrence for a small-town graveyard. All because the place had the good fortune to have a widow's million dollars bequeathed to maintain it in perpetuity.

Two miles north on Marshall Road is IN 47. One mile west is the entrance to **Turkey Run State Park**, the state's second-oldest park after McCormick's Creek State Park. Marshall Road becomes Narrows Road north of IN 47. Half a mile later the road approaches the scenic Narrows of Sugar Creek, a limestone pinch point that the 1882 Narrows Bridge leaps across. The Narrows Bridge is the only one maintained by the state due to its location in the state park.

The Narrows is part of Salmon Lusk's 1,000-acre government military grant and the site of his mill, which he built to the north of the bridge. His brick 1841

Sandstone canyons and hardwood forests highlight Indiana's second-oldest state park, Turkey Run.

house with a louvered cupola sits on the bluff overlooking the bridge site. It is said Lusk situated the bridge so he could watch the travelers crossing from his house.

His son, John, inherited the house and the 1,000 acres, living the balance of his life in melodramatic isolation. A man with strong tastes and a dislike of his fellow man, he harbored a particular distaste for members of the Masonic order, believing they wanted to poison him. Local legend says Lusk liked to climb on the roof of the covered bridge and rail at crowds of passers-by, inflaming himself to particular ire if he thought the group might include a few Masons. At the height of his fulmination, Lusk would leap from the bridge, ostensibly to cleanse himself from the imagined Freemason contamination.

Ironically, Lusk's need for isolation, and his love of the forest, saved the woods for generations of Hoosiers. In 1919, five years after John Lusk's death, the State of Indiana bought the property from the estate, and it became Turkey Run State Park.

20

Sugar Creek

From Thorntown through Shades and Turkey Run

General description: The 38-mile tour runs from Thorntown along IN 47 to IN 234 enroute to Shades and then down to Turkey Run on IN 47, paralleling Sugar Creek.

Special attractions: Crawfordsville, Shades and Turkey Run State Parks.

Location: Western Indiana.

Drive route numbers and names: IN 47 and 234; County Roads 600 West and 400 South.

Travel season: All roads are paved and in good condition, but heavy snow may make some of the roads difficult.

Camping: Shades State Park (765) 435-2810, Turkey Run State Park (765) 597-2635, Raccoon Lake State Recreation Area (765) 344-1884, Rockville Lake Park (765) 569-6541, all near Rockville; Cherokee Village Campground (765) 597-2029 near Bloomingdale; KOA Campground (765) 230-0965 near Crawfordsville.

Services: There are full services at Crawfordsville and gas and groceries in the vicinity of the parks.

Nearby attractions: Parke County (See Drive 19); Rotary Jail Museum in Crawfordsville; Gen. Lew Wallace Museum in Crawfordsville; Pine Hills Nature Preserve at Shades State Park; Wabash College in Crawfordsville.

The Drive

The drive begins in Thorntown on IN 47 where the confluence of Sugar and Prairie Creeks provided exceptional hunting grounds for the Eel River tribe of the Miami Indians. An Indian village here dates back to at least the 1700s, known as Kawiakiungi—"place of thorns." Local lore has it the name comes from an Indian maiden who, distraught over the deaths of two competing suitors, pierced her heart with the thorns that grew there.

In the eighteenth century French Jesuits established a mission at the village and made a European religious center for the territory to proselytize the Indians. Following the nineteenth-century Indian wars and the spurious treaties that uprooted tribes from their traditional homes, Thorntown became one of the principal Indian reservations west of Pittsburgh. In 1818 the federal government granted a 64,000-acre reserve to the Eel River Miami, centered on Thorntown.

Ten years later, the Miami tribe acceded to pressure from the American government and encroaching settlers and granted the land back to the government. The Miami retreated to another reservation near Logansport following the treaty signing. North of Thorntown on IN 47, a historical marker on the north side of

Thorntown through Shades and Turkey Run State Parks

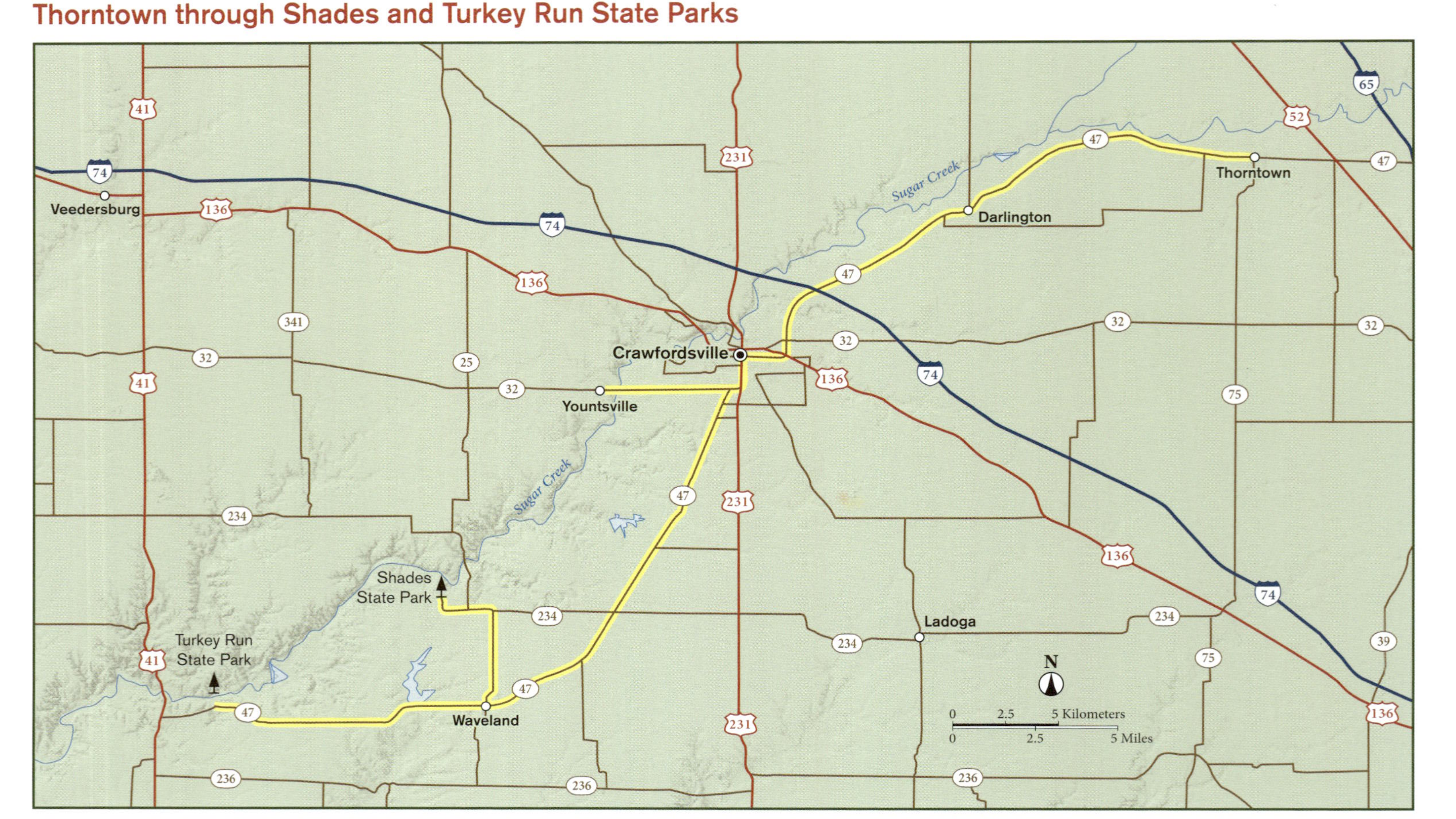

the road indicates the burial place of Chief Chapadosia and Chief Dixon, who fought to the death over the Thorntown treaty. They were buried in full ceremonial dress in a square grave, sitting facing one another.

Cornelius Westfall bought the land for $4 an acre the next year, and the first settlers lived in the abandoned Miami houses. The Thorntown Heritage Museum is in a Gothic structure at Main and Vine Streets and has history exhibits of the Thorntown area as well as Native American artifacts.

Proceed west on IN 47. The Montgomery County line is 4.9 miles down the road. The county was formed in 1822 in the western part of land taken from the Indians in the New Purchase treaty, which opened the central part of Indiana to European settlement. The flat prairie of the northern part of the county gives way to the heavily forested sections in the south. The route parallels Sugar Creek, a wild and scenic stream, in its lower sections.

Sugar Creek bisects the western edge of the flat, glaciated Tipton Till Plain, which extends far to the north. The creek begins many miles to the east near Tipton, Indiana, and rapidly becomes a broad, open stream, cutting a deeper streambed through sandstone and siltstone as it drains west toward the Wabash, forming the high bluffs and picturesque canyons of Shades and Turkey Run State Parks. It is considered the best canoeing river in the state and is certainly the most popular. Canoe rentals are available in Crawfordsville and in and near the state parks.

Darlington is 5 miles west, an early toll road town. The Darlington Toll Gate House on Main Street is a tiny 1880s gatehouse for the corduroy toll road made of felled timbers laid horizontal to one another, which made for a bone-bruising transit across the landscape. The Darlington Covered Bridge is 1 mile ahead on County Road 600 East. Built in 1868, the 166-foot bridge is still paved with wooden blocks. At one time, this peaceful scene was amid four factories and mills operating on Sugar Creek.

The Art Deco National Guard Armory on Franklin Street 2 blocks south of Main is from another era entirely, a product of the Works Progress Administration. Built at the height of the streamline craze in 1938, the building looks ready for a movie set but currently serves as a community center.

Crawfordsville is 7.3 miles west on IN 47. The town was platted in 1823. Since the mid-nineteenth century, the town has been a prosperous manufacturing center, making coffins, nails and wires, gloves, barrels, foundry items, and bricks. (See Drive 17 for more information on the cultural and educational side of Crawfordsville.)

Four miles west of Crawfordsville on Old Mill Road via IN 32 is Yount's Woolen Mill, an early industry on Sugar Creek. A 2 1/2-story brick textile mill is the last four buildings from a family business begun in 1843. During the Civil War and Spanish-American War, the textile mill was a major supplier of woolen uniforms, employing 300 workers. It closed in 1905.

Southwest of **Yountsville** is Stonebraker Cemetery and the gravesite of George Fruits, who died at the age of 114 years, 7 months, 4 days. Fruits was purported to be the last survivor of the Revolutionary War.

Return to Crawfordsville and turn south on IN 47. Drive 7.9 miles to IN 234, then 4.8 miles to CR W 800 S and turn west to Shades State Park.

Compared to nearby Turkey Run, Shades is relatively undeveloped, intended for the use of nature lovers who like to take their environments straight. There are 10 miles of hiking trails to park locations with exotic names like Devil's Punch Bowl and Maidenhair Falls. Sugar Creek has carved elaborate sandstone bluffs that provide spectacular vistas from the tops of places like Prospect Point, 210 feet over the stream, and the obligatory Lover's Leap.

The area's use as a recreational area dates to the 1860s when a mineral springs near Devil's Punch Bowl attracted health-seekers. A wooden inn was built in 1887. Today all the structures have long disappeared, and the only substantial development is the turfed Roscoe Turner Flight Strip for light airplanes.

The Pine Hills Nature Preserve at the east end of Shades State Park off IN 234 is a remarkable landscape of deep gorges and jagged hills. Rare ferns and fragile wildflowers prosper in the moist environs. Four slender stone ridges called "backbones" rise from the valley floor in humpbacked formation, Clifty Creek on one side of the sidewalk-width ridges, Indian Creek on the other. The two streams join

Devil's Backbone at Pine Hills Nature Preserve in Shades State Park belies Indiana's flat reputation.

at Honeycomb Rock and flow into Sugar Creek. Stands of massive white pines are the largest in the state.

While proposals to turn Pine Hills into a state park began in 1927, it took another three decades for it to transpire. The preserve was the first conservation project of The Nature Conservancy's Indiana chapter, purchased in 1960 and turned over to the state in 1961. The 470-acre plot is notable for its unique geological and biological features as well as the historical impact of humans. The Mill Cut Backbone was notched in the 1860s with a 20-foot cut for a mill flume. Giant-sized line drawings of passenger pigeons, last seen in Indiana in 1902, are atop Devil's Backbone along with a devil's face carved in 1910. The intent of the US Army Corps of Engineers to impound Sugar Creek and form a reservoir that would cover the white pines with 30 feet of water was squelched with citizen opposition. The preserve was named as a National Natural Landmark in 1968 and became Indiana's first state-dedicated nature preserve a year later.

Deer's Mill Covered Bridge is 0.6 mile north on IN 234, built by Parke County master builder J. J. Daniels in 1876. A canoe launch is adjacent to the bridge.

Return to IN 47 and turn south, driving through the towns of Browns Valley and Waveland, passing man-made Waveland Lake on the north side of the highway and Turkey Run Country Club on the south before reaching Turkey Run State Park.

Turkey Run is the second oldest in the state park system, established in 1916. When the state acquired adjoining land from recluse John Lusk, it acquired the intently stewarded land-grant virgin forests that he and his father, Salmon Lusk, had saved from timber interests for several decades. The park's 2,382 acres hold the state's largest stands of virgin forest.

It is by far the most developed of the string of Sugar Creek parks, with tennis, swimming, canoeing, horseback riding, bicycling, and picnic areas. There are 14 miles of hiking trails. A founding-era suspension bridge leads over Sugar Creek to the dappled wonders of the Rocky Hollow–Falls Canyon Nature Preserve, an alluvial forest with waterfalls and stands of old-growth hardwoods: towering black walnuts, hickory, sycamore, and stands of hemlock and other evergreens. An inn, cabins, and campgrounds offer a full range of accommodation.

Monuments to the "Father of the State Parks," Richard Lieber, and journalist Juliet Strauss stand near the inn. Both were instrumental in saving the forests for the park. Strauss wrote a column for the Rockville paper as well as national publications about the area. Lieber was the founder and director of the state park system after a successful business career. He died while visiting McCormick's Creek, the first state park, in 1944. His remains are buried in an old-growth forest near the pioneer log church. Another log cabin in the park overlooking Sugar Creek has an exhibit on his life.

NORTHERN INDIANA

21

Boilermakers to Indiana Beach

West Lafayette to Monticello

General description: The 35-mile drive covers the route of history that encompasses Indian battles and early commercial centers as well as vintage resort areas.

Special attractions: Purdue University in **West Lafayette**; Prophetstown State Park, Wolf Park, and Tippecanoe Memorial Battlefield in Battle Ground.

Location: Western Indiana.

Drive route numbers and names: IN 25 and 43, and US 421.

Travel season: Except when heavy snow can drift into huge banks covering the highway, the roads are fine year-round. Indiana Beach booms during the summer season.

Camping: Prophetstown State Park (765) 567-4919 in Battle Ground; IB Crow Campground (574) 583-4141, Indiana Beach Campground (574) 297-5130, Norway Campground (574) 593-9300, Tall Oaks Family Campground (574) 278-7181, Lost Acres Campground (574) 297-5043, all in Monticello.

Services: There are full services in Lafayette and Monticello: hotels, restaurants, shopping, movies, etc. Gas and food are available in Battle Ground, Delphi, and Americus.

Nearby attractions: Celery Bog Nature Area in West Lafayette; Columbian Park Zoo in Lafayette; Wildcat Creek Winery and People's Brewing Company, Knapptronix Brewing, all in Lafayette; Wabash & Erie Canal Park in Delphi; Lake Freeman and Lake Shafer.

The Drive

The drive begins in West Lafayette, home of the Purdue Boilermakers. (The university and town are covered in Drive 17.) By far the most locally momentous event happened in the early morning of November 7, 1811, when 600 Indian warriors crept through the mist to attack invading Territorial Governor William Henry Harrison's army of nearly 1,000 soldiers.

Led by the Shawnee prophet Tenskwatawa, or The Prophet, the brother of Tecumseh, warriors of fourteen allied Midwestern tribes sought to drive the Europeans from Native American land and protect nearby Prophetstown, the capital of the Indian Confederacy. While relatively untested in battle, Harrison's men repelled the attack, which lasted several hours. Although the outcome of the Battle of Tippecanoe was indecisive, it broke Tecumseh's alliance and earned Harrison the nickname Tippecanoe due to the battle's proximity to the Tippecanoe River.

West Lafayette to Monticello

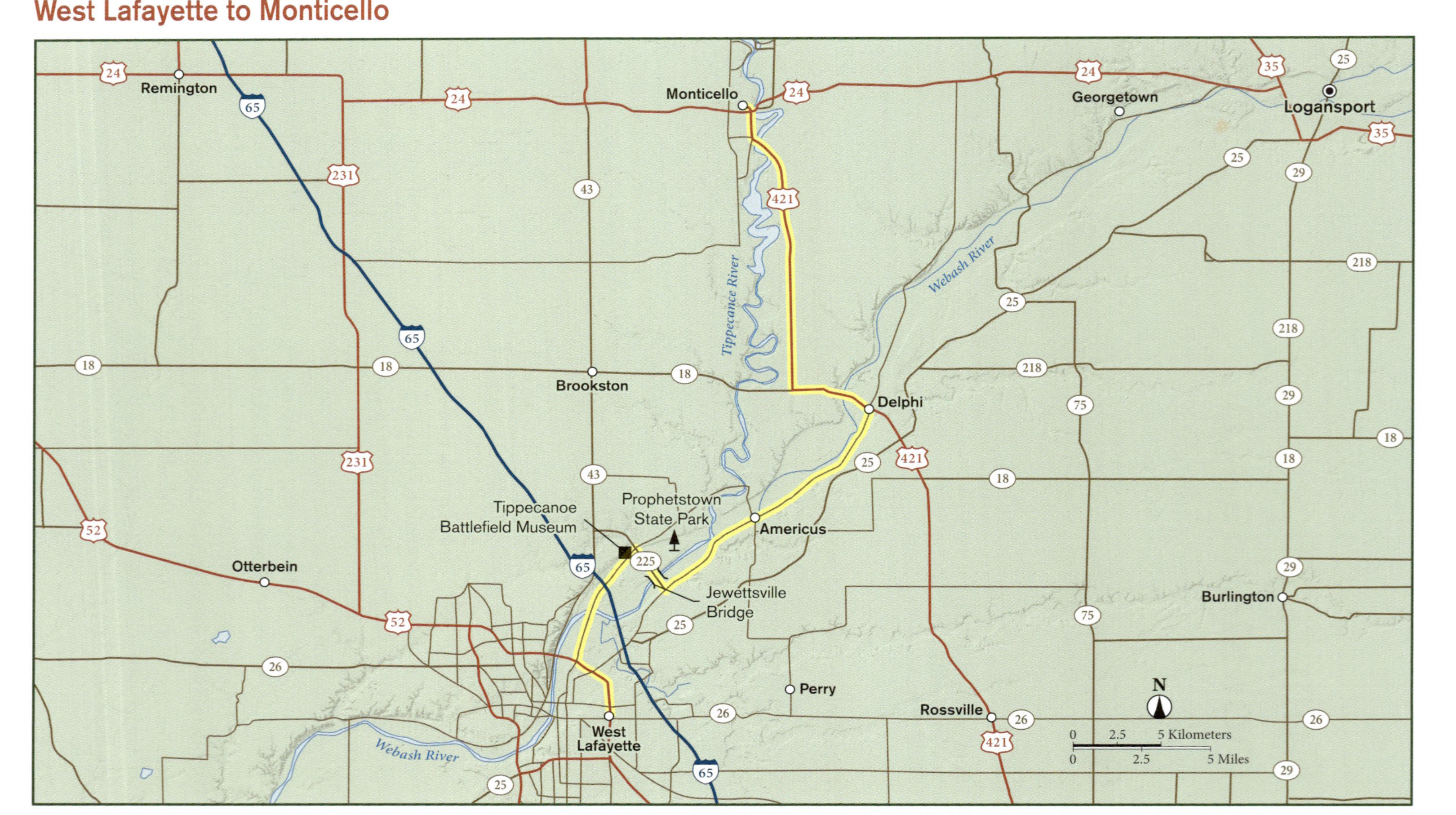

The nickname gave Harrison a slogan for his 1840 presidential campaign with running mate John Tyler—"Tippecanoe and Tyler Too." Drive north on IN 43 (River Road) from West State Street in West Lafayette. The Indiana State Soldiers' Home Historic District, 3.6 miles from West State Street, is a state property used for community gatherings. The grandiose Greek-Revival Indiana State Soldiers' Home dates to 1895 when Indiana established a home for destitute veterans and widows of veterans.

Proceed 1.6 miles on IN 43 to Burnett Road and turn right, then turn right again in 0.5 mile onto Ninth Street and drive 0.5 mile to Swisher Road. Turn left and continue for 2.5 miles to the **Prophetstown State Park** entrance. The park is tucked into a pocket bounded by the Tippecanoe and Wabash Rivers to the east and south, and the town of Battle Ground to the north.

The 2,000-acre park includes a meticulously restored prairie, a replica 1920s-era farmstead, and a reconstructed Native American village with a council house, granary, wigwam, chief's cabin, and medicine lodge. Toward the east end of the park is the **Circle of Stones**, a collection of fifteen large glacial rocks, each commemorating one of the fourteen tribes that were part of Tecumseh's confederacy, plus one for other Native Americans who were not affiliated with a particular tribe.

Prophetstown also offers modern amenities with a nature center, aquatic center, camping, and biking and hiking trails.

Prophetstown State Park rests on the site of the 1811 Battle of Tippecanoe. Indiana Department of Natural Resources

Backtrack to Ninth Street and turn right to reach the **Tippecanoe Battlefield and Museum**, recognized as a National Historic Landmark. The state purchased the battle site in 1836 and erected a 92-foot obelisk in 1908 that memorializes the army's casualties—188 dead and wounded. The Native Americans suffered at least 35 dead, though historians conjecture the number was much higher. The 96-acre site is now owned by the Tippecanoe County parks department and managed by the Tippecanoe County Historical Association.

A trail connects the Tippecanoe Battlefield with Prophet's Rock on a bluff where Tenskwatawa urged his forces to battle, exhorting them with promises of immunity from the soldiers' bullets with a magic potion he had made. The battleground also is the northern trailhead of the Wabash Heritage Trail, which runs for 13 miles along Burnett Creek and the Wabash River, passing through Lafayette and West Lafayette to Fort Ouiatenon.

Return to Ninth Street, turn left, and proceed through the town to Wolf Park on Jefferson Street just north of the IN 225 intersection. Begun by a Purdue professor in 1972, the park is home to a wolf pack that gathers to howl at the moon, most often in accompaniment with a gathered throng of homo sapiens. Visitors learn about pack behavior and social strata and can watch their interactions. The park's small herd of bison also allows visitors to watch the pack at work, testing the buffalo for weakness.

Return to Battle Ground and the intersection of IN 225. Turn left and go 1 mile to the one-lane, 632-foot-long Jewettsport Ford Bridge over the Wabash River, erected in 1912 and still in service. Upon reaching Old IN 25, turn left and look left for a glimpse of the **Tippecanoe River**'s confluence with the Wabash.

Upstream on the Tippecanoe, two mammoth dams create Lake Freeman and Lake Shafer, the terminus of this drive. Below the second dam, the Tippecanoe flows unimpeded between craggy bluffs until its junction with the Wabash.

The Tippecanoe is the largest tributary of the Wabash, stretching 166 miles up into Indiana's lake country and passing through two of the biggest natural ones, Webster and Tippecanoe. In the upper stretches it drains eighty-eight natural lakes and acts as a regulator for the whole watershed. It is one of the clearest streams in the state, where unique aquatic grasses and a profusion of waterfowl and fish prosper.

The nearby town of Americus hardly reflects the grandeur of its founding. Laid out in 1832, it was envisioned as the western terminus of the Wabash and Erie Canal. But the diversion of the canal to Lafayette left the dream high and dry, and it has survived since as a trading center for the area farmers.

The **Carroll County** line is 5.5 miles north of the mouth of the Tippecanoe, named for the Maryland Revolutionary War leader Charles Carroll, the longest-surviving signatory of the Declaration of Independence. The county was originally settled in the 1820s with a French trading post located just north of Rockfield near the Wabash. The dense forests and good canoeing rivers—the Wabash, Tippecanoe, and Wildcat Creek—made for good fur trading.

Today the county is overwhelmingly agricultural, with more than 95% of the land in cultivation. Despite that, picturesque Wildcat Creek as it flows through Carroll and Tippecanoe Counties is designated by the state as a Natural and Scenic River.

Delphi is a Wabash and Erie Canal boomtown. Established in 1828 as the county seat, the town's fortunes flared when the canal reached it in 1840. Until the last canalboat passed through in the 1870s, Delphi was an important port. As is the case in much of canal-era Indiana, the railroad came through in the 1850s, severely impacting canal commerce.

There are several imposing examples of fine period architecture, reflecting the town's former prosperity. The Barnett-Seawright House at 203 East Monroe is a Greek Revival structure built in 1857, with Italianate elements added later. The courthouse on Main Street was built in 1916. A courthouse bell used from 1841 sits under the stained-glass rotunda.

From the courthouse turn left on Washington Street and drive north to the Carroll County Historical Society's museum, housed in the **Stone Barn** built in 1904 by James Pierce. The historical society outgrew its space in the county courthouse basement and purchased the barn in 2016.

Cross the Wabash River 2 blocks farther north on Washington Street and turn left at Rhineland Trail to enter the Wabash and Erie Canal Park, which stretches on both sides of the old canal. Construction of the canal reached Delphi in 1840 and provided a brief boom, but the impact of railroads doomed canal operations by the 1870s.

The county has nineteen bridges deemed historically significant, including two covered bridges and four older stone-arch bridges to vintage steel Warren Pony and Pratt Thru Truss bridges. Maps to the historic bridges are available at the county museum, as are maps to the eleven Delphi Historic Trails that crisscross the town.

Deer Creek at the southern edge of town is another of Hoosier poet James Whitcomb Riley's fishing holes. It was here on the banks of the bluffed and sun-dappled stream that Riley got his inspiration for "On the Banks o' Deer Crick." Riley Park memorializes the peripatetic poet.

Return to US 421 and turn north. Pittsburg is another canal town, platted in 1836. The brick commercial structures of Main Street hark back to halcyon days when the townspeople thronged the dock at the sound of the boatman's trumpet.

Lake Freeman is 4 miles north on US 421. It was formed when the Insull Corporation—a.k.a. Indiana Hydroelectric Power Company, which later became

NIPSCO—dammed the Tippecanoe River with the 0.3-mile-long Oakdale Dam. The result was a 2,800-acre lake that quickly became a local fishing and boating favorite. Since the lake is privately owned, the shoreline is crowded with summer and weekend homes and cottages.

The lake stretches 7 miles along the highway north to Monticello, best known as a resort town. Monticello was platted in 1834 on a bluff overlooking the Tippecanoe River and named for President Thomas Jefferson's Virginia home. The town dozed for many decades, the major events seeming to be the tornadoes that swept down periodically. The 1872 Italianate-style James Culbertson Reynolds House at 417 N. Main St. obviously missed the tornado damage. James Reynolds was a successful farmer, merchant, and politician.

But the town's torpor lifted in the 1920s when plans were announced to build the two massive dams that created Lake Freeman and Lake Shafer north of Monticello.

The Insull Corporation erected the 1,200-foot-long Norway Dam north of the city in 1923. The resulting 1,291-acre Lake Shafer, ringed by 50 miles of shoreline and dotted with summer homes, stretches 4 miles up the river.

Continue north on Main Street to Rickey Road and turn left, then right on NW Shafer Road. Go 2.2 miles to **Indiana Beach Amusement Resort**, the premier lake playground.

Indiana Beach was opened under the name Ideal Beach in 1926 as "The Hoosier Riviera" by entrepreneur E. W. Spackman. The Riviera consisted of a bathhouse and sand beach where he rented ten small boats. Spackman erected the

Indiana Beach opened as Ideal Beach in 1926 and was dubbed "The Hoosier Riviera."

Ideal Beach Ballroom in 1930 to cash in on the Big Band craze. Musicians such as Duke Ellington, Louis Armstrong, Glenn Miller, Tommy and Jimmy Dorsey, and Benny Goodman played there.

As musical tastes changed, so did the acts. Bill Haley and the Comets, the Beach Boys, Janis Joplin, The Who, Chicago, Alice Cooper, and Sonny and Cher replaced the Big Band era in the venue, now called the Roof Garden Lounge. When Jefferson Airplane played in 1967, the admission was $3.25. Amusement rides along the beach, including a merry-go-round, Ferris wheel, and Rolo Plane, arrived in 1947. In 1951 Ideal Beach became Indiana Beach, and the growth hasn't stopped.

The Spackman family ran the amusement park until 2008 when it was sold to new owners, and then it was sold again in 2015. Indiana Beach was headed for closure in 2020 due to financial problems, but a new owner saved the day along with the advertising slogan "There's more than corn in Indiana."

Now there are seven roller coasters and giant waterslides among dozens of rides jammed into a man-made peninsula boardwalk that extends into the lake. Hundreds of hotel rooms and campsites are clustered around the amusement facility. *The Shafer Queen*, Indiana Beach's paddle wheeler, hauls nostalgic passengers around the lake daily in season.

22

Dance of the Cranes

Rensselaer and the Kankakee River

General description: The 68-mile route crosses the drained bed of the **Grand Kankakee Marsh** through some of the nation's most productive farmland. State Fish and Wildlife Areas strung along the Kankakee River like beads on a string are remnants of the historic wetland environment.

Special attractions: Hazelden in Brook; Willow Slough and LaSalle State Fish and Wildlife Areas and birdlife at Jasper-Pulaski Fish & Wildlife Area; Kankakee Sands.

Location: Northern Indiana.

Drive route numbers and names: US 231 and 41; IN 16 and 10.

Travel season: The fall and spring bird migrations are good times to explore this area. Winter can bring snowfall that will drift across roads, though snowplows are ubiquitous.

Camping: Willow Slough Fish & Wildlife Area (219) 285-2074 near Morocco; Tippecanoe River State Park (574) 946-3213; Little Creek Campground (219) 866-8807 near Rensselaer.

Services: There are full services in Rensselaer. Gas and food are available at the numerous gas stations/convenience stores that sprout at the area's highway intersections.

Nearby attractions: Kankakee Sands Preserve bison herd near Morocco; Tefft Savanna Nature Preserve and Coastal Plain Nature Preserve at Jasper-Pulaski Fish & Wildlife Area; Conrad Savanna Nature Preserve near Lake Village; Fair Oaks Farms in Fair Oaks; Carpenter Creek Cellars winery in Remington.

The Drive

The drive begins in Rensselaer, founded at the Falls of the Iroquois River, which never amounted to much in this case, given the unending flat landscape. The falls were a small rock ledge the river tumbled over. The first white settler made his way here in 1836, but within a few years sold out to enterprising Dutchman James Van Rensselaer from the upper Hudson Valley, who constructed a gristmill.

Van Rensselaer laid out the town as the county seat, and the Jasper County courthouse on Van Rensselaer Street is evidence that the town kept the honor. The Romanesque late Gothic-style structure was built from 1896 to 1898. Turn left onto IN 114 (Cullen Street) and proceed 1.9 miles. The Historical Log Cabin Museum is in the Jasper County Fairgrounds. The 1872 cabin has a collection of vintage county materials.

Collegeville, home of St. Joseph's College, is 0.3 mile south of Rensselaer on US 231. Founded in 1889, the college served as a seminary for priests at one time before becoming a four-year liberal arts school. The college closed in 2017 with

Rensselaer and the Kankakee River

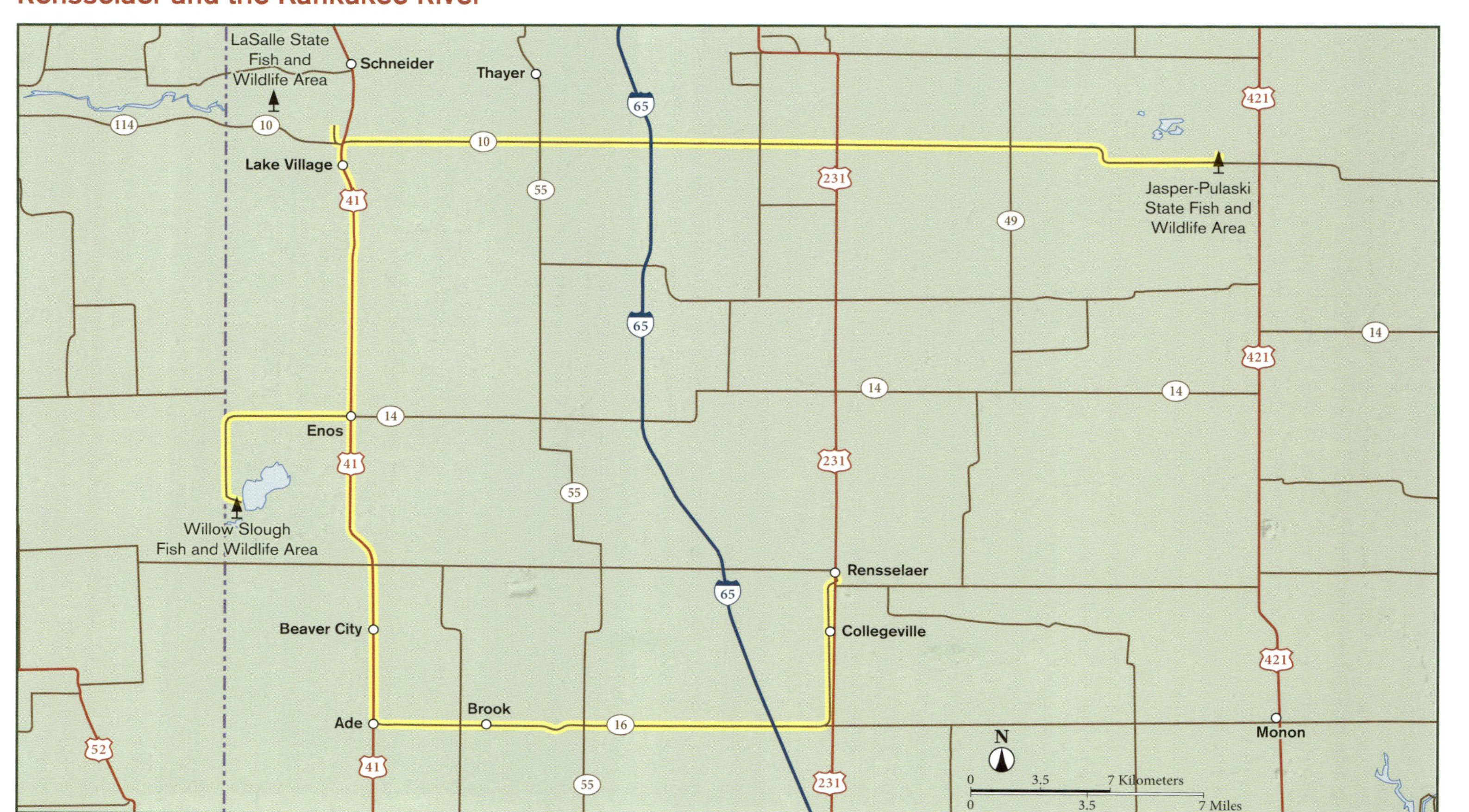

a debt of $100 million, but reopened as a junior college and since has expanded offerings in cooperation with other colleges and universities.

The Chicago Bears used the St. Joe campus for preseason training from 1944 until 1974 at the height of Coach George Halas's reign. Halas Hall is named after the coach, who was a heavy contributor to the school. The award-winning 1971 movie *Brian's Song* about Bears teammates Brian Piccolo and Gale Sayers was filmed on campus.

The three-story brick structure on the east side of the highway is Drexel Hall, the former St. Joseph's Indian Normal School. Young Native American students were brought from Michigan, Minnesota, Wisconsin, and the Dakotas to be taught "industrial" skills, such as farming, tailoring, and carpentry on the school's 420 acres. Philadelphia heiress Katharine Drexel funded the school with a $50,000 gift in 1888, but by 1896 the school was closed. The distance from their families caused few students to want to stay with the program. Only six out of the first class of fifty remained to graduate.

Rensselaer is the birthplace of James F. Hanley, who wrote musicals as part of New York's Tin Pan Alley scene in the early 1900s. He collaborated with Ballard MacDonald to write the popular "Back Home Again, in Indiana," which has been performed at every Indianapolis 500 since 1946.

Proceed 4 miles south on US 231 and turn west on IN 16. Continue west 11 miles to Brook. Hazelden, home of author George Ade, is on the south side of the

George Ade's Hazelden home hosted the likes of humorist Will Rogers and President Theodore Roosevelt. LEE LEWELLEN

road beside the Iroquois River. Ade was a prolific humorist, writer, columnist, and playwright. He and Neil Simon share the honor of having had three Broadway plays running simultaneously.

The sprawling Tudor-style mansion Ade built in 1904 sat on 417 acres alongside the Iroquois River. Ten acres of manicured lawns surrounded the house and formal garden. A baseball diamond, golf course, and swimming pool awaited his stellar guest list, which ranged from humorist Will Rogers and boxer Gene Tunney to General Douglas MacArthur and US presidents Calvin Coolidge, Theodore Roosevelt, and William Howard Taft.

Proceed west 3.7 miles on IN 16 to US 41 and turn north. Drive 9.7 miles across the low sand hills that separate the Iroquois's watershed from the Kankakee River to County Road 100 North to Willow Slough Fish and Wildlife Area. Opened in 1949, the 9,956-acre reserve is a haven for game and waterfowl thriving in the area's sand ridges and marshes. Willow Slough is the vestige of shallow Beaver Lake, part of the immense Grand Kankakee Marsh, which stretched for over half a million acres—5,300 square miles—in the northwestern corner of the state along the Kankakee River from today's South Bend to Momence, Illinois.

Beaver Lake stretched for 28,500 acres. Before developers drained the marsh in 1853, this corner of Newton County was covered by water 3.5 feet deep. In 1995 The Nature Conservancy's Indiana chapter purchased 7,200 acres to restore the native tallgrass prairie, dubbing it Kankakee Sands. The site has grown to 10,000 acres, taken on a small bison herd, and linked with other public lands for a 20,000-acre oasis.

Drive 10.5 miles north through fields of dark mucky soil along US 41 North to LaSalle State Fish and Wildlife Area. The LaSalle Fish and Wildlife Area contains remnants of the Grand Kankakee Marsh in its 4,500 acres.

Prior to the nineteenth century, the Kankakee region was a vast complex of swamp, marsh, slough, bayou, and slurry, the largest freshwater marsh in the country. Through it the Kankakee River crossed 90 miles of ground, writhing through 2,000 bends in 250 miles of stream. Six months of the year, half of Indiana north of the Wabash River was flooded. In high water, freight canoes could be paddled over the portages from one watershed to another.

The Kankakee marsh was a spectacular wildlife refuge where millions of furbearing animals lived in the wetland, joined by clouds of waterfowl: ducks, Canada geese, blue herons, and sandhill cranes. The fur-crazed French traders were the first to mine the swamp, and the Americans, including the tycoon John Jacob Astor, were right behind. By 1855 the Kankakee was overtrapped, and the stage was set for the next chapter.

The Indiana legislature passed the first motions to straighten the river and drain the swamp in 1848, and in 1858 developers formed the Kankakee Valley

Draining Association. Oxen began pulling enormous plows through the muck, digging V-shaped ditches 2 and 3 feet deep. By 1882 there were 30,000 miles of tile drain in the state, most in this near-aquatic corner.

But it took the arrival of the first steam dredge boat in 1884 to get the swamp drained. The Indiana State Legislature authorized $60,000 in 1893 to blast a limestone barrier across the Illinois border at Momence. When laborers finished their job, the ancient swamp began to give way to relatively dry land.

By the turn of the century, the straightening of the channel left 85 bends where 250 had been. The sluggish 5-inch drop became a brisk 15-inch fall down a 90-mile ditch from the headwaters to the junction with the Illinois River. Speculators created a land boom. Investors became wealthy raising muck crops like onions and potatoes, and grain crops in the sandy soils that slowly rose to the sunshine.

To add to the bounty, drillers found oil pooled a mere hundred feet beneath the onions at the turn of the century. The hamlet of Asphaltum remains as a memory of the short-lived boom.

Into the 1920s, the region remained a premier sporting destination for the country's hunters and fishermen, as it had since the 1870s. Up and down the stream, posh hunting clubs served a coterie of wealthy sportsmen from New York, Washington, Philadelphia, and Boston, as well as across the Midwest, drawn by the promise of up to a hundred birds a day. At Thayer (1.1 miles north on IN 55), hunting lodges stood along the winding banks—the Diana, Ahlgrim's Park, and the White Oak Outing Club among them.

By the 1920s bridges stood high and dry where the river once ran, and the legislature was busy, redrawing county lines that used to follow the curlicues of the river.

The fields, striated with the endless rows of crops following the neat grids of the government surveyors, stretched unchecked to the tree lines of the tamed and tidy river.

Crossing the quiet stream, its banks run straight as a die on a diagonal across the checkerboarded landscape. Kankakee River Ditch is the name given to it on the state maps.

Proceed 13.8 miles west on IN 10 to US 231 North. Drive 3 miles north to IN 10 East and drive 12.6 miles to Jasper-Pulaski Fish & Wildlife Area. The area—8,179 acres—provides an essential breeding and nesting ground for migrating waterfowl, including the spectacular sandhill cranes. More than 30,000 cranes arrive each fall in their migration to Florida and Georgia. Flocks of bird-watchers also arrive yearly to climb the observation deck and watch the curious dance of the cranes.

23

The Wild Life: Indians and Circuses

A drive along the Upper Wabash

General description: The 50-mile drive explores the Upper Wabash River, the spiritual home of the Miami Indian tribe.

Special attractions: Historic Forks of the Wabash and Quayle Vice Presidential Learning Center, both in Huntington; Mississinewa Battlefield in Marion; Circus Hall of Fame in Peru; Little Turtle Waterway Park and the Cass County Carousel in Logansport.

Location: Northern Indiana.

Drive route numbers and names: US 24; IN 124; and County Roads 500 East, 300 East, 200 South, 650 West; Division Road and Frances Slocum Trail.

Travel season: Peru Circus Days in the summer bring large crowds to the area. The roads are all in good condition, though winter can bring drifting snow.

Camping: Salamonie Lake (260) 468-2125 and Salamonie State Forest (260) 782-0430, both near Huntington; Mississinewa Lake (765) 473-6528 near Peru; France Park (574) 753-2929 and Tall Sycamores Campground (574) 753-4898, both near Logansport; Old Mill Campground & RV Park (574) 727-0869, near Twelve Mile; and Crooked Creek Trails (574) 643-9395 near Royal Center.

Services: There are full services at Huntington, Wabash, Peru, and Logansport. Gas and food are available at numerous places enroute.

Nearby attractions: Hathaway Preserve at Ross Run and Kokiwanee Nature Preserve, both near Lagro; Honeywell Center-Ford Theater, Charley Creek Garden, Charley Creek Falls, and Paradise Spring Historical Park, all in Wabash; Frances Slocum State Forest near Peru; Frances Slocum Monument near Somerset; Peru Amateur Circus, McClure's Orchard/Winery, 7 Pillars Brewery, Pipe Creek Mercantile, and Grissom Air Museum, all near Peru; Batman Museum, Longcliff Museum, and Cass County Historical Society Museum, all in Logansport.

The Drive

The drive begins on the west side of Huntington at the junction of US 24 and IN 9 at the Forks of the Wabash Park. It is where the Little River joins the Wabash at the southern end of the Long Portage, the historic link between the Atlantic and the Gulf of Mexico. Upriver at Fort Wayne, Indians and French voyageurs portaged from the junction of the Maumee over to the Little River, and in the process traversing from the great watershed of the St. Lawrence to that of the Mississippi.

A Drive along the Upper Wabash

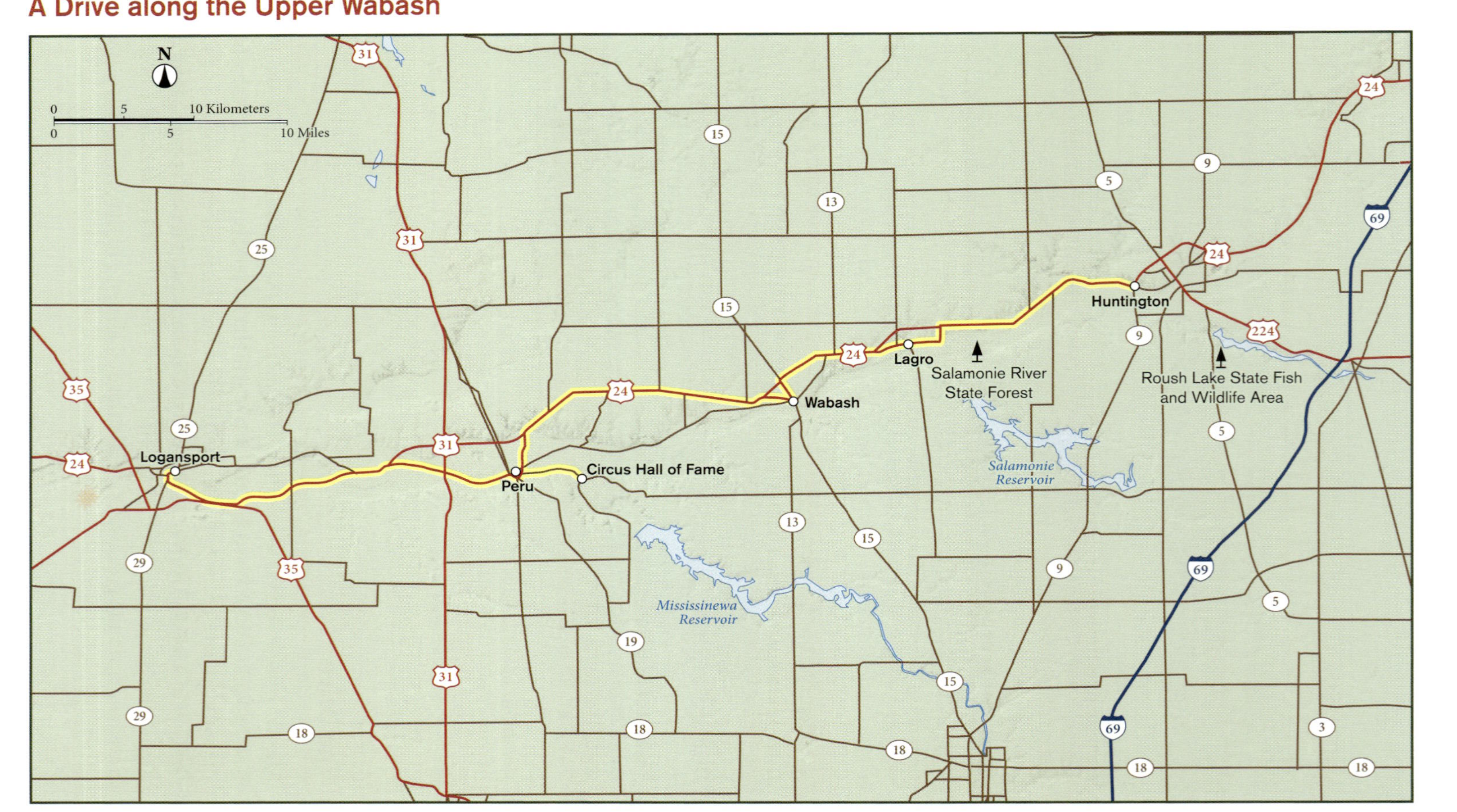

In high water the portage was a short distance, but for much of the year it was a long haul through wetlands from one river system to the other.

When the first French traders arrived, the Wabash was considered the home of the Miami Indians and their Algonquian kinsmen—the Delaware, Kickapoo, Potawatomi, and Shawnee. The relatively tolerant French coexisted with the Miami, also inveterate traders, for nearly a century, often using the forks as a convenient locale for commerce.

In the post–Revolutionary War period, white incursions seeking land for settlement precipitated several battles, with Miami Chief Little Turtle's Indian forces emerging victorious. But Little Turtle's defeat by General Mad Anthony Wayne in 1796 spelled the end of Miami hegemony in the Wabash Valley. A series of treaties increasingly ceded tribal land to the settlers. Miami chiefs and government negotiators signed the last treaty in 1840 here at the Forks of the Wabash. In 1846 the Miami, the last Indian tribe in Indiana, moved west of the Mississippi to Kansas.

The centerpiece of the park is the Chief Richardville House, home of Jean Baptiste Richardville, the Civil Chief of the Miami tribe from 1816 to 1841. A skilled negotiator, Chief Richardville received large tracts of land and a substantial

Miami chief Richardville's home is the centerpiece of Forks of the Wabash park. Phil Bloom

sum of money from the 1818 Treaty of St. Mary's, as well as sizable considerations from treaties signed at the Forks in 1834, 1838, and 1840. Richardville operated a trading post at Fort Wayne, and his son-in-law, Francis Lafontaine, controlled the porters that hauled the freight over the Long Portage.

The park re-creates the days of conflict and amelioration with festivals, interpretation, living history, and a visitor center with many exhibits. The park includes a reconstructed German settler house circa 1850s that displays the accoutrements of the day.

Huntington was once a Miami village called Wepecheange—"place of flints." Located on the Little River, it was platted as the county seat in 1834 and grew sporadically until the arrival of the Wabash and Erie Canal accelerated the town's development. Huntington was long known as a center of limestone production, earning it the nickname Lime City. At its peak there were thirty-one limestone kilns in operation, but the quarries were exhausted by 1900. It has been a small agricultural and manufacturing town since.

The best-known Huntingtonian is J. Danforth Quayle, vice president under George H. W. Bush. Quayle grew up in the river town, practiced law here, and helped publish the local paper.

The **Quayle Vice Presidential Learning Center** at 815 Warren St. is the only vice-presidential museum in the country. It offers exhibits and programs relating to the office of the vice president, since six vice presidents have come from Indiana.

The downtown is a redoubt of vintage brick and limestone commercial buildings, anchored by a neoclassical limestone Huntington County Courthouse with an Italian mosaic tile rotunda floor. The county museum is on the fourth floor.

The Federal-style 1844–45 Moore/Carlew Building at the northwest corner of Jefferson and Market Streets is a vestige of Huntington's canal days. It was the first brick building in the town.

Proceed west 12.5 miles on US 24 past limestone ledges and along the route of the Wabash and Erie Canal to Lagro. It was founded in 1829 and named after a Miami chief. Lagro was a major port on the canal, and the redbrick St. Patrick's Catholic Church at Main and Harrison is a remnant of the Irish canal workers who arrived to dig the ditch in 1834. The present church was dedicated in the 1870s.

The downtown is a down-at-the-heels memory of Lagro's brief heyday. Turn south on IN 524 to Washington Street and turn left. The small park 3 blocks away contains a cabin and the Kerr Locks, built from 1834 to 1838. Though now high and dry, the finely dressed stone lock walls remain, curved to ease the canal boats into the lock.

Lagro is best known for the Irish War, when warring Irishmen rioted in 1835 and state troops were called out to quell the battle, arresting more than 200 canal workers. The ringleaders were tried and jailed in Indianapolis, but the rest were sent back to their shovels and barrows.

Salamonie Reservoir and Salamonie River State Forest are located at the south edge of town. Hanging Rock is 2.1 miles south on Division Road. It's a 65-foot-high hunk of Silurian reef that towers above the countryside, providing a promontory for vistas. The small 780-acre forest has camping and trails for hikers, horses, and cross-country skiers. The reservoir is a 2,655-acre pool that stretches 17 miles and is surrounded by 12,555 acres of woodlands, marshes, and small ponds, plus hiking trails and campgrounds.

Proceed west 4 miles on US 24 to County Road 500 East, turn north, and drive 1.9 miles to CR 300 North. Hopewell Church is nature writer Gene Stratton-Porter's childhood church. Her brother, Leander, model for Laddie in her 1913 novel of the same name, is buried in the cemetery. Gene Stratton-Porter was born on a 240-acre farm 0.5 mile north of the church.

Return to US 24 West. Wabash, 1.5 miles west on US 24, is another canal town that hung on as a small industrial city and county seat. Some of the vintage structures still have doors on the canal side to facilitate loading onto the boats. Look behind the buildings at Canal and Wabash Streets to get a sense of Venice-style Wabash.

The 15-acre **Paradise Springs Park** at the corner of Allen and Market Streets re-creates the momentous treaty grounds where the American government in 1826 once again required the Miami and Potawatomi to cede more land. With the signing of the treaty, the tribes gave up a wide swath of their northern Indiana and southern Michigan land and acquiesced to the Wabash and Erie Canal to pass through their remaining reserve.

The current courthouse is a pastiche of Greek Revival, Italianate, and Romanesque styles, erected in 1878–79. Just west of the courthouse, the Wabash County Historical Museum houses artifacts of local resonance, including Native American materials, canal memorabilia, and a collection of war-related items including statues of a Union soldier and a sailor who stand guard at the entrance.

The canal in the upper valley did far better than farther south, in part because it operated in that halcyon canal period before railroads came down the tracks. Railroads reached Wabash in 1856, nearly two decades after the Wabash and Erie arrived. It is railroad history, however, that immortalized the town in song. "The Wabash Cannonball" celebrates the Norfolk and Western train that barreled through town and down the riverside track, running between Detroit and St. Louis.

In 1880 Wabash became the first electric-lit city in the world. Today Wabash is best known for its connection to the Honeywell Corporation, which began as a local heating concern in 1900, and the Ford Meter Box Company, maker of water meters.

Ford family scion Richard Ford moved home from Washington, D.C., in 1980 and embraced historic preservation initiatives both in Wabash and around the country. One of his highlight endeavors was restoring the 1920 Hotel Indiana and reopening it as a boutique hotel, Charley Creek Inn.

Downtown at Hill and Carroll Streets, the Honeywell Memorial Center is an architecturally significant civic center that boasts a fine collection of Hoosier School paintings, including works by T. C. Steele, Marie Goth, and C. Curry Bohm. The original exterior has some charming bas-reliefs of recreation-related objects like roller skates.

The requisite mansion of the local nabob, the Honeywell House, is located at 720 N. Walnut St. The home, built from 1959 to 1964, is furnished with fine Louis XIV and Louis XV pieces. Following a 1974 fire and the death of Eugenia Honeywell, the house was bequeathed to the Indiana University Foundation. The Honeywell Foundation, founded by Eugenia's husband Mark C. Honeywell in 1941, manages the home.

Continue 10.7 miles west on US 24 to Peru, "Circus Capital of the World." Platted in 1829, the city became the winter home of several major circuses such as Hagenbeck-Wallace, Sells-Floto, and the American Circus Corporation. In the golden age of the circus in the 1870s, twelve large circuses crisscrossed the continent, a traveling aggregate of wild animal acts, performers, clowns, grifters, and con men, leaving a path of delighted locals and disgruntled city fathers in their wake. They moved down the silver tracks, and Peru stood at a handy intersection with trains leaving in all directions.

Each winter, as many as seven troupes returned to roost in the small Indiana town, with many famous performers such as Emmett Kelly and Clyde Beatty using Peru as their permanent address. As their performing careers ended, many of the veterans of the big top returned to Peru to retire.

The Depression hit the circus world hard, and by the 1940s Peru's days as the winter home were over. The memories almost faded until 1956 when the National Convention of the Circus History Society met in Peru. Circus City Festival Inc., a nonprofit organization celebrating Peru's circus past, was formed in 1960 and the annual circus festival began. The yearly circus parade is now an eagerly awaited event. The Circus City Center where it all happens is in a renovated brick lumberyard at 154 N. Broadway. The building also houses a fine exhibit of Peru circus history.

East 2.5 miles on IN 124 at the confluence of the **Wabash and Mississinewa Rivers**, the International Circus Hall of Fame is the site of the largest winter circus quarters in the world. In its heyday the 3,000-acre farm had more than forty buildings and barns sheltering the animals and wagons of several circuses, including the American Circus Corporation and Buffalo Bill's Wild West Show. One

Circus City Arena's three-ring building celebrates the city of Peru's circus heritage. Phil Bloom

pasture held the herd of 100 zebras, another held 1,000 giant circus horses. Sixty elephants walked the grounds. Lions roared from the Hoosier barns. Today, an old sign that reads "Elephants–Big Cats" still hangs over the entrance to a looming yellow barn.

Behind it, another gargantuan structure, originally the circus wagon building, houses the Hall of Fame Collection, honoring the luminaries of the Big Top from the eighteenth-century beginnings to the 1920s Golden Days to modern performers like Gunther Gebel-Williams. The museum has more than forty wagons and calliopes, artifacts, props, costumes, posters, handbills, and lithographs from circuses around the world.

The winter quarters began in 1891 when Ben Wallace bought the farm of Miami Chief Francis Godfroy, who received the land as a government grant in 1826. The Greek Revival house was built in the 1870s. The Godfroy Cemetery where he and other Miami and their white spouses are buried is 5 miles east of Peru on IN 124 on the north side of the road.

The International Circus Hall of Fame hosts daily circus performances under the Big Top throughout the summer. The steam calliope burbles and whistles and the local animal trainer gives "tiger talks." The facility is a National Historical Landmark.

Return west toward Peru on IN 124, cross the Mississinewa, and turn south on Frances Slocum Trail. Cole Porter's parents' Southern Colonial house, Westleigh Farms, is in the first scene of the movie *Night and Day*, which told the life story of the Peru native. Just down the road, the bucolic white-frame "Old Fashioned Garden" farm is Porter's grandmother's house, and the inspiration for his first popular song, "Old-Fashioned Garden."

Cole Porter was a master of American popular song, famous for such Broadway hits as "Anything Goes," "Kiss Me Kate," and "Can-Can." He captured America's attention with songs like "Night and Day," "In the Still of the Night," "You're the Top," "I've Got You Under My Skin," and "Don't Fence Me In."

Return to IN 124 and proceed west to CR 300 East and turn south. The site of the Osage Village, one of the largest Miami tribe villages, is nearby, memorialized by a large boulder with a bronze plaque on the right side of the road. Tecumseh assembled the braves of a dozen tribes here in 1812, attempting to persuade them to join his confederacy in the War of 1812. Colonel J. Campbell burned the village in 1813. The brick house to the south is yet another of Jean Baptiste Richardville's homes.

Drive south 1.2 miles to CR 200 South and turn left. The Seven Pillars of the Mississinewa, a sacred site of the Miami Indians, is across the stream. The 25-foot-tall pillars symbolize "the Great Father" and figure prominently in tribal ritual and lore. Much of the area's land was part of the Miami Reserve until 1840, when the last treaty forced the tribe west of the Mississippi. The 6,000-member Miami Nation of Indiana, which is reasserting itself in the local area, recently bought the land across the river from the Pillars for tribal rites and festivals. ACRES Land Trust in Fort Wayne acquired the site in 1992.

Return to IN 124 and proceed east to CR 650 West and turn south. Drive 2.8 miles to Frances Slocum Cemetery. Slocum, "the White Rose of the Miami," was a Miami Indian woman, Maconaquah, who was kidnapped as a young girl from her Pennsylvania Quaker family by three Delaware braves. Raised by a childless couple, she became wholly integrated into tribal ways, later marrying a Miami chief. At an elderly age, she was reunited with her Pennsylvania family, but chose to remain with her Miami family. She died at the age of 74 and was buried in an upright position in the Miami cemetery. The flooding of the area for the Mississinewa Reservoir necessitated the relocation of the graves to this spot.

Return to Peru. At the Wabash River bridge at Broadway, the old Toll House stands on the northeast corner. The 1840 structure is the oldest in town.

In canal days, boats unloaded at the south end. The Wabash County Courthouse is a neoclassical structure built in 1911. Cole Porter's birthplace is located at 102 E. Third St.

Drive west 14.1 miles on US 24 to Logansport. The road twists and turns a bit as it winds through a forested section. Logansport is situated at the confluence of the Eel and Wabash Rivers. The city is named for a Shawnee warrior, John Logan, who died fighting for the American forces near Fort Wayne in the War of 1812. **The Wabash and Erie Canal** made the town flourish, and the railroad's coming in 1855 transformed it into a rail center. By 1860 it was one of the Midwest's main hubs and repair depots. The Iron Horse Museum on South Fourth Street is in the former Pennsylvania Railway Station, filled with railroad kitsch and memorabilia. The Cass County Historical Society Museum at 1004 S. Main St. is located in an 1853 Italianate home and has a large collection of Cass County pioneer and Native American artifacts.

Cass County is second only to Miami County in Native American population. They have celebrated the heritage with the well-designed Little Turtle Waterway along the Wabash. The monument features granite insets honoring the Miami and Potawatomi tribes and a granite map of the Wabash watershed showing the locations of 1812 Miami villages. A statue of Chief Little Turtle is planned.

Another Logansport park is located on the Eel River on 10th Street. The 1895 Riverside Park boasts a magnificent National Historic Landmark, the Cass County Carousel, a perfectly preserved Dentzel merry-go-round, carved by Gustav Dentzel and his artisans more than 100 years ago. It has delighted four generations of Cass County kids with its whirling charms and is one of only three intact Dentzel carousels left.

24

Indiana Lakeland

Warsaw to North Webster

General description: The drive proceeds from Warsaw past Tippecanoe Lake and winds around Lake Wawasee.

Special attractions: Winona Lake, Lake Wawasee, Tri-County Fish & Wildlife Area, Lake Webster, Barbee Lakes, Tippecanoe Lake.

Location: North Central Indiana.

Drive route numbers and names: IN 15 and 13; US 6; County Roads 775 East, 1300 North, 900 East, 850 East, 1000 North, and 500 North and East; and North Shore Drive.

Travel season: This is a longtime summer playground, so accordingly, the place hops from Memorial Day to Labor Day. The roads are drivable in all but the worst of winter weather.

Camping: Pike Lake Campground (574) 269-1439, Hoffman Lake Campground (574) 268-8997, Kosciusko County Fairgrounds (574) 269-1823, all in Warsaw; Camp and Fish (574) 551-1792 at Dewart Lake.

Services: There are full services in Warsaw, Syracuse, and North Webster, and gas and food at numerous places enroute.

Nearby attractions: Center Lake Beach, Pike Lake Beach, Nye Park, Warsaw Biblical Gardens, Ledgeview Brewing Company, Streven Distilling Company, all in Warsaw; Grace College, Winona History Center, Billy Sunday Home, Spring Fountain Park, all in Winona Lake; Oppenheim Woods, HopLore Brewing, and Tippy Creek Winery, all in Leesburg; Sacajawea Wetlands, Man Cave Brewing Company, and S.S. *Lillypad*, all in Syracuse; Conklin Bay Boardwalk on Lake Wawasee; *Dixie* paddle boat on Lake Webster; Tri-County Fish & Wildlife Area, near North Webster.

The Drive

The drive begins in Warsaw, the county seat of Kosciusko County. Following the Indian treaties that opened the land for settlement, the county was organized in 1835 and 1836. The county was named after the Polish Revolutionary War hero Tadeusz Kosciuszko, and the city after the capital of his homeland. More than ninety lakes dot the county, including Indiana's largest natural lake, Wawasee.

Settlers named Warsaw as the county seat in 1837. The courthouse is an 1880s Second Empire structure with a mansard roof, topped with an octagonal clock tower. The third-floor courthouse still retains the original fireplaces, though the heavy legal lifting is now done across the street at the modernist justice building that opened in 1982.

The 2-block courthouse area was designated a historic district in 1982, and the Saeman Building at Buffalo and Center Streets is the centerpiece. The

Warsaw to North Webster

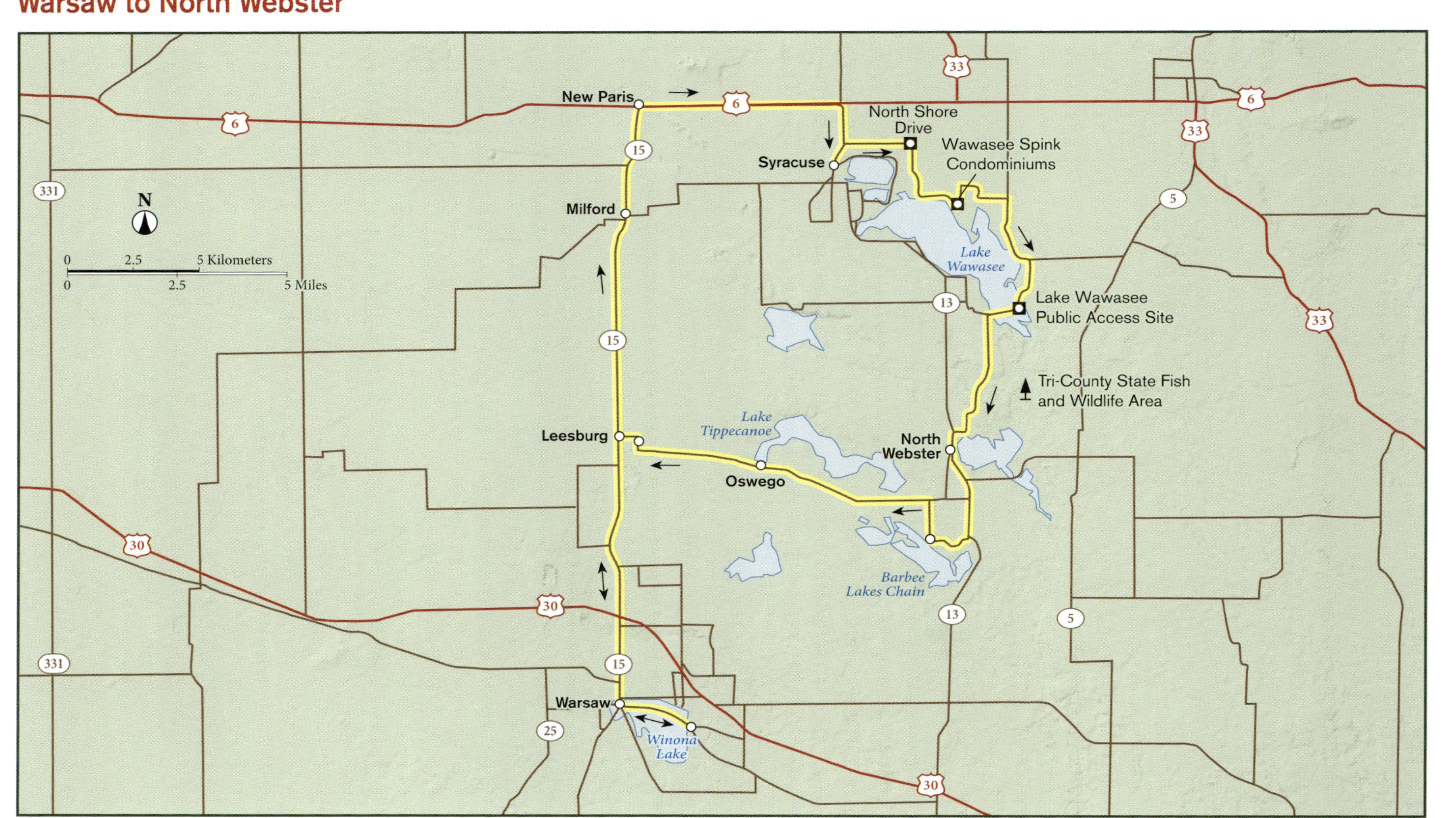

Italianate structure has retained its original cherry and walnut woodwork and stained-glass transoms.

One block south of the courthouse square on Buffalo Street is the **St. Regis Club**, home of the Anthology Whiskey Room, which features nearly 1,500 labels of bourbon, rye, scotch, and other whiskeys from around the world.

The old county jail at Indiana and Main Streets, 2 blocks west of the square, is also in the district. It houses the Old County Jail Museum, which has a large genealogical library and county mementos, with a particular focus on the Civil War.

Warsaw Biblical Gardens packs more than 100 plants referenced in the Bible onto less than 1 acre, from autumn crocus to zebra grass.

The town has a diversified industrial base but is a center of surgical prosthetics and artificial joints, a specialty that dates to 1895. The county is also known as the "Egg Basket of the Midwest," with millions of eggs laid yearly and sold to stores across the country. Mentone, on the county's western edge, celebrates its status with a 3,000-pound concrete egg on the main drag that is lit up at night.

Another vintage business is the Warsaw Cut Glass Factory, which has operated since 1911. Proceed 3 blocks east on Center Street to Detroit Street, then go south 4 blocks. The first floor has an exhibit of antique glass and a showroom of new material.

Winona Lake, southeast of Warsaw, was the western outpost of the Chautauqua movement. It is a summer resort and religious revival center. Each summer

Warsaw Biblical Gardens packs more than one hundred unique plants in a single acre.
KOSCIUSKO COUNTY CVB

thousands from Chicago, New York, and the Midwest traveled via the Pittsburgh, Fort Wayne, and Chicago Railroad to the lakeside town for elucidation and exhortations. An early twentieth-century evangelist in the area was Billy Sunday. His house, a small wooden bungalow, can be seen at 1111 Sunday Lane.

The Winona Christian Assembly dates to 1895, the result of the collusion of influential men like food-processor H. J. Heinz, auto manufacturer John Studebaker, and Dr. J. Wilbur Chapman, a famous evangelist. Following Sunday's death in 1935, the Free Methodist Church World Headquarters was established here, and the Grace Brethren Church followed, which also operates the nearby Grace College and Seminary. Tens of thousands still arrive annually for the services held in the Billy Sunday Tabernacle.

Return through Warsaw to IN 15 and drive north. The road crosses Tippecanoe River below Tippecanoe Lake, where it receives the waters of the seven-lake Barbee chain. It winds between tree-lined banks, with bluffs and grassy islands decorating the stream.

Drive north 6 miles to **Leesburg**, the oldest town in **Kosciusko County** and the first county seat. Twenty-one buildings bunched in a 2-block area make up the Leesburg historic district along Van Buren Street. **Maple Leaf Farms**, which began operations in 1958, is in its fourth generation of family leadership with annual production of 9 million to 12 million ducks. The company relocated its headquarters to Leesburg from Milford in 2015.

Milford, 6 miles north on IN 15, was first settled in 1836 as Pucker Huddle but didn't become an incorporated town until 1880.

Continue north 3 miles to the junction of US 6 East. Proceed 5 miles east to IN 13 and turn south. Drive 2 miles to Syracuse. Founded in the 1830s, the town was destined to be a resort town. The first hotel was called the Rough and Ready, and two distilleries and a barrel-making factory were among its first businesses. Today Syracuse is primarily a resort town with four lakeside parks that dozes through the winter. It sits at the end of Syracuse Lake, a 410-acre bay of adjoining Lake Wawasee.

Take IN 13 to Washington Street, follow it to North Shore Drive, and turn right. Follow this to East Shore Drive and go 0.7 mile across the railroad tracks, turn left, and continue 0.6 mile to Lake Wawasee. Named for Miami Chief Wau-was-aus-see, the 3,410-acre lake is the largest natural lake in Indiana. A dam built at Syracuse in 1834 raised the water to its present level.

A marker noting the boundary line of Chief Papakeechie's former reservations is on the right, Indian land that extended into Noble County. The nearly half-mile section of lakeshore that follows became a refuge for Indianapolis industrialists, most notably Indianapolis Motor Speedway co-founder James Allison and pharmaceutical giant Eli Lilly.

Next door is the former Spink-Wawasee Hotel. In its heyday it was a pink stucco destination for the moneyed classes, celebrities, gangster Al Capone, the Queen of Siam, and comedy duo Abbott and Costello. The Detroit Lions practiced there. Heavyweight boxing champ Joe Louis trained there. Built in 1925, the Spink-Wawasee offered 130 rooms equipped with private bathrooms, a restaurant, cocktail lounge, conference center, house band, clandestine casino, and luxurious amenities, including an eighteen-hole golf course across the road. After the hotel closed in 1947, it was purchased by the Fort Wayne–South Bend Diocese of the Catholic Church and operated as a Catholic seminary and prep school from 1948 until the 1970s. It resurfaced in 1984 as the Wawasee Spink Condominiums.

Around the corner on North Bishop Road is the Wawasee Golf Club, a nine-hole course that is half what it was when founded by Eli Lilly in 1891.

Turn right on CR 1290 North in 0.5 mile, drive 1.4 miles, and then turn right on NE Wawasee Drive. Proceed 1.6 miles to CR 1100 N and turn left. After 0.2 mile, turn right on North Turkey Creek road and proceed south.

The road changes names to East Hatchery Road at the public access site. Proceed to CR 850 East, turn left, and drive 1.3 miles to the headquarters of Tri-County State Fish and Wildlife Area. The 3,569-acre DNR property has ten natural lakes and several man-made ponds, used for wildlife viewing and mushroom gathering as well as hunting and fishing. Greider's Woods—a 10-acre nature preserve within the refuge near the Spear Lake—was part of Chief Papakeechie's reservation from 1828 to 1834. It features a self-guided nature trail.

Follow CR 850 East to North Hoss Hill Road, then west on East Epworth Forest Road to IN 13. Proceed south on IN 13. A marker noting the Continental Divide between the Great Lakes and the Gulf of Mexico is half 0.5 south—less dramatic than the one on top of the Rockies, but momentous, nonetheless.

North Webster is 5 miles south. It is another summer playground town, cutesied into a faux Camelot for the most part. Webster Lake is a deep kettle lake, reaching a depth of 45 feet, with a surface of 640 acres. *The Dixie*, a double-decker sternwheeler, churns around the lake as it has since 1929. Webster is Indiana's premier lake for muskie fishing.

Proceed south from North Webster on IN 13 to CR E 400 N and turn right to enter the heart of the Barbee chain of lakes. Seven smallish lakes are interconnected by natural channels, beginning with **Big Barbee Lake**. Situated on North Barbee Road between Big Barbee and Little Barbee is the **Barbee Hotel and Restaurant**. Originally opened as the Ormond Hotel in 1897, it has survived multiple ownership changes. Its heydays may have been the 1920s and '30s when it was reputed to be a hideout for gangsters Al Capone, John Dillinger, and Baby Face Nelson. Hollywood stars Carole Lombard and Clark Gable honeymooned there in 1939. Stories of paranormal activity persist with reports from hotel staff of cigar

Legend has it that gangsters Al Capone and John Dillinger frequented the Barbee Hotel.
KOSCIUSKO COUNTY CVB

smoke wafting from under the door of Room 301, Capone's preferred lodging choice because it had an escape door. Other ghostly rumors involve a screaming woman or a boy wandering the hallways after he died at the hotel. The Travel Channel explored the eerie tales on its Dead Files series in 2014.

Continue west on North Barbee Road and East McKenna Road for 2.2 miles to CR N 475 E. Turn right and go 1.2 miles to CR E 500 N, passing **Shoe Lake** on the right, the northernmost of the Barbee chain.

Proceed west on CR E 500 N. Tippecanoe Lake lies just to the north. One of Indiana's deepest lakes, it is secluded in a picturesque valley, an ideal place for a stroll, picnic, or boat excursion. **Tippy Dance Hall** on the lake's south shore was built in 1944. Louis Armstrong and Duke Ellington played there in the early years, and through the 1960s it drew acts such as Mitch Ryder & the Detroit Wheels, Grand Funk Railroad, and The Byrds.

Oswego at Tippecanoe's southern end is a small resort village that was an early settlement on the site of Chief Musquabuck's Indian village and tribal reservation. John Pound's Store located at Armstrong Road and Second Street is the oldest business in the county, established in 1838. It is now maintained by the county historical society as a museum and contains many original fixtures and furnishings.

Proceed west from Oswego on East Armstrong Road to Leesburg, then turn south on IN 15 to return to Warsaw.

Round Barn Theatre, built in 1911, stages six shows annually.

25

Wintertime Cheer to the Austere Life

Angola to the Indiana Amish homeland

General description: The tour starts in Angola and the heart of Indiana's glacial lake region. The drive continues through Auburn, famous for the Auburn-Cord-Duesenberg Automobile Museum, to Amish country at Shipshewana and home of one of the country's most famous flea markets.

Special attractions: Pokagon State Park and Lake James near Angola; Auburn-Cord-Duesenberg Automobile Museum in Auburn; Gene Stratton-Porter State Historic Site in Rome City; Pigeon River Fish & Wildlife Area near Mongo; Menno-Hof Mennonite-Amish Visitor Center and Shipshewana Auction and Flea Market in Shipshewana.

Location: Northeastern Indiana.

Drive route numbers and names: IN 827, 120, 127, 427, 8, 3, 9, and 5; and US 20 and 6.

Travel season: Summertime draws thousands to lakes both small and large for boating, fishing, and swimming. Wintertime is a special season here for winter sports opportunities. The region falls in the lake-effect snow belt, so be prepared for some storms.

Camping: Pokagon State Park (260) 833-2012, Buck Lake Ranch (260) 665-6699, Camp Happy Acres (260) 665-9843, Steuben County Park (260) 668-1000, and Lake James Campground (260) 833-9577, all near Angola; Trading Post Outfitters (260) 367-2493 in Mongo; Grand View Bend Campground (574) 575-5927 and Twin Mills Campground (866) 862-3212, both near Howe; Shipshewana North Campground (260) 768-4324 and Shipshewana South Campground (260) 768-4609.

Services: There are full services in Angola, Fremont, Auburn, Albion, Rome City, LaGrange, Howe, and Shipshewana. Gas and food are available at numerous places enroute.

Nearby attractions: Trine University, Steuben County Soldiers Monument, Old Steuben County Jail, Indiana Rail Experience, all in Angola; Wild Winds Buffalo Preserve and Satek Winery, near Fremont; Auburn Brewing Company, Byler Lane Winery, Martha's Popcorn Stand, and National Auto & Truck Museum, all in Auburn; Albion Ale House in Albion; Sarge's Tavern and Mongo Country Store in Mongo; former Howe Military Academy in Howe; numerous shops and restaurants in Shipshewana.

The Drive

The drive begins in Angola, the Steuben County seat. The New England–flavored courthouse reflects the Yankee origin of many of the town's earliest settlers, who migrated from New England, New York, and the Western Reserve areas of Ohio

Angola to the Indiana Amish Homeland

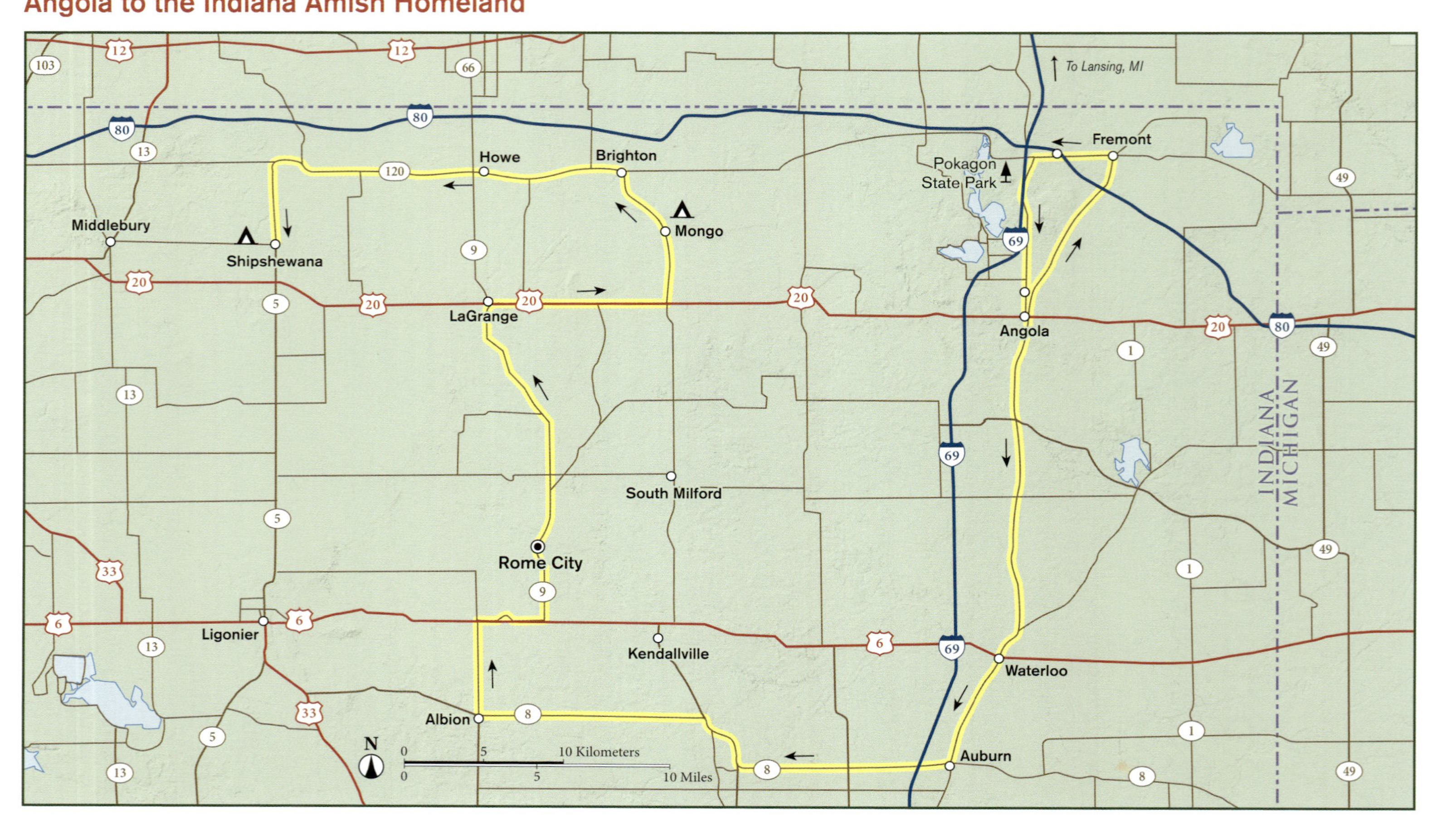

that were the home of New Englanders after the Revolutionary War. The two-story courthouse with its elaborate cupola and Italianate brackets was built in 1867 and 1868. It is on the southeast side of the town square. A statue of abolitionist and suffragist Sojourner Truth stands in front of the courthouse where she gave a speech in 1861. The center of the square features a 70-foot-tall monument and four figurines built in 1917 as a tribute to 1,278 men of Steuben County who served in the Civil War.

The jail just behind the courthouse was finished in 1877, also with local materials. Local laborers dredged the marl and blue clay from nearby Lake James to make the bricks for the jail and courthouse.

Five blocks west of the square is the entrance to Trine University, across the street from the T. Furth Center for Performing Arts, a $7.8 million facility that preserves the **Angola Christian Church** built in 1910. Trine was founded in 1884 as Tri-State Normal College and currently offers associate to doctorate degrees in fifty fields of study.

Just southwest of the campus, Fox Lake has been a playground for Midwestern Black families since the 1920s when strict segregation plagued Indiana. From the Roaring Twenties until today, it primarily has been used by African Americans, and most of the lakefront property is still owned by Black families.

There are 101 lakes in Steuben County and two popular waterways for paddling—Fawn River and Pigeon Creek. Nine state-dedicated nature preserves are open to nature enthusiasts daily. The lake-effect of Lake Michigan and prevailing westerlies can bring snow to the region. Accordingly, locals and visitors take advantage of the natural assets to turn it into a four-season playground. Fishing, boating, swimming, and hiking enliven the warm months, and cross-country skiing, tobogganing, snowmobiling, ice-fishing, and traipsing through the winterland trails spice up the cold ones.

Three blocks east of the **Angola square** is the historic Cline House, built in 1891 and now the home of the Steuben County Historical Society Museum.

Just past the museum, turn north on Williams Street. The road becomes IN 827. Drive 7.5 miles to **Fremont**, passing the Erastus Farnham House on the south side of town at East Feather Valley Road. Farnham was an abolitionist and advocate of the Underground Railroad, which enslaved African Americans used in the early to mid-1800s to seek freedom. Farnham designed the home to be a stop on the escape route.

Fremont is on the Vistula Road, which traversed from Lake Erie at Toledo to Lake Michigan at Chicago, the route for traders, French Jesuits touting Christianity to Native Americans, and Mormons trailing Brigham Young to the West.

Turn west on IN 120 and drive west 2 miles to Van Guilder Road, then turn north to visit the small but award-winning **Satek Winery** (pronounced like *attic*). The winery is producing ten times as much wine as it did when opening in 2001.

After returning to IN 120, turn west, go 1.4 miles to IN 127, and turn south. The entrance to Pokagon State Park at IN 727 is 1.8 miles south. Established in 1925, the 1,260-acre park is located on Lake James, one of the largest lakes in Indiana. The park offers a variety of recreational facilities, including a unique toboggan run that is open from late November to late February. The two-track refrigerated run covers a quarter mile at speeds reaching 40 mph. The vintage Potawatomi Inn has 126 guest rooms and 12 cabins and has been ranked as one of the top 25 resorts in the Midwest.

Proceed south on IN 127 through the Angola square, taking the second, or south, exit to pick up Old US 27. Drive 20 miles south through Pleasant Lake to merge with IN 427 as it winds through **Waterloo** to downtown **Auburn**. Each Labor Day weekend more than 200 Auburns, Cords, and Duesenbergs—the Grand Trinity of luxury roadsters synonymous with the Roaring Twenties high life—return to their birthplace in Auburn, along with 200,000 people celebrating the Golden Age of Motoring with a festival and a classic car auction. The Auburn-Cord-Duesenberg Automobile Museum at 1600 S. Wayne St. is housed in the Auburn Automobile Company's Art Deco administration building and showroom, built at the height of the streamline era. The chandeliers, elaborate terrazzo floors, and grand staircase are all original, as are the hundred classic automobiles housed there.

Proceed west 20 miles on IN 8 through a land of rolling glacial moraines to Albion. One of the smaller towns in the county, Albion's central location gave it county seat honors. The Richardsonian Romanesque courthouse was built in

The ACD Museum features the Roaring Twenties Grand Trinity of luxury autos: Auburns, Cords, and Duesenbergs.

1888–89. The Old Jail Museum next door is housed in an 1875 jail. Turn north on IN 9 and proceed 4 miles to US 6. Turn east 1.4 miles to IN 9. Rome City and the Gene Stratton-Porter State Historic Site are 3 miles north.

The town is situated on Sylvan Lake, an 1830s reservoir for a canal used to connect Lake Michigan with the Wabash and Erie Canal, another of the projects that went bust in the canal days. French and Irish workers each took a side of the canal-in-progress as their home.

The Gene Stratton-Porter State Historic Site honors the naturalist and author who wrote *Freckles* and *Girl of the Limberlost* among many others. She designed the two-story cedar log cabin and lived here from 1914 to 1919. The adjacent Wildflower Woods were the inspiration for many of her stories.

Proceed north on IN 9 through lake and northern moraine country. LaGrange County is home to a large Amish community, which began relocating here from Lancaster County, Pennsylvania, in the 1840s. About half of the county's population is Amish. Be alert for slow-moving buggies and wagons. Also, please refrain from photographing the Amish.

The town of LaGrange is the county seat, 11 miles north of Rome City. The brick and sandstone courthouse in the heart of LaGrange was built in 1879 in a Georgian and French Second Empire style with a 125-foot-high bell tower. Along the west side, Amish tie their patient horses to the hitching posts.

After checking out the courthouse, backtrack on IN 9 (a.k.a. Detroit Street) 1 block to Foltz Bakery, which serves traditional sweet things to local townspeople and visitors. Continue south on IN 9 to US 20 and turn east to drive 11 miles to IN 3.

Turn north on IN 3 and drive 3 miles to **Mongo**, a town that has garnered regional fame for succulent honeydew, muskmelon, and cantaloupe melons that thrive in the sandy soil. Originally named Mongoquinong, Potawatomi for "Big Squaw Village," the town straddles the Pigeon River at the mill pond. The river sweeps out of sight around a willow-lined bend on its way to a confluence with the St. Joseph's River 36 miles away. It is considered one of Indiana's best canoeing and float streams, and rental places abound.

The Potawatomi were the original inhabitants of the area, and French and American fur traders joined them in the 1830s. The historic Olde Store at the northwest corner of Mongo's main intersection was built in 1832 and has served as a post office, distillery, informal courtroom, and general store. Thc Greek Revival two-story structure was built in 1832 by John O'Ferrell and was added to the National Register of Historic Places in 1975.

Across the main intersection is a 1915 Mongo Bank Building, now Sarge's Tavern, with Prairie-style stained glass and fine detailing. To the east, the now empty Olde Mongo Hotel stands resolute with an ornate Victorian cupola on top.

Mongo is centered in the sprawling Pigeon River State Fish and Wildlife Area, an 11,800-acre property managed by the state Department of Natural Resources. The area was established in 1956 when three reservoirs—Mongo, Nasby, and Ontario—in the Pigeon River valley were given to the state. The DNR's Curtis Creek Trout Rearing Station, which annually raises and releases thousands of rainbow trout into Indiana waters, is located on the property. A nature preserve in the area has the largest tamarack bog forest preserve in Indiana. Shallow Lake is a waterfowl production area that has helped nurse Canada geese back to healthy levels after near extinction.

Proceed north 3 miles on IN 3 to IN 120 in **Brighton**. Turn west at Brighton and drive 6 miles to Howe. It's a quintessential small Indiana town, with scrupulously mowed lawns and well-maintained older homes nestled in shady yards. The Kingsbury House on the square on Third Street is a finely wrought yellow brick hotel built in 1863, replacing another hotel that dated back to 1835 but burned.

The former Howe Military Academy is a block north of the IN 120/IN 9 intersection. The small school closed in 2019 after 135 years and was sold a year later to World Olivet Assembly, a New York–based evangelical religious denomination. The new owner plans to reopen the campus as Great Commission University to educate and train current and future ministers and missionaries.

Continue 8 miles west from Howe on IN 120 to IN 5 and turn south. Go another 3.5 miles to **Shipshewana**, the heart of Amish country. The town was founded in 1889, named after a local Potawatomi chief. The town is best known for the Shipshewana Auction and Flea Market, where auctioneers simultaneously

Shipshewana is both a tourist attraction and the heart of the Amish community.

holler out their cadences to rings of intent bidders. Goods range from '50s junk to high-end country antiques that make their way to the big-city antique shops and dealers. The flea market, billed as the largest in the Midwest, features more than 700 vendors offering their treasures every Tuesday and Wednesday from May through September. Workhorse and livestock auctions happen throughout the season.

In the auction-barn restaurant, diners share communal tables as Amish girls in prayer caps and shin-length dresses whisk plates of farm food to the patrons. Antique dealers and tony mavens pass the salt to bearded farmers with Red Man Tobacco belt buckles, and chats about original paint and resale get mixed in with gimlet-eyed discussions of feeder calves and workhorses.

Other popular restaurants serving Amish and Mennonite food include the Blue Gate and Wana Cup. In the evening the Wana Cup becomes a happening place, the hitching posts filled as the young courting couples gather for soft-serve ice cream and a little post-chores chat. Shopping opportunities abound at small shops as well as the Davis Mercantile, Yoder's, and E&S Sales.

The 1,500-seat Blue Gate Theatre draws national acts such as the Oak Ridge Boys, the Temptations, Emmylou Harris, Jeff Foxworthy, Red Hot Chili Peppers, and Herman's Hermits.

The Menno-Hof Mennonite-Amish Visitor Center is one of the nation's most respected interpretive centers. Within the barnlike museum, visitors can learn about the history, customs, and lifestyles of the Amish and Old Order Mennonites that make the region their home.

The Amish trace their origins to the early 1500s when a priest named Menno Simons preached against the non-scriptured teaching of the Dutch church. He taught that only willing adults should be baptized, and there should be a strict delineation between church and state. A movement known as the Anabaptists rose from his beliefs.

In 1693 a conservative Swiss, Jacob Amman, preached an even more austere brand of Anabaptism, urging beards for married men, plain dress for both sexes, and shunning from the community for those not adhering to the rules. Amman's preaching split the Anabaptist community, and those that followed him became known as Amish.

Eventually both the Mennonites and Amish were driven from Europe for their beliefs, particularly their resistance to military service, as both sects are pacifistic. Many moved to the early Pennsylvania colony, invited by Quaker William Penn.

The Amish and Old Order Mennonites share many beliefs including pacifism, adult baptism, and plain lifestyles. The Amish, remembering their days of persecution, have no central religious authority, electing their local deacons, ministers, and bishops from the congregation. There are no Amish churches, as they continue to meet in homes every other Sunday.

A south German dialect called Pennsylvania Dutch is used in the home and church, though it has evolved into its own parlance, enlivened with colloquialisms and English words. Northern Indiana Amish can no longer converse in German with their southern Indiana brethren, being forced to use English instead. The families are large, and divorce is almost nonexistent. Farming is still the preferred vocation, though many men now work in the area factories (particularly woodworking and the RV industry) and on construction crews.

The Amish educate their children in small Amish schoolhouses scattered through the region, with an Amish woman most often serving as teacher. Children are educated up to the eighth grade when they leave to pursue their traditional occupations. Until school consolidations in the 1960s, the Amish children were educated in public schools, but the Amish opposed their children being bussed to faraway institutions and instead choose to set up their own facilities within a buggy ride of home.

26

Indiana Amish Heartland

Nappanee to Goshen

General description: This 55-mile drive explores the northern Indiana heartland of the Old Order Amish, beginning in Nappanee and running through Amish farmland to Bonneyville Mill.

Special attractions: Amish Farms, Amish Acres, The Bag Factory, and Bonneyville Mills.

Location: Northern Indiana.

Drive route numbers and names: IN 119, 4, and 5; and County Roads 16, 34, 37, and 250 West.

Travel season: The roads are drivable in all but the worst of winter weather. There are many Amish buggies on the roads, so caution is vital.

Camping: Shipshewana North Campground (260) 768-4324 and Shipshewana South Campground (260) 768-4609; Foxwood Hills (574) 825-3152 and KOA Campground (800) 562-5892, both in Middlebury; Eby's Pines Campground (574) 848-4583 in Bristol.

Services: There are full services in Nappanee, Goshen, and Middlebury. Gas and food are available at Bristol.

Nearby attractions: Coppes Commons and Hoosier Cabinet Museum in Nappanee; Goshen Brewing Company, Which Craft Brewery, Goshen Historical Museum, South Side Soda Shop, Ox Bow County Park, Pumpkinvine Nature Trail, all in Goshen; Fruit Hills Winery & Orchard in Bristol; Blue Gate Restaurant, Blue Gate Theatre, Menno-Hof Amish-Mennonite Museum and famous flea market and auction are just east; Middlebury Community Museum in Middlebury; Quilt Gardens, Midwest Museum of American Art, Wellfield Botanical Gardens, RV and Motor Home Hall of Fame, all in nearby Elkhart.

The Drive

The drive begins in Nappanee, a railroad town founded in 1874. The town has capitalized on the allure of the plain Amish, and there is an abundance of black buggy art painted on local signs. Area strip malls all seem to have Amish and country themes and crafts, and it's hard to ignore the fact that this is Amish country.

The **Barns at Nappanee**—home of Amish Acres, an 80-acre re-creation of a working Amish farm—has given the town its lodestone. The farm began in 1874 when Christian and Moses Stahly bought it. The farm includes the original house with appropriate furnishings, the smaller Gross Dawdy Haus where the grandparents lived, and several vintage farm buildings including the grand Schweitzer barn. It operated as a working farm among the Stahly, Nissley, and Kuhns family until 1969 when the current owners purchased it on the auction block to prevent it from being turned into an industrial site.

Nappanee to Goshen

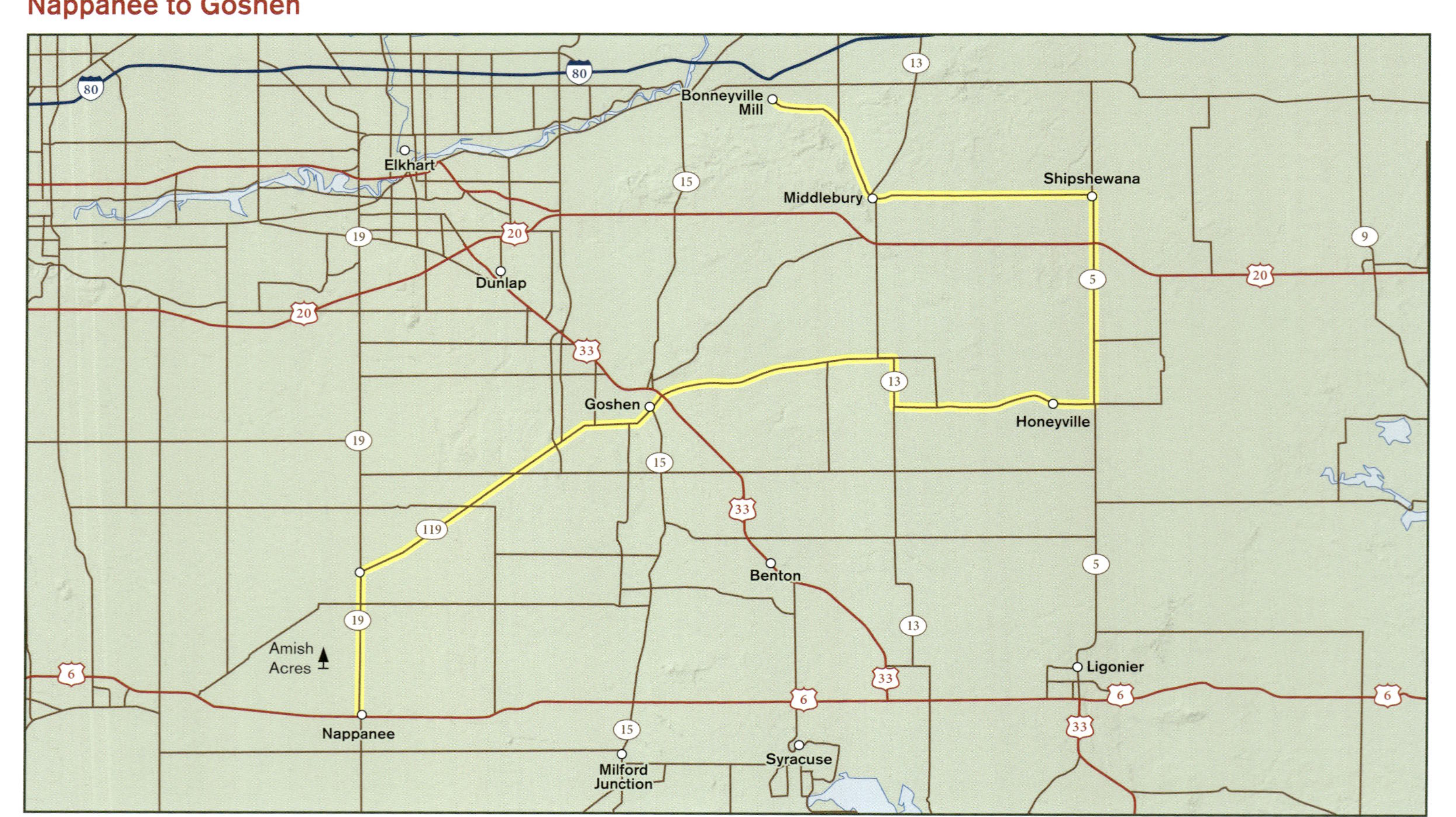

Thousands of people a year visit the farm, experiencing the rustic life of the Amish of yesterday (and today, for that matter, since things don't change much on an Amish farm). The place still exhales the air of a calm yesterday, even with a 400-seat restaurant, a musical theater operating in a restored 1911 round barn, and relocated log houses serving as shops for crafts, soda, meat and cheeses, and homemade fudge.

The farm acts as a living museum. Women carry out everyday tasks such as candle making, quilting, and outdoor baking, while the men engage in maple sugaring, cider making, and animal husbandry. The farm is listed on the National Register of Historic Places and served as a heritage tourism pilot area for the National Trust for Historic Preservation.

Proceed to the east edge of town and turn north on County Road 7. The road passes several Amish farms, where bearded farmers work the fields with draft horses, and teams of as many as a dozen are used in spring plowing. Herds of cows lay in leisure beside great white barns. Tall silos hold the provender of the year to satisfy the herds in the winter. Austere farmhouses sit beneath towering windmills spinning in the breeze.

Proceed north 5 miles to IN 119 and turn to the northeast. Black buggies with bonneted women trip down the road, pulled by horses with dark shining coats, some crossing the highway like moving silhouettes. Young Amish men with snappy fedoras ride behind horse-drawn cultivators like charioteers.

To the southwest, rolling hills are dotted with small woodlots. Tree-lined streams wind through the fields. The air is tinted with the smell of hay and manure—livestock's "useful byproduct" according to the local tourism brochures.

A hummocky golf course with a requisite gated golf course "community" announces the outskirts of affluent Goshen. City fathers platted Goshen in 1831, but it took a while to boost its fortunes enough to warrant incorporation in 1854. It is still primarily an insular agricultural trading town, in character if not in revenues. The growth of the locally owned recreational vehicle industry has created a burgeoning class of nouveau riche who are responsible for the bloated lakeside homes that ring the region's many lakes.

The 1870 Elkhart County Courthouse at the center of town reflects the town's suspicions. An octagonal limestone booth with a carved frieze at the corner of Main and Lincoln Streets was built by the WPA during the Depression at the behest of the town fathers.

Originally settled by Mennonites, the town retains a strong connection to the sect. Goshen College at Ninth and Main Streets is a four-year liberal arts college. Although 30% of the student body is Mennonite, the school admits students of all religions. With a strong tradition in peace movements, the college offers several courses, as well as encouraging understanding of the developing world by offering their students a fourteen-week sojourn in a Third World country.

The annual Michiana Mennonite Relief Sale held at the Elkhart County Fairgrounds draws thousands. Besides the three large auctions of handmade quilts, the sale features crafts from Mennonite relief villages in thirty-three different countries including baskets, figurines, toys, rugs, and wooden ware. Online bidding on auction items has been added to the sale, which dates to 1968 and annually raises more than $400,000 to support Mennonite ministries worldwide.

Quilts are a burgeoning cottage industry in the Amish area, often a substantial second income in Amish homes. Beginning in the 1870s the Amish women began to make bold geometric designs from blocks of solid-colored fabric, then embellished with elaborate quilting in feathered scrolls, florals, grids, and cables. They still use solid fabrics for their quilt blocks as prints are considered too worldly, though much of the piecing is done on treadle sewing machines. The quilting is still done by hand. Quilt shops advertising their wares are scattered through the area and welcome visitors.

Of course, the quilt sale offers barrels of traditional food like headcheese and mush, apple butter, dumplings, strawberry shortcake, and whole hog sausage. Haystacks, an Amish favorite, are a big seller. It is kind of an Amish taco salad, a layering of crackers, ground meat, rice, lettuce and tomato, peppers, olives, and corn chips, with cheese poured all over it. It is often the dish served at fundraising Amish pitch-ins when a disaster has struck one of the insurance-shunning Amish. The haystack becomes whatever the congregation brings.

From the intersection of IN 15 and Westwood Road near the college campus, drive west 0.3 mile to the Elkhart River and Shoup-Parsons Woods Park, known for record numbers of bird species. The rich natural area is used by Goshen College professors and local ornithologists.

The Bag Factory at Indiana and Chicago Avenues is a rehabilitated turn-of-the century industrial complex that has been reborn as a shopping destination. The structures began life in the 1890s as the Cosmo Buttermilk Soap Company followed by the Chicago-Detroit Bag Factory (later Chase Bag), which made burlap bags until 1982. "Bagology" is emblazoned on the side of the building. It was reborn as a high-end hardwood furniture workshop and showroom and artisan gallery. Unlike repetitive malls selling the same thing across the country, the Bag Factory features one-of-a-kind arts and crafts made by premier resident artisans and craftspeople. Goods include quilts, pottery, metal sculpture, furniture, glass windows, toys, European-style breads and pastries, hand-carved cameos, and gourmet chocolates.

Take IN 4 east from Goshen through rolling farmland. Grazing ponies and well-cared-for horses are alongside the road. Buggies clop down the road. Spotted cows graze and lay chewing their cud in farm lots. Because of the high proportion of Amish farmers, Elkhart County ranks second in the number of cows and the amount of milk produced in the state. The farms are smaller than average—105 acres versus the state average of 272. Almost 65% of the county's farms are less than 50 acres.

Change is coming to the Amish world. Half of the men now work in non-farming occupations. Where the plainest of porch rail spindles used to be, turned and adorned spindles now stand. Previously most of the shopping was done at country stores. Now there is a hitching rack at the Walmart in Goshen, and there is a small local industry of van drivers who do nothing but provide taxi service for Amish shopping trips and medical visits.

Proceed east from Goshen on CR 34 for 13 miles through a popcorn-growing region (a popular and profitable crop in the area) to IN 5 North. Go north 6.5 miles to CR 250 West on the north side of Shipshewana and turn west. (See Drive 25 for information on Shipshewana.) At the west edge of town, the Brown Swiss Dairy octagonal barn was built by Manuel Yoder and his sons in 1907 and 1908. Yoder determined that the shape would give additional strength as well as usable space.

Small signs along the road advertise honey, eggs, cheese, maple syrup, and popcorn for sale, but not on Sunday. As involved and active as the Amish are in agriculture and commerce, they resonate to a divine spiritual reality. They see their duty to keep "un-spotted from the world" and separate from the desires, intents, and goals of the worldly people. An Amish cemetery, a *graabhof*, is beside the road, as plain and simple as their lives.

Middlebury, 6.5 miles west of Shipshewana, is another center of Amish culture and related kitsch. County Road 250 turns into CR 16 on the way to Middlebury. Main Street offers an old-time hardware store. Like many towns in the northern part of the state, Middlebury was founded by Yankees. It was named after Middlebury, Vermont, by Vermonters who arrived in 1830.

Das Dutchman Essenhaus, considered Indiana's largest family restaurant, with over a thousand seats, is west of town at IN 20 and Wayne Avenue. It is more hearty farm fare—noodles, biscuits, dressing, potatoes, roast beef, fried chicken, ham, and pies—of course, pies. It is the Land of Happy Calories. "Would you like noodles on those potatoes?" as the local joke goes.

Take Bristol Avenue northwest out of town where it becomes CR 8 along the Little Elkhart River. The road curls over the rocky glacial moraines left from the last great ice age 15,000 years ago, and twists through forests past small streams before re-entering open ground. Most of northern Indiana was part of the Michigan Territory but was ceded to Indiana to give the state a port on the Great Lakes.

This area, as most of the state, was wrested from the indigenous Indian tribes in a series of treaties in the first 40 years of the nineteenth century.

Recreational vehicles are a vital part of the **Middlebury** economy, with four major manufacturers—Coachmen, Grand Design, Jayco, and Winnebago—but food products have a significant role as well. **Meijer Central Kitchen** makes everything from cookies to salads for the Meijer department store chain while the Rise 'n Roll Bakery chain opened its first location here in 2004.

Old Hoosier Meats is another Middlebury staple, with offerings of fresh-cut beef, chicken and pork, tasty smoked versions of the same, along with cheeses, side dishes, and a variety of seasonings. Adding to the appeal of Old Hoosier Meats is its location: the old Middlebury High School gym.

Bonneyville Mill, built in the 1830s, is the oldest continuously operating gristmill in Indiana. Elkhart County Parks Dept.

Bonneyville Mills is 4.5 miles northwest of Middlebury on CR 8. Established in the 1830s, Bonneyville Mills was envisioned by Edward Bonney as the beginning of a great Midwestern metropolis centered on his grist and saw mills. The mills were near the Toledo to Chicago Trail and canals were sure to follow the Little Elkhart. But the railroad passing the mills by deflated any of those dreams. Bonney sold the mills, ran a tavern, and later fled as fugitive from a counterfeiting charge. Bonney landed in Chicago, where he joined the 127th Illinois Infantry in 1863 and specialized in tracking down deserters from the Union army.

The gristmill was never modernized into a roller mill, remaining an old-style stone gristmill. In the Depression the mill owners added hydroelectric generation to their offerings, providing forty-five customers with electric current. It hung on until the 1960s, producing livestock feed and "Famous Buckwheat Pancake Flour." In 1968 a county group bought the mill and continued the tradition of slow mill grinding. The rustic mill remains as Indiana's oldest continuously operating gristmill, now surrounded by a 222-acre park, offering trails through meadow, marsh, hillside, and valley, and dozens of picnic sites.

27

Lake Maxinkuckee Loop

Plymouth to Lake Maxinkuckee

General description: The 35-mile drive loops from Plymouth around Lake Maxinkuckee and back to Plymouth.

Special attractions: Plymouth downtown and northside historic districts, Chief Menominee Monument, Lake Maxinkuckee, Culver Academies, Potawatomi Wildlife Park.

Location: North Central Indiana.

Drive route numbers and names: US 30 and IN 17, 117, 10, and 331.

Travel season: This is a summer playland from Memorial Day to Labor Day. Graduation weekends at Culver Military Academy can fill up the area. The roads are drivable in all but the worst of winter weather.

Camping: Hidden Lake Paradise Campground (574) 936-2900, Campers Roost (574) 936-9350, and Yogi Bear's Jellystone Park (574) 936-7851, all in Plymouth.

Services: There are full services in Plymouth and Culver. Gas and food are available at several convenience stores enroute.

Nearby attractions: Marshall County Historical Museum, East LaPorte Footbridge, and River Park Square, all in Plymouth; Culver Commercial Historic District and Forest Place Historic District, both in Culver; Argos downtown historic district; Bourbon Commercial Historic District and Bourbon Residential Historic District, both in Bourbon; Bell Aircraft Museum in nearby Mentone; South Bend and the University of Notre Dame are 20 miles north of Plymouth.

The Drive

Deep natural lakes dapple Marshall County, and the Yellow and Tippecanoe Rivers cut across the county. Marshall County sits at the eastern edge of the Grand Kankakee Marsh, which stretched for 5,300 square miles southward from South Bend in the pre-settler days. Much of Marshall County's agricultural land is drained soil, and the primary produce are muckland crops: onions, potatoes, hay, corn, oats, and mint. Across the mucklands of northern Indiana, mint was a major crop. Cut like hay, it was stomped in a Hoosier version of a grape crush, and then distilled in specially made outbuildings. The glacial moraine highlands around Culver, Pretty Lake, and Twin Lakes are the home of many orchards that thrive in the well-drained soils.

Tourism and resort life are a major part of the lake economy. Many of the state's most attractive lakes are tucked into the county—Lake of the Woods, Twin Lakes, and Lake Maxinkuckee to name a few.

The loop begins in Plymouth, the Marshall County seat. Settlers organized the county in the 1830s on land that the Menominee tribe previously owned. The

Plymouth to Lake Maxinkuckee

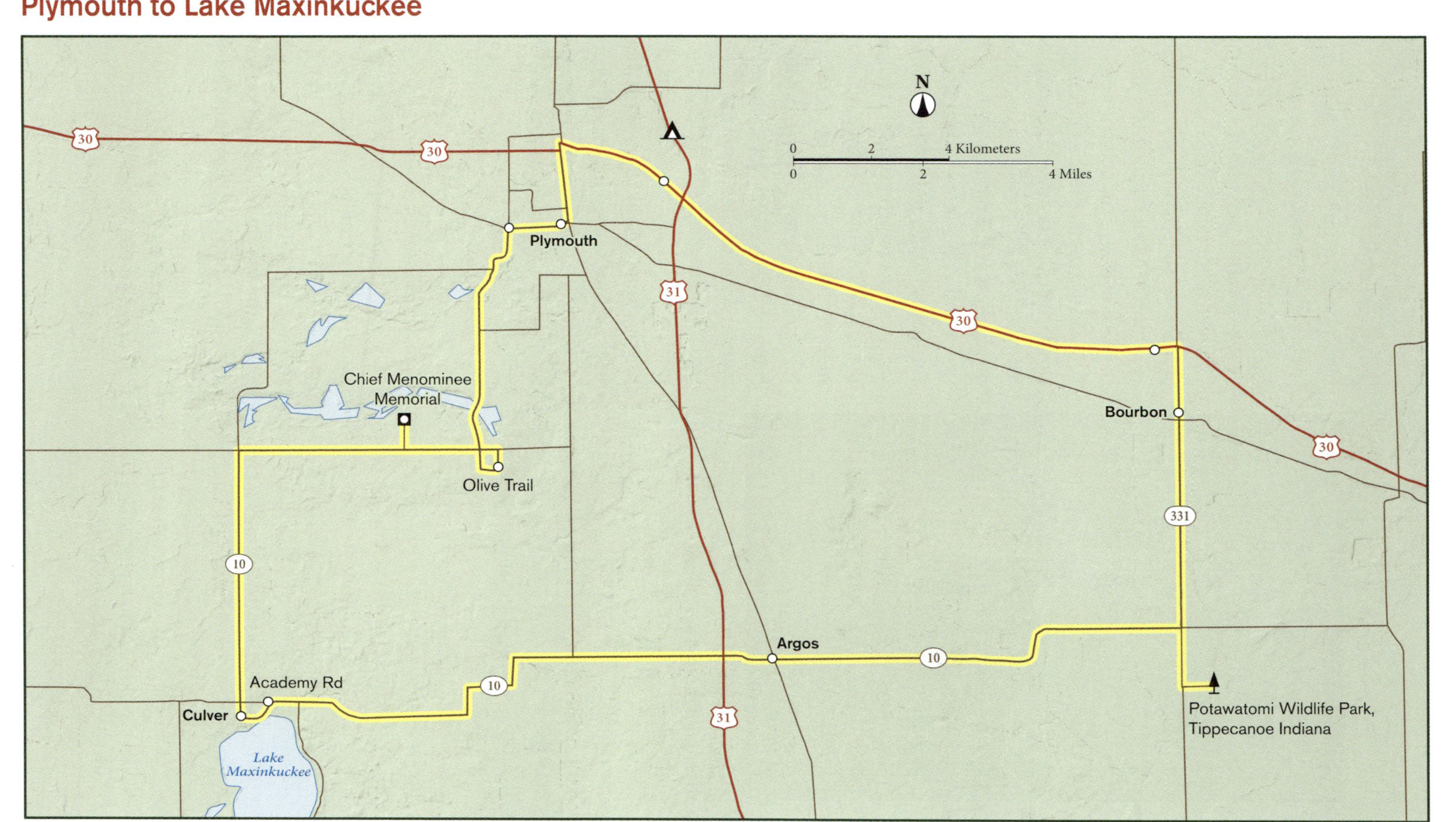

An impressive clock tower highlights the Marshall County courthouse in Plymouth.
PHIL BLOOM

nearby swampland caused endemic outbreaks of malaria, and periodic fires retarded the town's growth. But as the wetlands were drained and the city sorted out its fire department, the small town stabilized. It was incorporated in 1851 and reached city status in 1873. Besides producing automotive and plastics parts, the area is known as a top pickle producer, the county being among the top 3% in cucumber production in the nation.

Another big thing in **Marshall County** are barn quilts. The county tourism bureau promotes the trail as the first of its kind in Indiana with more than seventy different colorful "quilts" painted on plywood and hung on barns and houses. The county courthouse is an Italianate and Renaissance Revival structure with Corinthian columns and an impressive clock tower, completed in 1872. Somewhat incongruously, the square is ringed with residences rather than businesses. One residence that doubles as an essential business is located at Madison and Walnut Streets—the Simons House is now the Deaton-Clemens-Van Gilder Funeral Home.

The Marshall County Historical Museum is in the historic Lauer Building, also located in downtown Plymouth, at North Michigan and Garro Streets. It houses exhibits on local history, gristmill wheels, farm implements, a schoolhouse bell, Potawatomi artifacts, and decorative arts. Period rooms depict life between 1870 and 1910, including a child's room, a kitchen, and a vintage parlor.

Drive along the east side of the courthouse square south for 2 blocks to Center and Washington Streets and the Plymouth Fire Engine House, which is on the National Register of Historic Places. Built in 1875, the station has a redbrick watch tower and served as Plymouth's only fire station until a new one was built in 1980. A preschool is the current tenant of the old firehouse.

One block east and south is the historic Lauer Building at 123 N. Michigan St., home to the Marshall County Historical Society and the Marshall County Convention & Visitors Bureau.

East of downtown 3 blocks on LaPorte Street, the cantilevered East LaPorte Street Footbridge lightly leaps over the Yellow River. Erected in 1898 to help develop the area across the river, the "footpath of iron" is only 6 feet wide. There was an adjacent iron vehicle bridge, but it was replaced in the 1920s.

Centennial Park, the flagship of the municipal park system, is north on Michigan Street, just south of US 30. Depression-era WPA workers built the rustic entrance gate to the park. Rich in labor but short on money for materials, the workers used stones scavenged out of riverbeds and farmers' fields to construct the arch.

By far the town's biggest yearly event is the Blueberry Festival, which sprang out of Plymouth's 1966 celebration of Indiana's sesquicentennial. Blueberries made sense as a festival theme since Marshall County produces one-third of the delicate fruit grown in the state. Over 500,000 people throng the streets for the four-day event over Labor Day weekend each year. The parade lasts 2 hours, the fireworks display is one of the Midwest's largest, and 300 craft vendors and 100 food vendors offer their wares.

From Centennial Park drive south on North Michigan Street to Oakhill Avenue and turn right. Stay on Oakhill Avenue, which becomes Glenn Overmyer Drive, to South Olive Trail. Turn south and proceed 3.1 miles to 13th Road, turn west, and drive 1.2 miles to South Peach Road. The Chief Menominee Monument is 0.4 mile north in **Twin Lakes**. The Indiana state legislature appropriated $2,500 in 1909 for the life-sized granite statue that was erected here. It is said to be the first monument erected by a state to a Native American.

In 1832 Potawatomi Chief Menominee signed a treaty that guaranteed "forever" 14,000 acres to the Potawatomi for their many villages along the region's lakes and streams. There were more than one hundred wigwams at Twin Lakes alone.

In the spring of 1838, the government lured several chiefs to a treaty parlay and convinced them, with the help of threats and whiskey, to sign over their land and migrate west of the Mississippi. With the Treaty of Yellow River, the government bought the 14,000 acres the Potawatomi had in perpetuity for $1 an acre. Menominee protested that he had not signed the document and the young chiefs were drunk when they signed.

Because of the resistance of the Potawatomi, the governor sent General John Tipton to remove the Indians from the land. Tricking the tribe into meeting for a counsel at the Catholic mission, troops were able to then place the Indians under arrest. The tribe was eventually forced on a sixty-one-day march to Kansas, with little water and detestable food. Along the way, sixty escaped and made their way home. But forty-two died due to the horrible conditions. The march was known as the Trail of Death.

Return to 13th Road and turn right. Proceed west 2.5 miles to IN 17. Drive south across the Yellow River through Burr Oak to IN 10 and Culver.

Yellow River is another sluggish meandering northern wetland river that has been drained, straightened, and pacified, particularly in the reaches to the west where it contributed to the Grand Kankakee Marsh. East of Knox and into Marshall County, the river is allowed to roam free in its original banks as it cuts through the massive Maxinkuckee Moraine, a high bank of land left by the retreating glaciers 15,000 years ago. The river winds through a green, scenic valley with calming hills and glittering lakes.

Culver, just off IN 10, has been a resort town since the nineteenth century, and its wide streets and comfortable homes reflect the presence of old money. A fine new park stretches along the lakefront. Culver sits on the shores of 1,864-acre Lake Maxinkuckee, the state's second-largest natural lake.

Follow Lakeshore Drive to Academy Road. Turn left and the road leads into the 1,850-acre campus of Culver Academies. The campus buildings are designed to lend an air of medieval Europe, with Tudor-Gothic, Italian Renaissance, French, and Belgian aesthetics worked into structures.

When Henry Culver founded the academy in 1894, his goal was to make men out of boys through the rigors of the military system. A girls academy was started in 1971. Accordingly, the school is renowned for the pageantry and pomp of its military ritual and ceremony. Alumni include playwright Joshua Logan, Olympians Molly Engstrom and Kayla Miracle, New York Yankees owner George Steinbrenner and his son Hal, Dodgers owner Walter O'Malley, actor Hal Holbrook, film critic Gene Siskel, and Indianapolis Speedway owner Roger Penske.

The academy is best known for the Black Horse Troop, the largest remaining cavalry in the United States. Public appearances of the troop began in 1898, and it participated in President Woodrow Wilson's inauguration parade in 1913. Since then, the troop has performed in seventeen other inauguration parades and hundreds of other events. The troop has drills almost every summer Sunday.

The Vaughn Equestrian Center on campus is the largest indoor riding hall in the nation, at 300 × 90 feet, with grandstands for 800 people. The east portion of the center has stall space for ninety-four horses and tack rooms with equipment custom-tailored for each animal. Built in 1917, the center received a $10 million facelift in 2009. The Armory north of the Equestrian Center houses blacksmith and leather smith shops and private boarding stalls for the students' horses from home.

Proceed 10.1 miles east on IN 10 to Argos. The leafy town was a stagecoach stop on the old Michigan Road (US 31 today), named by Vice President Schuyler Colfax in the Grant administration. It is a traditional dairy farming area.

Culver Acadamies' Black Horse Troop has appeared in presidential inaugural parades since 1913. Culver Academies

Proceed 7.2 miles to IN 331. The Potawatomi Wildlife Park, located 2.5 miles south of IN 10, is a 300-acre privately owned facility that has wetlands, fields, ponds, and forests bordered by the Tippecanoe River. There are 5 miles of trails and excellent birding and wildlife viewing.

Potawatomi villages extended along the Tippecanoe, including the largest, Aubbeenaubbee, which was near the southern county line. The 166-mile-long Tippecanoe River, known as Kethtippecanunk to the Potawatomi, was an important early waterway. It flows through two of the state's largest lakes—Tippecanoe and Webster—and helps regulate the levels of the eighty-eight lakes it drains.

Proceed north on IN 331 through Old Tip Town and Tippecanoe to Bourbon. Founded in 1836 by a native of Bourbon County, Kentucky, the town was a lumber and woodworking center after the railroad arrived in 1856. The small town continued the woodcrafting tradition with butter tub, boat oar, and furniture manufacturing for many decades before switching to artificial-joint manufacturing with a medical technology company.

At Sit Park on the northwest corner of Center and Main Streets, the Old Town Pump is a re-creation of a town landmark. The colored rock monument memorializes popular drinking fountains used from the 1860s into the 1900s. The monument was built in 1929 featuring a drinking fountain and statue of the original wooden pump. An estimated 2,000 people attended the dedication ceremony.

US 30 is 1 mile north on IN 331. Turn west and proceed 9.3 miles to Plymouth.

28

Dunes and the Big Lake

Indiana's Lake Michigan shoreline

General description: The 25-mile drive covers the lakeshore from Gary to Michigan City.

Special attractions: Indiana Dunes State Park, Indiana Dunes National Park, Paul H. Douglas Center for Environmental Education, Bailly Homestead, Chellberg Farm, West Beach, Homes of Tomorrow, Kemil Beach, and Mount Baldy.

Location: Northwestern Indiana.

Drive route numbers and names: US 12, and County Roads 500 East and 1400 North.

Travel season: Each season seems to offer a different delight for the Dunes area, from the holiday bustle of summer to the quietude of winter. The roads are drivable in all but the worst of winter weather.

Camping: Indiana Dunes State Park (219) 926-1952 near Chesterton; Dunewood Campground at Indiana Dunes National Park (219) 395-1882; Sand Creek Campground (219) 926-7482 at Chesterton.

Services: There are full services in Miller and Michigan City. Gas and food are available at numerous places enroute.

Nearby attractions: Marquette Park in Gary; Duneland Distillery, Hunter's Brewery, and Running Vine Winery, all in Chesterton; historic Barker Mansion, Washington Park Zoo, Brincka Crossgardens, Michigan City Beach, Blue Chip Casino, Friendship Botanic Gardens, Old Lighthouse Museum, Michigan City Lighthouse and Pier, Shoreline Brewery, Zorn Brew Works, Burn 'Em Brewery, Shady Creek Winery, all in Michigan City.

The Drive

The Indiana Dunes National Park enchants people. The wind piles the sand into wandering mountains, carving it into arabesques and curlicues and calligraphic etchings of air. The light dances endlessly on the lake, a bowl of gray-green glass moving kinetically to the blue horizon as the beach grass bows to the lake breeze, a tableau of mustard, pewter, and pale green.

But the Dunes sit in an odd juxtaposition to one of the world's great industrial complexes, the great steel-making factories of the Calumet Region. Look down the beach from the dunes and a vast assemblage of black and rust-colored elevators and mill buildings and spuming and flaring smokestacks hulks on the lakeside. Beyond them, the tall towers of Chicago levitate in the haze. It is certainly a unique national park.

Thanks to many decades of dedicated conservation work, there are more than 15,000 acres of state and national parks and natural areas that stretch 18 miles

Indiana's Lake Michigan Shoreline

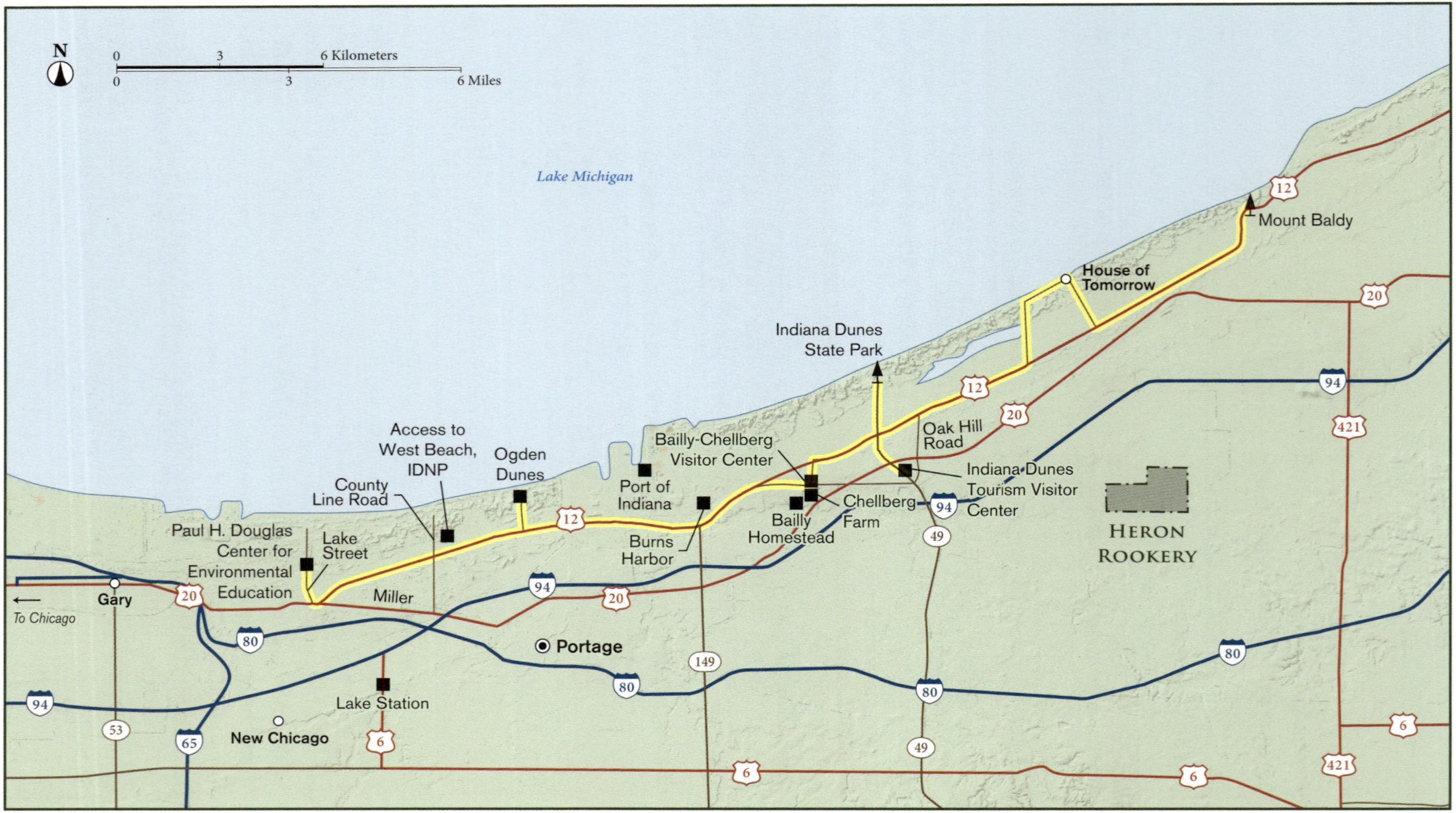

A summer sunset at the Michigan City lighthouse pier.

along the Indiana lakeshore, with the most diverse flora and fauna in the entire Midwest. Among all of the national parks, the Indiana Dunes National Park is the fourth highest in plant and animal diversity. The prairie meets the eastern deciduous and northern conifer forests at the southern end of Lake Michigan and the topographic relief of the Dunes offers a variety of altitudes and habitats for plants to thrive in lusty diversity.

In 1916 National Park Service director Stephen Mather envisioned the area as a national park, but World War I intervened and it was the state that moved first by establishing Indiana Dunes State Park in 1925. It wasn't until 2019 that Mather's dream came true when Indiana Dunes National Lakeshore was elevated to national park status. The state and national parks offer an array of educational facilities and activities, including fifteen nature trails to quaking bogs, moving dunes, ponds, savannas, prairies, and beaches.

The Dunes tour begins at the junction of US 20 and 12 east of Gary. US 12 follows the route of the Calumet Beach Trail, a major Indian route between the Great Lakes and the Mississippi River. Later the US military used the road between Chicago and Detroit, and in the 1830s a stage line ran along the lake. US 12—the Dunes Highway—opened in 1923.

Take US 12 to South Lake Street and turn left to the national park's Paul H. Douglas Center for Environmental Education. It offers interactive exhibits and an animal room with many of the area's representative species. Behind the environmental center, the Miller Woods Trail leads past cattail ponds to the rare black

Indiana Dunes National Park is among the most ecologically diverse in the federal park system. National Park Service/Jeff Manuszak

oak savanna, a great place to see woodland wildflowers in the spring and prairie flowers in the fall.

County Line Road, 2.2 miles east of Lake Street off US 12, leads to West Beach. It is a winding road through a varied terrain of towering dunes, low marshes, and scrub forests. West Beach is one of the national park's most popular beaches. Dune Succession Trail offers a glimpse into the life cycles of dunes. Long Lake is the largest of the interdunal ponds, reached by a hiking trail.

The Indiana dunes are the result of windblown sand that was left from ice-age lakes that predate Lake Michigan. Until the glaciers melted enough to open the Straits of Mackinac, the lakes drained down the Illinois River. When the straits opened, the lakes found their present level and the wind blew the remaining sand into the piles that abound yet today.

The national park proceeds east and surrounds the town of Ogden Dunes, an upscale bedroom community of the Calumet and Chicago region.

A South Shore Line Station is on US 12 at Hillcrest Road. The electric commuter line extends from South Bend to the Randolph Street Station in the Loop of Chicago, hauling millions of commuters annually.

Proceeding east on US 12, the Midwest Steel complex at the Port of Indiana is just east of Odgen Dunes, which adjoins Bethlehem Steel and a large Northern Indiana Public Service Company power plant at Burns Harbor. Midwest and Bethlehem are two of the largest steel producers in the Calumet Region.

The Calumet Region sits at the intersection of the coal of Appalachia and the iron ore of the Lake Superior Mesabi Range. The lakeside location and the availability of cheap land drew developers, industrialists, and capitalists early in the century.

Hammond got its start as an enormous slaughterhouse town. Whiting became the home of the gargantuan refinery that rolled its first tanker of kerosene out in 1890. The refinery, the sixth largest in the country, still looms over the town. In 1901 Inland Steel began at Inland Harbor in East Chicago, and in 1905, US Steel began in Gary.

Today, the mills are highly automated and buffeted by competition from abroad and domestic mini-mills. The armies of steelworkers that used to march into the mills are sharply diminished, and the steel output is far below the peak years.

But the flames still flare from the steel furnace stacks, and the 285-ton ladles of liquid steel still pour golden flows. And the thousands of red-hot steel slabs still race down the lines at 45 miles per hour on their way to the rolling mills, where immense pressure squeezes them into coils 1/16th of an inch thick and 4,000 feet long.

The historic isolation and intense industrial development combined with the eastern and southern European, Southern African American, and Mexican settlement gives the Calumet Region a distinct flavor that is closer in affinity to the big-shouldered bravado of Chicago than the agricultural ethos of the rest of Indiana.

Across from the Burns Harbor complex, turn right on CR 1350 N, which becomes Oak Hill Road, and drive 0.3 mile to **Augsburg Swensk Skola**, a tiny Swedish chapel and school built by nineteenth-century Swedish immigrants. It was originally built as a large tool shed but was given in 1889 to the local Lutheran congregation for use as a school. In 1930 it was dedicated as a church, now considered Indiana's smallest.

A steep staircase highlights West Beach at Indiana Dunes National Park.

Continue east on Oak Hill Road to Mineral Springs Road. Turn south to the 1835 Bailly Homestead and the Chellberg Farm. French-Canadian pioneer Joseph Bailly settled in the area in 1822 on the Little Calumet River, where the Sauk and Potawatomi Trails joined, the first white man to settle in northwest Indiana. For a decade it was one of only two trading posts between Detroit and Chicago. The Bailly family occupied the 42-acre homestead until 1918 when it became a Catholic retreat. In 1971 it became part of the national park.

The adjacent Chellberg Farm is a restoration of a turn-of-the-century Swedish homestead. The area had a Swedish settlement when Anders Chellberg arrived in 1863. His descendants continued to operate the farm until 1972. It includes the 1885 farmhouse, a Swedish-style post-and-beam barn, chicken house, corncrib, and sugarhouse. Like the Bailly Homestead, it is now part of the national park.

Return to US 12 on Mineral Springs Road and proceed across the highway to the Cowles Bog Nature Preserve. The bog is where botanist Henry Chandler Cowles conducted intensive studies of plant succession in the early 1900s that became pioneering work in the science of ecology. Trails wind through the wetlands and over dunes to a secluded beach.

A mile east of Mineral Springs Road, US 12 meets IN 49. Go left to the entrance of Indiana Dunes State Park, then right to the national park's visitor center.

The 2,200-acre state park contains a long sand beach, a nature center, a restored pavilion, and an accessible bird observatory. Mount Tom is the highest point along the Indiana shore at 192 feet. Mount Holden and Mount Jackson are nearby, only a few feet smaller. The park has several "blow-outs" where wind currents from the lake have eroded the land and created desert depressions devoid of vegetation.

When industrialists wanted to mine Mount Tom for its sand in 1916, the uproar created the "Save the Dunes" movement. The Indiana legislature voted to purchase lakefront land in 1923, and the park was established in 1925.

The state park nature center is particularly strong in children's programming. Trail 9 leads through forested sand dunes, past the rim of the Beach House Blowout, and then along the ridge of the first dune inland from the beach. There are some wonderful views of the lake though the last virgin pines in the region. The Dunes Pavilion was built in 1930 but fell into disrepair over the ensuing decades before a public-private partnership brought it back to life in 2021 with a major renovation that now offers a restaurant, snack bar, an event room, and an adjacent bathhouse for beachgoers.

The national park's **Indiana Dunes / Dorothy Buell Memorial Visitor Center**, 2 miles south on IN 49 from the state park gatehouse, is the best place to pick up informational brochures for the area, souvenirs from the gift shop, or tips and pointers from national park rangers.

Three miles east of the US 12/IN 49 intersection, turn left on East State Park Boundary Road and proceed north to Kemil Beach and Dunbar Beach on West Lake Front Drive. Continue northeast to the Century of Progress Historic District in Beverly Shores. The district features five remarkable homes that look oddly out of place, an architectural compendium of Art Deco, sci-fi, and Florida. Built for the 1933 Chicago World's Fair as examples of innovative materials and construction techniques, they were floated and trucked to Beverly Shores after the Fair.

The town of Beverly Shores dates to 1947, though two colonial-style structures, the Old North Church on West Beverly Drive and the Wayside Inn on Jameson Avenue, look much older. They too were built for the World's Fair as part of the colonial exhibit and barged over to Beverly Shores after the show.

On the lakeshore at the east end of the national park, 126-foot-high Mount Baldy offers the combination of a scenic beach and a giant wandering dune. Pushed by wind and waves, the massive dune migrates southward about 4 feet a year. When the winds are right, the moving dunes make a sound like a deep bass viola, what locals call the singing sands. Climbing **Mount Baldy** is no longer possible without a national park ranger escort as the park attempts to protect the fragile environment.

Five Century of Progress homes from the 1933 World's Fair were relocated to Beverly Shores.

Index

S

T

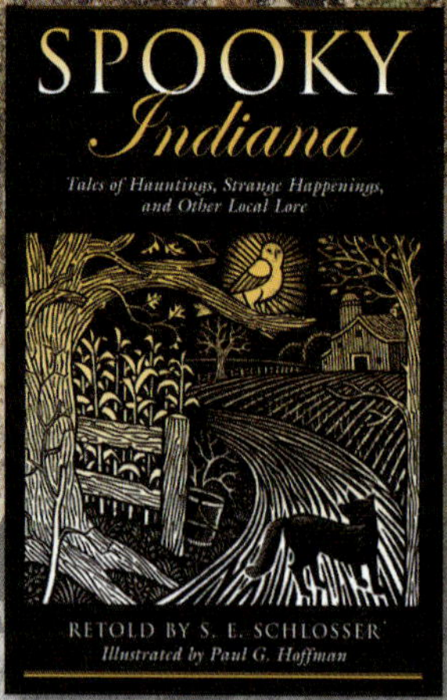